TH
GUIDE
TO THE
LAKES

HUNTER DAVIES

Chief Researcher – Colin Shelbourn
Assistant Researcher – Pam Williamson

Published by Forster Davies Ltd. Loweswater and London

The Good Guide to the Lakes by Hunter Davies
Chief Researcher, Colin Shelbourn
Published by Forster Davies Ltd., Loweswater and London.

1st edition, 1984 (white cover) 11,000 copies;
2nd printing, 1984, 15,000 copies; 3rd printing, 1985, 5,000 copies.

2nd edition, 1986 (blue cover) 15,000 copies.

3rd edition (red cover), edition, 1989, 15,000 copies.

This is the 4th edition, 1993 – note fashionable green cover – 10,000 copies.
ISBN 0 9509 190 8

Created, printed and published in Cumbria, of course.
Typeset by Cardtoons Publications Ltd., Windermere.
Printed and bound by Titus Wilson & Sons, Kendal.

STAR RATINGS

☆☆☆ Not to be missed
☆☆ Highly recommended
☆   Interesting

Throughout this book, we have used star ratings for almost everything, from mountains to restaurants, as a way of indicating those places or services which we think are worth experiencing. Listings with no stars at all are there mainly for reference.

CONTENTS

Introduction

Hello and Welcome to the Fourth Edition, totally revised, lavishly researched, expensively reprinted, and once again, all published and printed in Cumbria. We do try to keep our local printer people off the streets. And as ever, we have taken no bribes, accepted no free meals, nor charged anyone for inclusion, unlike some guide books we could mention. Sorry about the delay. I meant to produce a new edition every two years, as the demand is huge, the book sells as brilliantly as ever, but things happened, though can't remember what.

A gap of four years means there have been some important changes in Lakeland. The Mountains and Fells haven't changed much, how can they, did not Nature design them that way, nor the Lakes and Tarns, another of God's gifts to us, though hold on, what if a 10 mph speed limit is introduced on Windermere? Yes, that could see a spectacular change by the time the next edition is due.

At present, there are 14,000 powered boats registered for Windermere. In theory, they can whiz around at 300 mph, should they be capable of it, but the ban currently being proposed by the Lake District Planning Board on anything whizzing over 10 mph would see them all disappear, plus several large boat businesses, water ski schools and a lot of jobs. The Cumbria Tourist Board, ever mindful of the tourist trade, and the investments of their members, appears to be against the ban. The Friends of the Lake District is for it. The Government will doubtless have to sort it out, probably with a public enquiry. Ah well, that'll mean nothing will be resolved for a few years yet.

Coming down the scale a bit, from our largest lake to one of our largest but lesser known tarns, there has been some good news about Overwater. It annoyed me for years, when I lived near Caldbeck, that Overwater, a tarn of 54 acres, was so unapproachable, sparkling and alluring from afar, the only stretch of decent water in the Northern Fells, yet inaccessible when you got near. Now it is no longer in private hands. It has been given to the National Trust by Lord Schon, well done, plus 14 acres of marginal land. Let's hope it will soon be opened up, for us all to enjoy.

Meanwhile, stand by your bunks. The important changes for this edition mainly concern Museums, Galleries, Hotels and Restaurants. These are always the hardest sections to research, as places will close, go off, change their format the moment after you've been there. (So always ring in advance, just to check.) The closures, on the whole, have been few and relatively minor, such as the demise of the little railway museum in Keswick, though it is sad to report that Belle Isle is now closed to the public.

The openings, however, have been many – some of them major. Who would have thought that in such a short space of time, and in a period of recession, so many new ventures would have started. In the last edition, we had no mining or mineral museums – now there will be three in Lakeland. One in Cockermouth, one in Caldbeck and a big outdoor one opening at Threlkeld. Of specialist interest, certainly, but very worthwhile.

There are also some big new projects, all doing good business. Tullie House Museum and Gallery in Carlisle is the biggest, but it's partly a revamp, extending an existing site at a cost of £5 million. It's already a spectacular, award winning success, with 300,000 visitors in its first year.

Then there are three completely new enterprises which deserve individual applause. Clap, clap, clap for:

The Old Laundry, Bowness-on-Windermere

This was at one time a laundry, then latterly a disused boat house, till in 1991 a couple from Sheffield, Charlotte Scott – originally from Bowness – and Roger Glossop, decided to buy and convert it, using private money and bank loans. They are both set designers, so they know about knocking stuff about. He has worked for the Royal Shakespeare Company and Alan Ayckbourn's theatre at Scarborough. They call their new venture a Visitor Centre, which is a bit misleading, smacking of council involvement.

It's a 3D trip round the world of Beatrix Potter, leading you along a sylvan path passed tableaux from her lovely books, plus a video and film show. Very well done, state of the art design, compared with those dusty, musty old sets they used to have at Brockhole. Highly commercial. You enter through the caff, then come up into the souvenir shop, before you've even got to the exhibits, but very professional. And incredibly popular. In their first year, starting from scratch, they had 117,000 visitors. Eat your heart out, Dove Cottage, Hill Top and Brantwood, Lakeland's 'real' literary shrines.

A quarter of their visitors are Japanese. Should you be watching the film, and the majority of the audience happens to be Japanese, don't be confused when the sound track comes on in Japanese. English speakers will find English on their head phones.

They have also built a brand new theatre, which is usually a quick way of losing money, especially in Lakeland where trade is so seasonal. It's a theatre in the round, holding up to 300, and they hope to put on a new Ayckbourn every summer, plus other companies and local shows. So, a welcome addition to Bowness's attractions. Shame about the parking. If you don't happen to be already based in Bowness, you have to use the council parking lot nearby, which is very expensive.

Cars of the Stars, Keswick

In 1987, a young dentist called Peter Nelson was driving along in his 1946 MG TC from his home at Applethwaite, just under Skiddaw, to his surgery in Keswick when he was flagged down by a stranger. Not the cops, or a hold up, but a researcher from Granada TV wanting to use his car in a film series called Spoils of War. He let them rent it, for a suitable fee, and after it was over he began to think – what happens afterwards to all those cars which appear in films and TV? So began a hunt which took over his life. And his bank balance. He's the son of a policeman, born in Carlisle, brought up in Whitehaven, with no private means, apart from his dental work.

He tracked down one of the two original Chitty Chitty Bang Bangs to Australia - and found the asking price was around £200,000. Gulp. He came back, took his wife out to dinner, and said he had to buy it - but the only way was to sell their house at Applethwaite. Which they did, moving into rooms above his Keswick surgery.

He now has 25 original vehicles, as seen in TV and films, including three James Bond cars, the Batmobile, a Laurel and Hardy Model T Ford, Thunderbird's pink Rolls Royce and Del Boy's Reliant Van. The latter cost him only £995, bought through a classified ad. When the BBC decided to make another series of Only Fools and Horses, he rented it back to them.

His cars are on show at his recently opened museum in Kewsick, housed in a converted garage. Last year, they attracted 50,000 visitors. His Mum and Dad help out, and so do his brothers. He hopes to add at least one new car every year, and is aiming for 80,000 visitors. The exhibit is unique, not just to Lakeland, but the world. He's still a dentist, by the way, but he takes a day and a half off each week to track down cars.

Senhouse Roman Museum, Maryport

By comparison, this newcomer is a more modest affair, but it provides an opportunity to see the country's oldest private collection of Roman remains. It was begun in 1570 by John Senhouse who collected bits and pieces from the site of Maryport's Roman Fort. William Camden visited him in 1599 and commended 'that worthy Gentleman' for saving so many inscribed stones. For twelve generations, members of the Senhouse Family preserved and added to the collection, displaying it for their friends in their local stately home, Netherhall. The house has now gone, and the direct family died out, but the collection was kept together and finally put on public show for the first time in 1990. It is now housed in The Battery, a Victorian naval building on a cliff just outside Maryport. There are only three rooms, and despite the sexual nature of their magnificent Roman altars (spot the phallic symbols), they are unlikely to attract the mass market. So far, they are averaging 6,000 visitors a year, which is good going, considering. "Every day I pray for rain", says Lindsey William, BA (Cantab), the museum's manager. "That always brings in people".

Tourism

As I write, the recession is still with us and hotels and restaurants everywhere have been complaining about the decline if not the death of their business. Even Miller Howe has felt it. In the Eighties, they were 96% full, every year, all year, from opening day in March till closing in December. Amazing. Last year, they had their first drop for over a decade – down by 18%.

Lakeland had not suffered as much as the rest of the country, but it's been hard luck on any new places trying to attract customers. Two hotels at the top end of the market spent around £1m each on refurbishments – Underscar and Tarn Hows – and reopened with great and lavish hopes. Plus quite a few empty bedrooms. If they can survive in lean times, they should do well in the future. It's about time Sharrow Bay and Miller Howe had a bit of competition in the luxury market.

The Time Share boom seems to be over. Keswick Bridge has suffered serious financial troubles. The brave new Marina at Maryport also hit problems. Let's hope this will not hold back the general development of the harbour site.

There have been two interesting changes in the pattern of Lakeland tourism. The attempt to move people away from the honeypot areas, especially at the height of the season, is at last succeeding. The pavements in Bowness, Ambleside, Grasmere and Keswick will probably be hell in August for another few decades yet, but there are signs that sensible people are making more expeditions to the West Coast or the Eden Valley to escape the hordes. Carlisle, now that it has been cleaned up and become culture conscious, has hit a mini boom. The Tourist Information Centre in the Old Town Hall had 200,000 visitors last year.

The other trend is more surprising. In our last edition, we published a survey which revealed that only 7% of visitors came to Lakeland in January, February and March. Given the generally accepted image of Lakeland weather, who can blame them. The latest figures show that now 14% of visitors take a winter visit. Why the sudden jump? Hard to say. There are more facilities available, such as winter services on Windermere and Derwentwater. Dove Cottage does winter courses and other cultural centres now offer winter programmes. It all helps.

Lakeland is romantic in frost and snow. All our hotels are built for bad weather. So think on. Far better than a winter break in fog bound Gatwick.

Residents

Farmers are moaning, so what's new, as their land and stock decline in value, but some are showing unusual enterprise. A farmer near Keswick has starting selling off his dry stone walls to builders – 1,500 metres for £15,000. This is clearly reprehensible, tut tut, as these walls are part of Lakeland's heritage. Lakeland slates are also highly desirable, selling for £1,000 a ton, thanks to the Planning Board insisting on their use. This has resulted in barns and even occupied houses having their roofs stripped in the middle of the night by slate robbers.

A much better solution for any farmer having financial problems is to do Sunday lunches. Farm teas don't make much profit, and are hardly worth bothering with, but a full scale meal in a real farm house can have punters queueing round the farm yard. I know one at Uldale where you have to book up three months ahead and another near Greystoke where the meals are better than most restaurants. The farmer is still a full-time farmer, but on Sundays he and his family put on their best shirts, carve the best joints, make the yummy puddings which Cumbrian wives have always made, and create for themselves a handy cash crop.

Another source of rural income is to spruce up your old barns for people wanting cheap accommodation. These camping barns, or stone tents as they are known, had 4,500 guests last year. I had the great honour of unveiling one at Loweswater. Look out for the Plaque.

House prices in Lakeland, best parts, have not collapsed the way they have in the rest of Britain, thanks to the competition from outsiders wanting a Lakeland escape. This is accentuating the old problem of dead villages, lived in only part of the year. Even in a fairly remote village like Bassenthwaite, 32 out of its 180 houses are now second homes. In Langdale and Patterdale, the proportion is much higher, around 40%. Where will it end? Villages as museums?

Meanwhile in the towns, locals are ever welcoming. Outside the Rembrandt Restaurant in Keswick, I saw a notice saying 'No shirt, no service'. And at the back of the Oddfellows Arms a sign said 'Eat you own fish and chips on my tables and I will charge you £5 per person. Thank you'. It was the thank you bit I liked.

Finally, some words of warning. At Whitehaven magistrates court a youth on a drugs charge had in his possession what the police thought were some white amphetamine tablets. When analysed, it turned out to be Kendal Mint Cake. So, if you are buying any bars as presents to take home, do keep the wrappers on. Enjoy.

Hunter Davies
Loweswater, 1993

Chapter One

Planning

BASSENTHWAITE LAKE AND SKIDDAW
LAKE DISTRICT NATIONAL PARK
CUMBERLAND
GO IN COMFORT—BY TRAIN

Things to know before leaving home – or bear in mind when you have just arrived.

Location Is that all it is, that little hilly region up in the top left hand corner of the map of England? How can so much fuss have been made for the last 200 years over such a small area? Ah, but in that pocket handkerchief are all nature's delights, plus quite a few man-made wonders. As you will quickly discover.

The Lake District is all in the County of Cumbria, formerly Cumberland and Westmorland, which is now England's second largest county in terms of acreage. There is a large circle inside the county which is called the Lake District National Park, a boundary line which at times appears perverse, cutting out some parts of Cumbria which are equally beautiful, but this inner circle contains the jewels in the crown. The National Park area is only thirty miles across, not much bigger than Greater London.

It is bordered today on its east side by the M6 motorway. If you were driving fast, you could pass the Lake District in half an hour and never know it was there. What a tragedy that would be.

What is it? It's a load of very old lakes and mountains covering an area of some 880 square miles. The mountains are high compared with other British mountains, and there are four over 3,000 feet, and the lakes are big in British terms, with one being 10 miles long, but as far as the world's biggest mountains and the largest lakes are concerned, they are but pimples.

It has been called lots of things. The Cumbria Tourist Board, having billed it for years as "English Lakeland - the Most Beautiful Corner of England" then changed it, according to the slogan on their envelopes, "Lakeland - the Roots of Heaven". It is also known as the English Lakes, The Lakes, Lakeland. You can use a permutation of several

9

words. We intend to call it the Lake District, or sometimes LD if space is short, meaning that part of Cumbria designated as the Lake District National Park.

How to Get There

Road   Most visitors zoom up the M6 by car from the South. As Motorways go, it can be surprisingly attractive, far less crowded than those horrible race-track stretches further South, around Manchester and Birmingham. After Lancaster, you begin to see real scenery, then once into Cumbria, hurrah, there are real mountains. Watch out for the police. Empty stretches of Cumbrian Motorway can make the mind wander, the heart soar, and the speedometer rise above 70mph.

From London, the distance by Motorway to Kendal, the Southern gateway to the Lakes, is about 260 miles. Turn left at Junctions 36 or 37. For the Northern Lakes, heads

down for Penrith, another 20 or so miles, then turn left at Junction 40 for Ullswater or Keswick. Mad drivers can get to the Lakes in four hours from London. We generally take six hours on family trips, with two stops, one for a picnic and one for watering the animals.

The M6 proper peters out just north of Carlisle, but those coming down from Scotland, from Glasgow or Edinburgh, do have reasonably good dual carriageways most of the way till they reach the Motorway. There are two useful Tourist Information Centres on the Motorway, when you're heading to the Lakes. On the northern stretch, just south of Carlisle, there's one at Southwaite Service Station. From the south, drivers can stock up on free literature at Forton Service Station, just south of Lancaster.

If you're approaching the Lake District from the East, then it's hard cheese. The roads over the Pennines are pretty, and the one over Hartside Pass, via Alston, is sensational, but they can take forever as they are narrow and twisty, even some of the so-called main or A roads. First timers should never try a short cut or attempt a minor road. You might never be seen again.

Rail There is no direct train into the Lakes. You have to change at Oxenholme, and even then you can only travel as far as Windermere, the only railway line inside the Lakes. There were others, but they have all gone. It means that Oxenholme, a toy town station, hardly more than a halt, becomes in the summer a meeting place for all the rucksacks in the Western World. But Oxenholme is on the main intercity route, from Euston up to Carlisle and Scotland, and you can get there by train from most British cities, far quicker than by roads. Best train times:

> **London** - 3 hours
> **Birmingham** - 2 hours 15 minutes
> **Manchester** - 1 hour 30 minutes
> **Liverpool** - 2 hours
> **Glasgow** - 2 hours 15 minutes
> **Edinburgh** - 2 hours 15 minutes

Other Stations Penrith also has a station, but you then have to transfer by bus or other means to the Lakes. Carlisle is a main line station and connects with the amazing Cumbria coastal route - however did Beeching never kill it? - which hugs the west coast. Very handy for exploring the western Lakes and Furness, though it never actually touches any of the Lakes. (For transport *inside* the Lakes, see Chapter Three.)

By planning ahead, you can take advantage of *large* savings with a special saver ticket, or a Student Railcard, but it can take a large amount of time, working out all the conditions, most of which seem to have been dreamed up for your inconvenience.

Airport There is no large Lakeland airport, though Carlisle does have a little one. Contact the airport manager, 'phone 0228 573641. If you own a private plane, this would be the handiest place to land. (And if you own a private plane, would you also like to buy a private publishing company?).

Blackpool also has an airport, 'phone 0253 43061. The nearest international airports are Newcastle, 'phone 091 286 0966, or Manchester 061 489 3000.

Sea   Despite all that water which surrounds Cumbria on three sides, there are no regular passenger boats these days to any Cumbrian ports. The nearest is Heysham in North Lancs, 'phone 0524 853802.

Coming from Abroad   Before arriving in Britain, it is possible to get information and advice about a holiday in the Lakes by contacting the nearest local office of the British Tourist Authority. Most major cities in the US and most capital cities elsewhere have a BTA office.

Coming from London English Tourist Board, Thames Tower, Black's Road, Hammersmith, London W6 9EL. 'Phone: 081-846 9000.

Tourist Information in Cumbria

Cumbria Tourist Board, Ashleigh, Holly Road, Windermere, Cumbria. Phone: Windermere 05394 44444.

When you are planning your holiday, tell them in advance your special interest or problem. This is their HQ address, where you can write or telephone, but don't call in person.

When you actually get to Cumbria, there are lots of local tourist information offices you can visit in the flesh. We'll come to them later in Chapter two.

Tourist Information   A 24 hour service of recorded events information is available on 05394 46363.

Radio Cumbria broadcasts tourist information on 397m (AM) and 95.6 (FM), or if you're in South Cumbria try Radio Furness on 358m (MW) and 96.1 (FM).

Weather Weather forecasts for the Lake District are available each day after 0800 on 05394 45151. These are usually reliable and essential if you are planning a day's walking. An outlook for the following day is given after 1600. During the winter the same number gives walking conditions on the fell tops.

Also Met. Office 'Weathercall' line for Cumbria – 0891 500419. General picture and outlook.

Guide Books

Guide books to the Lakes first appeared around the 1770s. Since then, over 5,000 books have been published about the Lakes, more than on any similar sized region in the UK, so the choice is enormous and still growing.

Beware the over-glossy booklets with chocolate box covers with unbelievably blue skies and lakes. They have probably put their money and energy into colour reproduction at the expense of the words and new information. Also be wary of publications taking advertisements. How can they possibly give you real opinions?

Historic Books

☆ William Wordsworth, **Guide to the Lakes**. This was first published in 1835 but is now available from OUP in a facsimile edition. Fascinating reading, after you have had your holiday. Don't try to plan anything from it in advance. Notice how many subsequent Lakeland writers have pinched ideas and even phrases from Wordsworth, trying to capture the essence of Lakeland scenery.

☆☆ Dorothy Wordsworth, **Journals**. OUP. This is a facsimile of the Journals which Wordsworth's sister Dorothy kept of their life together at Dove Cottage in 1800-1802. It pays to know something of Wordsworth's life beforehand, to understand exactly what is going on, as it is very confused in parts but charming and illuminating descriptions of day to day life with her Beloved Brother, either helping him with his muse or baking his pies. Also now available in illustrated editions.

Educational Books

☆☆☆ **GCSE Resource Guides**. An ambitious series of books, aimed at GCSE students. Full of facts, information and ideas, presented in a lively manner. Four titles. Additional backup available in the form of fact sheets, video tapes and computer material. Published by the National Park Educational Service, Blencathra Centre, Threlkeld, Keswick 07687 79764.

☆☆ **Field Studies in Cumbria.** Published by Cumbria Education Committee - invaluable guide for all teachers looking for sites in Cumbria which they can visit for environment-based educational purposes.

☆☆ Susan Denyer, **Traditional Buildings and Life in the Lake District,** Gollancz, 1991. Best of the academic style books on the history of Lakes and buildings and every day life in the past. Full of human interest.

All Change! Published by the National Trust and Cumbria County Council. A teacher's pack on landscape conservation, for use in schools.

Walking Books

☆☆☆ **A. Wainwright, Pictorial Guide to the Lakeland Fells,** seven volumes previously published by *The Westmorland Gazette*, Kendal now acquired by Michael Joseph. Essential for all walkers. Wainwright divided the Lakes into seven areas, so buy the one you will be visiting most, or buy them all to take home and wonder at. In his own words and with his own pen (for there is not an ounce of printer's type in any of his books), he draws and describes exactly every walk up every fell you could possibly make. He spent thirteen years on his walks and though the first volume came out in 1955, they reprint endlessly and are still up to date, although you would hardly recognise some paths now from his descriptions. Each is a work of art, full of wit, wisdom and love of the Lakes. The first editions are collectors' pieces. Buy them **now** as they keep going up in price. They will be a joy for ever.

N.B. Joan Newsome, has devoted her retirement to providing index to all W's guides: "A companion to W's Lakeland Fells" pub. 1992.

☆☆ John Parker, **Walk The Lakes,** Bartholomew. A peculiar-looking, spiral-bound book (it's easy to mistake for a calendar) describing forty, easy low-level walks. Excellent for the less ambitious walker. Each of the forty walks is graded, described in detail (including what you can expect to see around you) and is accompanied by a one inch to the mile colour map of the area described. Warning: because of the idiosyncratic binding and layout, it is worth spending some time at home getting to know your way round the book *before* you set off on the walks. (Follow up book in 1983 **Walk the Lakes Again** - reissued in 1988 as **More Walk the Lakes** - different title, different cover, same contents. Naughty.)

☆ A. Wainwright, **Fellwalking with Wainwright,** Michael Joseph, 1984. Topped the British non-fiction lists but more a book to display on your coffee table so your friends all know you go walking in the Lake District.

☆☆ Colin Shelbourn, **Great Walks in the Lake District,** Ward Lock, 1987. Another coffee table book - when will publishers ever learn? - but superb colour photographs by David Ward and twenty-eight walks ranging from dead easy family strolls to day-long mountain hikes.

☆ Bob Allen, **On High Lakeland Fells,** Pic Publications 1987, plus **On Lower Lakeland Fells,** Michael Joseph, 1990. Real walkers stuff. Brilliant for ideas and route planning, with a good mix of personal anecdote and detailed route descriptions. Be wary of his estimates of time and exertion level – he must be very fit.

☆ **Rocky Rambler** L.D.N.P. 1992. By Iain Peters, illustrated by Colin Shelbourn. 'Wainwright for Tots' – a walking guide that puts the children in charge and lets them make the decisions. Good selection of walks, wonderfully presented and illustrated. Adults should definitely sneak out and buy it, and do the walks themselves.

General Books

☆☆ Norman Nicholson, **Portrait of the Lakes**, Hale. The late Norman Nicholson has been our most recent poet of the Lakes, born and bred in Millom. Good on history and geology. Perhaps the best-written present day book on Lakeland. Now out of print so look in second hand bookshops.

☆☆ AA - **Ordnance Survey Leisure Guide, Lake District**. First class production, excellent maps and very handy potted guides to the main places, arranged alphabetically. Short on comments but has almost all the facts that any beginner might want.

Stephen Kelly, **Victorian Lakeland Photographers,** Swan-Hill Press, 1991. All about the early photographers such as Abrahams, Mayson, Pettitt. Original research and fascinating illustrations..

☆ John Wyatt, **The Shining Levels**, Penguin. Not a guide book, but the story of one man's return to nature, amongst the Lakeland fells. A nice book to take home and read once the holiday is over.

☆ Norman Nicholson, **The Lake District - an Anthology**, Penguin. Marvellous selection of stuff written about Lakeland, from the 7th century onwards. (But no Beatrix Potter - couldn't he get permission?) Ideal for literary buffs and browsers.

☆ W. Rollinson, **Life and Tradition in the Lake District**, Dalesman. A most original work of non-fiction. Describes and illustrates the vanishing or vanished folk culture of Lakeland, from stone walls, sports, dialects to diet and folk medicine.

Hunter Davies, **A Walk Around the Lakes**, Dent. Dreadfully out of date, why do they keep buying it in their millions? But a joy to read, the most loved general book on the Lakes ever written. Unquote.

Maps

The ordinary Ordnance Survey Landranger maps (1:50 000 series), are not much good for the Lake District. They're detailed enough for walking, yet you have to buy seven to cover Cumbria. You could go mad, trying to work out the overlaps. So find a good map or bookshop and go for the more specialised maps.

☆☆☆ **OS Outdoor Leisure Maps** (1:25 000 scale 2 1/2 inches to the mile). They divide the Lakes into four - SE, SW, NE, NW. Worth investing in all four. A pity the cover drawings have been dumped in favour of gaudy photographs.

☆☆ **OS Lake District Touring Map** (1 inch to the mile). This does at least give you the whole of the Lakes on one map. (Well almost. They have cut a nasty slice off the top of Caldbeck.) Good detail, but a bit cumbersome to use for those who are only exploring one area of the Lakes.

OS Six Inch Maps (1:10 000 and 1:10 560). For the absolute specialist, wanting to know a lot about a very little chunk, 5 x 5km square, down to individual fields, they usually have to be ordered. Only available as flat maps.

☆☆ **Cumbria - English Lake District**, Cumbria Tourist Board's Touring Map. Revised in 1992. Has tons of tourist info on the back (though if you've already bought this book you won't need any of it).

☆☆☆ **The A-Z Lake District**, published by the A-Z map people in London. 1 inch to the mile but a lot easier to read on the move than the OS 1 inch and with visitor attractions and places to visit marked out and *named* on the map (no confusing symbols as on the CTB). Excellent for road touring.

☆☆ **Town Trails**. Available from TIC's. Visually pleasant. Jolly useful.

☆☆ **Lake District Lap Map**, published by Cardtoons Publications Ltd. A small, easy-to-use road map, designed for those who don't want the fuss and expense of larger-scale sheets. Loads of tourist info and suggested road tours on the back. Incredibly good value. (End of advt.)

Hint - A good source of local street maps are the estate agents - they usually have free ones available which are reasonably accurate.

Magazines

Lakeland magazines come and go. They tend to be short on opinions and true guidance, very cosy and old fashioned, but are normally reliable when it comes to listings. Being magazines, they are generally more up to date than any proper book with the latest details of Lakeland events. Even this wonderful book.

☆ **Cumbria**, monthly. Dalesman Publishing Co, Clapham, via Lancaster, Lancs. Rather old-fashioned.

☆ **Lakescene**, monthly, Townfoot Ind. Estate, Brampton. Folksy, but useful.

☆ **Cumbria Life**, quarterly, 32 Lowther Street, Carlisle. Gone glossy. Some good reading.

Newspapers

Best of all, for the *very* latest information, are the local papers. Here are the seven main ones, together with the areas they cover:

☆ **Whitehaven News** (Thursday) - Whitehaven and west coast of Cumbria. Queen Street, Whitehaven.

☆☆ **Cumberland News** (Friday) - Carlisle and N Lakes. Dalston Road, Carlisle.

☆☆ **Westmorland Gazette** (Friday) - Kendal and S Lakes. Stricklandgate, Kendal.

☆ **Barrow News** (Friday) - Barrow and Furness areas, round to Grange-over-Sands. Abbey Road, Barrow-in-Furness.

☆ **Cumberland & Westmorland Herald** (Saturday) - Penrith and E Lakeland. 14 King Street, Penrith.

☆ **West Cumberland Times & Star** (Friday) - Cockermouth and Workington. Oxford Street, Workington.

Keswick Reminder (every Friday) - Keswick and North Lakes. Station Street, Keswick. Worth it just to admire the prehistoric lay-out.

The Lakeland Echo - S. Lakeland free sheet, published Thursdays. Not so hot on news (the editorial wears money-tinted spectacles) but has a weekly listing of local events. 0539 730630.

The Lakes Leader - new competitor to the Echo, published Wednesdays. Far better on news, less good on events listings. Good for small ads. 0539 720555.

National Park Publications

☆☆☆ **The Lake District Guardian** - another freebie, published annually in vast quantities by the National Park Authority. Interesting articles plus a listing of visitor activities organised by the Park; guided walks, days with a ranger, farm open days. Available from TICs throughout the area. Residents get one delivered free with their local paper.

Events '93 - a useful NP publication (we'll leave it to you to guess the title for coming years). NP events for the whole of the season, including useful listings of talks and slide shows. Free from TICs.

When to Come?

If you have school age children, then you are lumbered with coming in the school holidays. August is always a wicked month. For pretty scenery, May and June, then September and October are the best months. May and June are also the driest months, whilst September and October are the most colourful, with the bracken and trees finally turning from green to brown to gold.

The winter snows can be dramatic, and the views sensational, but apart from the fells, which never close, most man-made Lakeland things shut in winter. 'The Season' in the Lakes is shorter than the so called summer season elsewhere in England where most things open up at Easter for the visitors. In Lakeland, you'll find that many of the major attractions are not fully operational until Whit.

The Weather

Fascinating. Yes, that's what I think. There are few places in the world where you can get such variations from place to place, from day to day, in such a short distance. If you don't like it, move on a few miles, or come down a few thousand feet. Naturally, it could be *worse*, but at least it is unlikely to be the same.

Now for some hard facts about Lakeland weather. South Devon gets more rain than Carlisle. Honestly. It's the high bits at the head of the valleys which give the Lake District a bad name for rainfall. Elsewhere in Lakeland, the rainfall is normal-to-dry for Britain.

Seathwaite, at the head of Borrowdale, is admittedly the wettest place in England, with 130 inches a year, but if you go to Keswick, just eight miles away, it drops dramatically to 51 inches a year. Move on another 20 miles, into the Solway Plain at Carlisle, then it is only 30 inches a year. Positively arid.

Keswick has milder winters than London - and it's sweltering in the winter compared with really cold places like New York or Berlin. Though there is a great variation from day to day in Lakeland villages and valleys, there are not enormous seasonal *extremes*. You will notice that shepherds and farmers tend to wear the same clothes all the year round - usually a jacket and trousers that don't match and old shoes or boots, which sometimes don't match either. Inside their cottages, the fire is often lit all around the year.

The summer can be hot - but don't bank on it. There has not been a summer in which I have not had a bathe in a Lakeland beck, if only for a few minutes, but it is best to come prepared, especially if you intend to do any climbing. It's always colder up top. And look out for mist. But note well, there is *never* any fog in the Lakes.

The nicest bonus of all for Lakeland lovers is that you get three quarters of an hour more daylight every summer's evening in the Lakes compared with London or the South. The weather often gets better as the day wears on and, with luck, you can have two days in one and organise two different expeditions. Climbers, even serious ones like Chris Bonington, often set out at six in the evening and get a day's climbing in before dark.

What to Wear

Clothes, they're terribly useful. They don't like you going naked in the Lakes. It frightens the sheep. As for *what* clothes, then that's up to you. The experts and the officials and the organisation men would have you dressed for a simple fell walk as if you are going up Everest, with oxygen masks and ice picks and very bright colours.

The most important rule for walkers, and I stress walkers not climbers, is that Comfort is All. The second rule is that it won't last. So it is best to take a pullover, even setting off in the sun, and some sort of raincoat or water-proof anorak. Shell suits are all the rage at the moment. At least they make you easier to spot if you get into diffi-culties on the fells. In the winter, or obvious bad weather, I take leggings as well. Third rule - always tell someone exactly where you are going and when you plan to return. Fourthly, take a whistle.

Climbing is a specialist sport, for which some partici-pants dress like space explorers, but we'll discuss that later. Walking is natural. There's no secret. All you do is put one foot in front of the other. Easy peasy.

As for footwear, I walked happily for twenty years on the fells with plimsolls in summer and wellingtons in winter. Now, for winter and bad weather, I have to admit I've recently changed to lightweight boots. After two cartilage operations, caused by football not walking, I found that wellingtons hurt my calves. I now love my boots, but there is no need for you to buy them, if you don't want to. Nor any need to buy fancy climbing socks, pretty though they look, or those natty plus fours in that thick hairy tweed. I once got a pair as a present, and I looked terrific in them, but they itched like hell and I now never wear them. Have a second glance at the next shepherd you see working on the fells. How many are wearing climbing boots, plus fours and carrying ropes? Well then.

Accidents

What do you do if something awful happens? In the first edition of this book we gave no advice, but since then the accident rate has enormously increased. (Not our fault, I hope.) In the second edition, we reported that 1984 saw the highest number of deaths on Lake District Mountains since records began. Sadly, that record was broken again in 1991, with a total of 27 deaths. The Mountain Rescue teams were called out for a total number of 368 incidents in 1991 including 48 with helicopters. Often the call outs are due to people being lost, or coming down in the wrong place and not notifying base. A large number of the injuries, however, can occur on wet grass, when it is very easy to slip. Plimsolls and wellingtons aren't much use here.

Rock climbers and specialist sportsmen and women have their own set of rules and guide lines. However, all users of the fells and mountains should take great care. In the events of a serious accident, do the following:

Summon help by six long whistle blasts, or torch flashes if you have one, then repeat after a minute. This is the recognised distress signal on mountains.

Go for help, if one of your party is able to, having made the injured person comfortable and administered any first aid. It is vital to memorise the exact spot, working out on the map the grid reference if possible.

Telephone for help, when you can find a box or the nearest farm. Dial Police 999. (You don't call out the Mountain Rescue Teams. The police will do this.)

You will be asked location of injured person, time of accident, nature of accident - they need to know this to decide if a helicopter is necessary. The vital information is you will be asked to stand by the telephone, so the rescue team can reach you first.

The police will then contact the nearest Mountain Rescue team. There are fifteen in all, based at Keswick, Coniston, Cockermouth, Ambleside, Kendal, Furness, Penrith, Patterdale, Wasdale, Millom, Kirkby Stephen, plus two Outward Bound Rescue Teams, a Dog Team (Search & Rescue Dog Association – SARDA – English Lakes Section) and RAF Helicopter team based in Humberside and Northumberland. When the leader is contacted he goes to his base HQ and puts out an emergency call to all his members. As soon as the first four arrive, usually including a doctor, they set off by Land Rover, taking first aid and radio equipment. They do a brilliant job. All voluntary. Please support them.

Winter Walking Increasingly, people are taking to the fells in winter and it is worth carrying and *knowing how to use* an ice axe if you plan to go on the high fells in snow conditions. The National Park runs a training scheme - details from Brockhole or one of the specialist outdoor shops.

Grid References Just in case you have forgotten, tut tut, this is how you work them out. They are always given in a group of six figures, such as 342 152, which in this case is the summit of Helvellyn, and they refer to a precise if 'imaginary' small square on an OS map.

To find the exact site taking the example above, look firstly for 34 on the top or bottom margins of your Ordnance Survey map. Because the third figure is 2, you must look right two tenths of a square.

Now look for the 15 on either of the side margins and from this line count up two tenths of a square.

Hospitals

Assuming the accident is not too serious, and you can hobble or somehow get back on your own to your own transport, you might still want medical attention. Be careful. You might look up the nearest hospital in the telephone book and be unaware that it's only a titchy one, a cottage hospital perhaps, without any X-ray facilities or even doctors on the premises. This recently happened to a reader from Nottingham. She had been walking round Ullswater, as recommended by this very wonderful guide book, when a six year old in the party fell on a flat piece of grass, and appeared to have broken her leg. They looked up Hospitals in the *Good Guide* (first edition, alas, which didn't have them), so they worked out that the nearest town must be Penrith. They raced to Penrith, found the hospital, but were told the X-ray machine operator had gone off as it was after three o'clock. So back in the car and a mad dash up the M6 to Carlisle where they eventually found the Cumberland Infirmary. The leg was X-rayed, found to be broken, and treated. "They were very kind to us stupid trippers."

Here's a list of hospitals, just in case it happens to you. Hospitals starred have doctors available 24 hours a day and can cope with major accidents (though Kendal may refer people to Lancaster). The others all call on local GP's or refer to nearest large hospital. Again, they will do this

24 hours a day, but for minor accidents, GP's are often available at the hospital where times have been indicated.

South Cumbria:

☆ **Furness General Hospital,** Barrow-in-Furness
Tel: 0229 870876

☆ **Westmorland General Hospital,** Burton Road, Kendal. Tel: 0539 732288

West Cumbria:

☆ **West Cumberland Hospital,** Hensingham, Whitehaven. Tel: 0946 693181

Cockermouth Cottage Hospital, Isel Road, Cockermouth. Tel: 0900 822226

Victoria Cottage Hospital, Ewanrigg Road, Maryport. Tel: 0900 812634

Workington Infirmary, Infirmary Road, Workington. Tel: 0900 602244. (GP available 9am-12 noon, Mon-Fri)

North & East Cumbria:

☆ **Cumberland Infirmary,** Newtown Road, Carlisle. Tel: 0228 23444

Keswick Cottage Hospital, Crosthwaite Road, Keswick. Tel: 07687 72012. (GP and X-ray available, GP. 9.30-12 noon, X-ray 9.30-12.30)

Penrith New Hospital, Bridge Lane, Penrith. Tel: 0768 63647. (X-ray Dept. 10am-12 noon, 1pm-3pm, Mon-Fri).

Early Closing and Market Days

Unlike London and most Southern towns, Lakeland shopkeepers still often have one half day off every week when they close at lunch time. There is no geographical consistency. The favourite half day tends to be Thursdays, though several choose Wednesday and a handful opt for Tuesdays. It does not mean that *every* shop in that particular town or village will be closed. Many of the big ones and chain stores stay open. But you have been warned.

Market days are worth noting. They are often in covered market halls, selling mainly local vegetables and produce, clothes and domestic stuff. Often very colourful and full of country folk. Rarely something exotic to buy, but the faces are studies in themselves. Especially the egg ladies.

Early Closing (EC) and Market Days (M)

Alston: EC Tue; No Market. **Ambleside:** EC Thu (winter only); M Wed. **Appleby:** EC Thu; M Sat. **Arnside:** EC Thu; No Market. **Askam-in-Furness:** EC Weds; No Market.

Aspatria: EC Thurs; No Market. **Barrow-in-Furness:** EC Thu; M Wed, Fri and Sat. **Brampton:** EC Thu; M Wed. **Brough:** EC Thu; M Mon. **Broughton-in-Furness** EC Thu; M Tue. **Carlisle:** EC Thu; M Mon to Sat (except Thu pm). **Cleator Moor:** EC Wed, M Fri. **Cockermouth:** EC Thu; M Mon. **Coniston:** EC Thurs; No Market. **Dalton-in-Furness:** EC Wed; M Tue. **Egremont:** EC Wed; M Fri. **Grange-over-Sands:** EC Thu; No Market. **Grasmere:** EC Thu; No Market. **Hawkshead:** EC Thu (Winter only); No Market. **Kendal:** EC Thu; M, Wed and Sat. **Keswick:** EC Wed; M Sat. **Kirkby Lonsdale:** EC Wed; M Thu. **Kirkby Stephen:** EC Thu; M Mon. **Longtown:** EC Wed; No Market. **Maryport:** EC Wed; M Fri. **Millom:** EC Wed; No Market. **Milnthorpe:** EC Thu; M Fri. **Penrith:** EC Wed; M Tue and Sat. **Sedbergh**: EC Thu; M Wed. **Shap:** EC Thu and Sat; M Mon. **Silloth**: EC Tue; M Sun. **Ulverston:** EC Wed; M Thu and Sat. **Whitehaven:** EC Wed; M Thu and Sat. **Wigton:** EC Wed; M Tue. **Windermere:** EC Thu; No Market. **Workington:** EC Thu; M Wed and Sat.

Calendar of Events

Check with the local newspapers, or with any of the tourist information centres for the precise dates each year of the following Big annual events. Bear them in mind when planning your holiday.

Note Don't worry if you can't understand some of the words at this stage. No, Egremont Crab Fair has nothing to do with fish. We'll come to fuller descriptions of the major events and activities in Chapter Fourteen.

April

International Festival of Mime and Dance, Kendal - late April. Contact Brewery Arts Centre for details.

May

Model Boat Rally, Windermere.
Cartmel Races - Bank Holiday weekend.

June

Appleby Horse Fair - second Wednesday.
Warcop Rushbearing - St Peter's Day (June 29) or preceding Saturday if the 29th is a Sunday.

July

Ambleside Rushbearing - first on 2nd Saturday.
Great Musgrave Rushbearing - first Saturday.
Lakeland Rose Show, Grange-over-Sands - 2nd weekend.
Lake Windermere Festival - one week, early July.
Cumberland Show, Carlisle - next to last Thursday.
Penrith Show - Saturday (date flexible).
Keswick Convention - religious convention, two weeks, mid-July.
Wordsworth Summer Conference - late July or early August. Details from Dove Cottage.

August

Ambleside Sports - Thursday before the first Monday.

L.D. Summer Music Festival, Ambleside - early August.

Cockermouth Show - Saturday before the first Monday.

Grasmere Rushbearing - Saturday nearest St Oswald's day (5th).

Cartmel Show - Wednesday after first Monday.

Gosforth Show - third Wednesday.

Grasmere Sports - third Thursday after first Monday.

Lake District Sheep Dog Trials - Thursday after first Monday.

Rydal Sheep Dog Trials - second Thursday after first Monday.

Skelton Agricultural Show Penrith - third Saturday.

Carlisle Great Fair - third Saturday for about ten days.

Patterdale Sheep Dog Trials - Bank Holiday Saturday.

Keswick Show - Bank Holiday Monday.

Ennerdale Show - last Wednesday.

Lake Artists' Society Annual Exhibition, Grasmere - August and first week in September.

Lowther Horse Trials and Country Fair - weekend in early August.

Kendal Gathering - late August (date flexible).

Hawkshead Show - late August.

Kendal Folk Festival - August Bank Holiday. Contact Brewery Arts Centre.

September

Westmorland County Show, Kendal - second Thursday.

Egremont Crab Fair - third Saturday.

Loweswater Show - third Thursday.

Urswick Rushbearing, Ulverston - Sunday nearest St Michael's Day (29th)

Eskdale Show - last Saturday.

Borrowdale Show - 3rd Sunday

October

Wasdale Show - second Saturday.

Wigton Horse Sales - last Wednesday.

Windermere Power Boat Record Week - late October. Contact Low Wood Hotel on Ambleside 33338.

Kendal Jazz Festival - late October. Contact Brewery Arts Centre for details.

Windermere Marathon - Sunday in late October. Contact Bowness Bay or Windermere TIC.

November

Biggest Liar in the World Competition, Santon Bridge. Contact Civic Hall, Whitehaven.

Chapter Two

Background Briefing

The Promenade, Bowness.

All you need to know about Lakeland geology and history, plus the National Park today and its wonderful services . . .

Having arrived in the Lakes, the first thing is to try to get your bearings, not just how to get out of the bedroom or undo the tent flap, but to work out the shape of things to come, as well as the history and background and organisation of the area you will shortly be exploring.

It was Wordsworth who first likened the shape of the Lakes to a wheel, with the lakes and dales radiating from the centre like the spokes of the wheel. It's a good description. Things do radiate from a centre and it is very hard jumping from one spoke to another. To get to the outer spokes, especially on the West, you still have to make some very tortuous journeys.

But a handier image in your head is to think of the Lakes as *two* wheels, one in the North radiating from Keswick and the other in the South, radiating from Ambleside. Though the two towns are only fifteen miles apart, separated by the pass at Dunmail Raise, they often seem to be in different countries. They even talk differently, with the folks round Windermere and Coniston sounding almost Lancashire, while the rougher folks up North appear to have a Scottish influence in their dialect, at least to Southern ears.

The natives hardly move between the two divisions, but then Cumbrian natives have traditionally hardly moved anywhere. They often consider the folks in the next dale as foreigners. Most visitors who stay in the Northern Lakes, with Keswick as the nearest town, tend to stick there, exploring the lakes and mountains nearby. In the South, they look towards Ambleside and Windermere. Deciding to cross Dunmail Raise then becomes a major expedition.

Start by acquiring a general feeling of Lakeland as a

whole, then concentrate on the names and places and character of the area where you are based. In a week's holiday, you will probably hardly venture into the other section. That will be for your next visit.

Geology

Yes, a tough subject to take in for absolute beginners, but come on, we can zip through it quickly. It's well worth it.

Roughly speaking, there are three major rock bands running across the Lake District and they have created three different types of scenery and buildings.

In the North, there are the Skiddaw Slates which give rounded, smooth hills and gentle horizons with not a great deal of colour. One result is that Skiddaw is relatively safe to climb with no dangerous crags. Skiddaw Slates were formed under the sea about 500 million years ago from shales and mudstones and are inherently weak. Skiddaw is considered to be the oldest mountain in Europe and the Lakeland hills as a whole are amongst the oldest in the world, more ancient even than the Alps or Himalayas.

The central zone is dominated by a band of Borrowdale Volcanic rocks which came just as the Skiddaw Slates had been laid down. Violent volcanic explosions threw up a much harder, more jagged rock and created dramatic, angular sky lines, such as Scafell and the Langdales. They're perfect for rock climbers. Something to get hold of, yet not fall off. They hope. The rocks and resultant vegetation are very colourful, rich in reds, pinks and greens, and provide technicolour autumn views for the photographers as well as the best rock climbs in England.

Next came the Silurian period, about 400 million years ago, and this resulted in a band across South Lakeland known as the Silurian Slates. These again have left more rounded hills. The distinctive green slate of the Coniston area, which you see in walls and roofs, are from this period. Around the edge of the Lake District, there are two other distinctive rock formations which should be mentioned - sandstone on the West Coast and in the Carlisle and Eden Valley area, which can clearly be seen in the local buildings, and limestone in the South and towards the Pennines.

Just to mess up these rather neat divisions, along came the Ice Age. It was quite recent really, under 2 million years ago. Everything was then put in the melting pot, or in this case the freezing pot, and the final shape of the Lakes eventually emerged. The effects of glaciation are easy to see, and much loved by school teachers on field courses. The valley floors were swept clean, tarns and lakes scooped out, valley heads built up, debris dumped, deltas formed, and all those cwms and corries created, the sort we all learned about at school. The variety, once again, is incredible for such a small area. Little wonder that for the last 200 years, the Lake District has become an adventure playground for geologists.

History

If there were inhabitants before the Ice Age, they left no clues, not even an ancient Kendal Mint wrapper. The earliest evidence possibly suggests some sort of primitive Stone Age settlements on the West coast, round about 4,000 BC.

There are quite a few definite Bronze and Iron Age remains scattered throughout the Lakes, such as stone circles and burial areas, but none as dramatic as elsewhere in England. Several are popular tourist attractions, notably Castlerigg near Keswick and Long Meg near Penrith.

The Romans They came, saw and conquered, led by Agricola who marched north to Carlisle, but stuck mainly to the plain. You will see on the OS maps of Lakeland numerous references to Roman remains but they are mostly small, though some are fairly interesting. To actually see first class Roman remains, you must go to Hadrian's Wall. Fortunately for all Lake District visitors, the Wall is quite near and has the best Roman military remains in the whole world.

The Celts After the Romans departed, around 400AD, the natives were left to their own devices, till the hordes of invaders from the coasts of Western Europe started arriving.

The ancient Celts clung on to their old ways for a long time in Central Lakeland, just as the Celtic people did in Wales, and there are strong connections between them. They each called themselves Cymry, or Cymri, hence Cumbria. There are many Celtic place names in Cumbria to this day which sound Welsh - such as those beginning with *pen*, meaning head or hill, as in Penrith or Penruddock; or *blaen* meaning summit, as in Blencathra or Blencow. Helvellyn *sounds* decidedly Welsh, though so far the experts have failed to explain its derivation.

The Invaders The Anglo Saxons invaded mainly the softer and easier Eastern coasts of England, though they did reach some of the fertile plains on the western slopes of the Lakes and their characteristic Anglian name endings of *ham* or *ton* can be seen in Brigham and Dearham, Dalton and Alston.

It was the Norse, rather than the Danes or Saxons, who colonised Cumbria, coming down the West Coast of Scotland to Ireland and the Isle of Man and establishing settlements in Cumbria. Some of the most typical Lakeland words have Norse origins - dales coming from *dalr*, fells from *fjall*, becks from *bekkr*, tarns from *tjorns*, and force (meaning waterfall) from *foss*. The ending 'thwaite', which you see everywhere, is Norse, meaning a clearing in the forest.

The Borders

The northern half of present day Cumbria, the old Cumberland, has had its history, and its personality, fashioned by the very fact of being on the border between England and Scotland. For several centuries, there was constant conflict, looting and pillaging. Families and villages would swap loyalties, depending on who they thought would win. Much of Cumberland was in fact part of Scotland for many years. It has been romanticised by the novels of Walter Scott, but until as recently as the 18th century, it was a dangerous place in which to live. Many isolated North Cumbrians, even today, can be suspicious folk, preferring to winter you, then summer you, and winter you again. Then if you're lucky, they might say hello.

The legacy of all this Border conflict has been a large number of castles, fortified houses and pele towers, not beside the Lakes and Mountains themselves, but well away in the surrounding towns and plains such as Carlisle, Penrith, Cockermouth and Kendal. This was where the nobs lived and they were very keen on protecting themselves. Up on the fells, there was really not much worth stealing. Life, such as it was, went on, whether it was Agricola, William the Conqueror, Bonny Prince Charlie or Henry VIII who was out there causing all that nuisance, starting wars, leading rebellions or pinching land. The people who lived in the Lakes were 'statesmen', small time farmers with small estates and small farmhouses, much as they are today.

A Lakeland Cottage

Trades and Industries

You'll see an awful lot of sheep in the Lakes, and not all of them are wearing orange anoraks. The four footed versions might well be Herdwicks, the native Cumbrian breed, which is supposed to have originally come from

28

Spain, 400 years ago, when an Armada galleon was wrecked on the Cumbrian coast. Only a legend. Latest research indicates they were here in Roman times. They have white faces and only the males have horns. They have black wool when young which gets greyer with age. They never get fat and no wonder, living the life they lead out on the most barren of fells in the most barren of winters. They are reputed to be the hardiest breed of all sheep and when really hungry will eat their own wool to stay alive. (Well, they suck out the oils, just to keep themselves going.) There are fewer Herdwicks than there were and they are now in danger of becoming a rare breed. The more common breed are the Swaledales which are darker faced, with a light nose, and both sexes have horns.

Naturally, with all those sheep the woollen industry has always been strong in Cumbria. Kendal was the heart of it for six centuries and local cloths were known throughout the land. Shakespeare in Henry IV refers to a material as Kendal Green. It was a cottage industry in those days, with endless strings of pack horses carrying the raw and finished goods in and out of the town.

With the industrial revolution, Carlisle became a busy manufacturing centre for the cotton industry, till the main mass trade eventually moved to Lancashire and Yorkshire, though Carlisle today still has some high quality mills.

Mining in the Lake District is equally ancient and the Romans exploited the lead mines round Alston. All over the Northern fells you will find old mines, and round Coniston, one or two of which come back into temporary use as the price of the minerals goes up, or close when the prices fall. There is also extensive quarrying.

Heavy industry in Cumbria has always been restricted to the West, round Barrow and Millom, or up the coast around Maryport, Workington and Whitehaven, an important centre for many years for the coal and iron industries as well as shipping. At one time, around 1780, Whitehaven was the second port in the land after London - ahead of Liverpool and Bristol. It was one of the earliest planned towns in Europe.

The West Coast is now in decline, with heavy unemployment rather than heavy industry, though since the war some success has been made with new chemical and lighter industries, and the arrival of BNFL has been a huge financial boost to the area.

Today, the main industry of the Lake District is tourism, whatever the farmers will have you believe. Keswick, Ambleside and Windermere are largely tourist towns yet surprisingly, the towns just a few miles away are still *real* towns. Places like Penrith and Cockermouth, and to a lesser extent Kendal, are all market towns with old industries, hardly ruffled by slate lamps and signs boasting B and B in every second window.

Cumbria

The County today has a population of just under half a million (483,163 at the last count) and an area of 2,682 square miles. The County Council's main offices are in Carlisle (The Courts, Carlisle, telephone Carlisle 23456). There are six District Councils, four of which share the National Park between them - Copeland, Allerdale, Eden and South Lakeland.

District Councils

Barrow-in-Furness Borough Council, Town Hall, Duke St., Barrow. Tel: 0229 825500.

Carlisle City Council, Denton St., Carlisle. Tel: 0228 23411.

Copeland Borough Council, Catherine Street, Whitehaven. Tel: 0946 693111.

Allerdale District Council, Allerdale House, Workington. Tel: 0900 604351.

Eden District Council, Town Hall, Penrith. Tel: 0768 64671.

South Lakeland District Council, Head Office, Kendal. Tel: 0539 733333.

Lake District National Park

The National Park is that nice bit, right in the middle of Cumbria, but what *is* a National Park? Yes, visitors are always asking that. Read on.

There are eleven National Parks in England and Wales and the Lake District National Park, set up in 1951, is the biggest, covering 880 square miles. It is looked after by the Lake District Special Planning Board (also likes to call itself the National Park Authority, or NPA) which protects the area for both farmers and holidaymakers. It doesn't own the land (the single biggest landowner is the National Trust with nearly a quarter of the land within the Park boundary) but has control over planning and development. They are very strict about all new buildings and are currently trying hard to restrict any more second homes (which currently account for nearly one fifth of all homes in the Lake District) and to limit the number of timeshares and leisure centres invading the area. People feel quite proud to be residents of the National Park, as if they were living in one of nature's listed buildings - until they want to add a new window or put a bed in the barn and they come up against the battle to get planning permission and they wish they were just a few feet outside the boundary. But they do a worthwhile job in protecting the Lake District for us all, keeping an eye on developments, protecting footpaths and open land. Once you get above the field line you can walk almost anywhere in the Lake District. The open fell is common land, still owned by someone but where the freedom to walk unhindered has been enjoyed for generations. There is no need to ask permission.

National Park Rangers The National Park also provides a bevy of nine full-time Rangers. They patrol the Park giving help and advice to visitors, working on Board properties, policing the bye-laws or leading parties doing a variety of jobs from litter-sweeps to repairing footpaths and dry stone walls. There are also around 350 Voluntary Wardens who help Rangers.

Lake District National Park Statistics

	acres
Area of National Park	554 245
Area covered by lakes and reservoirs	16 062
Area under crops	9 227
Area under grass	188 446
Area of rough grazing	153 652
Area of common land	151 225
Area of broadleaved woodland	25 698
Total area of woodland	60 540

Who owns the National Park?

	acres
Areas of National Park Authority access land	20 554
Area owned and managed by NPA	18 723
Area leased to and managed by NPA	2 261
Area owned by National Trust	140 000
Area owned by Forestry Commission	31 466
Area owned by North West Water Authority	38 450
Area owned by Ministry of Defence	1 139
(MOD have firing rights over a further	1 196)

Population The population of the National Park is small, just 41,000, and is not growing. It doesn't include Carlisle, the county's biggest town, or Penrith, or the West Coast or - more surprisingly - either Cockermouth or Kendal, yet the Lake District Special Planning Board has its HQ offices in Kendal. (Lucky them, not having to apply to themselves for every planning permit.) They are still looking for premises inside the Park, so they say, but last time they considered it they came up against one of their own planning regulations which stopped them from changing a large country house from a dwelling place into offices.

Address The administration offices of the Lake District Special Planning Board are at Busher Walk, Kendal. Phone 0539 724555. Enquiries to the National Park Officer.

But note well: the NPA has applied for planning permission to turn the old Sock Factory in Kendal into its new headquarters. Gives a whole new meaning to 'putting a sock in it . . .'.

☆☆ The National Park Visitor Centre

In addition to running nine tourist information centres throughout the area, the National Park also provides a Visitor Centre at Brockhole, Windermere. Telephone 05394 46601.

The NPA's aim is to get you to start your holiday here, stock up on information and then sally forth among the lakes and fells, a better informed person. There are also things to amuse and entertain, especially aimed at family groups. A good place to wander around mid-week on a sunny day, when it can be less crowded (it gets very busy on wet days - Saturday is another quiet day, for some reason).

It's easy to miss, despite its size. From the name 'Visitor Centre' you might expect something modern, but it is in fact a stately home, a large detached building in its own grounds on the shores of Windermere, about two miles south of Ambleside on the A591. Keep an eye out carefully for the signs. Once inside the car park it is still confusing, as you can't tell the way to the house. Go through a little house - then to the Big House.

In the 19th century, Brockhole was the country home of a Lancashire cotton magnate, one of the many who built imposing residences along the shores of Windermere. It was converted in 1969 to its present use.

In 1990, there was a major refurbishment, aimed at updating their rather dusty Lakeland exhibition and bringing back some of the crowds they had lost. Their numbers had dropped from a peak of around 150,000 in 1984 to under 100,000, thanks to competition for family parties from places like Holker Hall and Sellafield. The refurbishment, alas, was not all that major. They had hoped to spend £1 1/4 million, but didn't have the money, and had to make do with £1/4 million, mainly on doubling the size of the restaurant. There is a new Lakeland exhibition, rather thin and photographic - once you've seen it, there's little need to return. They have made even more effort to attract and entertain families with new trails, quests, demonstrations and searches, plus their adventure playground, putting, croquet, bookshop and audio visual presentations. The best things are often the special daily events and talks by local experts. Check beforehand to see what's on.

Excellent grounds of 30 acres, all open to the public, with picnic spots and play areas. There are special launch trips, to and from Brockhole, and a regular daily service up and down Windermere, linking Brockhole with Bowness and Waterhead, from late May to September. Details from Bowness Bay Boating Company, tel: 05394 43360.

The cleverest thing Brockhole did, to bring back the crowds, was to make admission free. (Yah boo to Sellafield). In 1992, this brought attendances back up at once to the 150,000 mark. There is a slight catch - parking is expensive, if you happen to be alone, though families will still find it cheaper than it was. Admission: Free - but parking is £2 per car. House and grounds open daily 10-5 from April to October - plus late opening, till 8, from June-August.

Tourist Information Centres

Also referred to as TICs, these provide information on what to see and do; entertainments and events; places of interest; travel and transport and where to stay; even where to walk.

All the following tourist information centres should have information on local accommodation. Most provide a free local booking service for personal callers. Centres offering the Book-A-Bed-Ahead scheme can make a provisional reservation for you at any other town which has a centre also operating the scheme (anywhere in the country).

All the centres operate a local bed booking service. Some centres open only during the summer months - these are indicated with a * .

Alston
Railway Station
Tel: 0434 381696

Ambleside
The Old Courthouse,
Church Street
Tel: 05394 32582

Appleby
Moot Hall, Boroughgate
Tel: 07683 51177

Barrow-in-Furness
Civic Centre,
Duke Street
Tel: 0229 870156

Bowness-on-Windermere *
Bowness Bay
Tel: 05394 42895

Brampton *
Moot Hall,
Market Place
Tel: 06977 3433

Carlisle
Old Town Hall,
Green Market
Tel: 0228 512444

Cockermouth
Riverside Car Park,
Market Street
0900 822634

Coniston *
16 Yewdale Road
Tel: 05394 41533

Egremont
Lowes Court Gallery,
12 Main Street
Tel: 0946 820693

Glenridding *
(The Ullswater Centre)
Main Car Park
Tel: 07684 82414

Grange-over-Sands *
Victoria Hall,
Main Street
Tel: 05395 34026

Grasmere *
Red Bank Road
Tel: 05394 35245

Hawkshead *
Main Car Park
Tel: 05394 36525

Kendal
Town Hall, Highgate
Tel: 0539 725758

Keswick
Moot Hall, Market Sq.
Tel: 07687 72645

Killington Lake
Road Chef Service Area,
M6 Servics (South),
Killington Lake
Tel: 05396 20138

Kirkby Lonsdale
24 Main Street
05242 71437

Kirkby Stephen
Market Square
07683 71199

Longtown
Memoriall Hall
Community Centre
Tel: 0228 791876

Maryport
Maritime Museum,
1 Senhouse Street
Tel: 0900 813738

Millom
Millom Folk Museum,
St George's Road
Tel: 0229 772555

Penrith
Robinson's School,
Middlegate
Tel: 0768 67466

Pooley Bridge *
The Square
Tel: 07684 86530

Ravenglass *
Ravenglass & Eskdale
Railway Station
Tel: 0229 717278

Seatoller *
Seatoller Barn Dalehead
Base, Borrowdale
Tel: 07687 77294

Sedbergh *
72 Main Street
Tel: 05396 20125

Silloth-on-Solway *	Ulverston	Whitehaven
The Green	Coronation Hall	Civic Hall,
Tel: 06973 31944	County Square	Lowther Street
	Tel: 0229 587120	Tel: 0946 695678
Southwaite	Waterhead *	
M6 Service Area,	Main Car Park, Water-	Windermere
Southwaite, Nr Carlisle	head, Nr Ambleside	Victoria Street
06974 73445/6	Tel: 05394 32729	Tel: 05394 46499

Also if travelling M6 from south and between junctions 32 and 33, Gateway to Cumbria TIC, M6 Service Area, Forton, 0524 792181. It belongs to Lancashire but we won't hold that against them since it's good and helpful for Lakes information.

National Trust Information Centres

These are basically recruitment centres cum gift shops and don't deal with general information. That can be obtained from their regional office at The Hollens, Grasmere 05394 35599.

Ambleside - The Bridge House, Rydal Road
Grasmere - opposite St Oswald's Church, 05394 35621
Keswick - at the Boat Landings, Lakeside, 07687 73780
Shops and cafes in:
Sizergh Castle 05395 60070, Kendal, **Wordsworth House**, Cockermouth and **Fell Foot Country Park**, Newby Bridge 05395 31273, **Acorn Bank Garden,** Temple Sowerby 04683 61281.

The National Trust also has two shops, at The Square, Hawkshead 05394 36471 and Main Street, Cockermouth 0900 824805 (actually offshoot of WW's house - mentioned above).

The Friends of the Lake District

Anyone interested in protecting the area could do no better than contact the Friends of the Lake District. They've been going for 50 years now and do a lot to protect the area by lobbying MPs, stirring up the press and generally keeping an eye on what is going on. Now have their own permanent HQ at Number 3, Yard 77, Highgate, Kendal 0539 720788.

You don't have to live in the area to be a member. Subscription details from the secretary.

Chapter Three

Transport

Travelling around inside the Lake District .

Train

There is not much scope for travelling by train inside the National Park, as the only BR line is the branch from Oxenholme to Windermere. But there are four main railway routes which skirt the Lake District:

☆☆☆ **The Lakes Line** This important route runs from Preston through Lancaster, Oxenholme and Penrith up to Carlisle. The Lakes branch starts at Oxenholme, running through Kendal, Burneside and Staveley to Windermere. The following are all manned stations and the telephone numbers are for passenger and timetable enquiries:
Preston (0772 59439); Lancaster (0524 32333); Oxenholme (0539 720397); (for Windermere times, ring Oxenholme); Penrith (0768 62466); Carlisle (0228 44711). Also recorded timetable for London-Carlisle services. Mon-Sat. 0228 47046.

Windermere Station The original site was sold and developed into a tasteful new supermarket (apparently the NPA has no jurisdiction over BR property in the Lake District). There is now a sweet little railway station round the back. It was developed after much local pressure, BR extracting £15,000 from the local community in the process. To combat any threat to the line, a Lakes Line Action Group was formed (their slogan is: "Helping BR to get there").

Kendal Station The latest good news on Kendal Station is that the exterior looks wonderful; the bad news (at least for rail travellers) is that it has been bought by a developer. Its facade has been retained (as a listed building) but its interior has been completely revamped to includes a chemist, doctor's surgery and offices. Travellers have to wait under a shelter - still, if they get hypothermia, medical help will be handy . . . .

☆ **The Furness Line** Runs from Preston and Lancaster through Carnforth up to Barrow-in-Furness. Telephone numbers for the manned stations: Carnforth 0524 32333; Barrow-in-Furness 0229 20805.

☆☆ **The West Cumbrian Line** This almost forgotten service, which is second class only, meanders along the length of the Cumbrian coast from Barrow-in-Furness to Carlisle. Along the way it passes through Askam, Kirkby-in-Furness, Foxfield, Green Road, Millom, Silecroft, Bootle, Ravenglass, Drigg, Seascale, Sellafield, Braystones, Nethertown, St Bees, Corkickle, Whitehaven, Parton, Harrington, Workington, Flimby, Maryport, Aspatria, Wigton and Dalston. Of these, you'll not be too surprised to learn that only two are manned: Workington (0900 602575) and Whitehaven (0946 692414). And at most of the others the train won't even stop, unless you ask the guard in advance.

To save time trying to ring Cumbrian stations (even the manned ones never seem to answer) pick up the latest timetables from the nearest Tourist Information Centre. They also have good leaflets about rail/bus/ferry links.

☆☆☆ **Settle to Carlisle Railway** This famous railway line runs the length of the Pennines to provide one of the most scenic rail routes in Britain. The line crosses the spectacular Ribblehead Viaduct (all 24 arches of it), and is the only way of reaching Appleby and the east Cumbria towns by train.

BR put it up for sale, moaning about the lack of passengers and the expense of repairing the viaducts, but for the moment it has been saved. For time table details ring Settle (0729 823536) or Carlisle (0228 44711). Or why not join the Friends of the Settle-Carlisle line, help to keep it alive and find out about guided tours and other delights - send sae to Membership Secretary, 16 Pickard Court, Leeds LS15 9AY.

Apart from British Rail, there are three other short railway lines in Cumbria. All are popular tourist attractions, and all use steam locos.

☆☆☆ **The Ravenglass and Eskdale Railway**
This runs from Ravenglass on the West Coast of Cumbria up to Dalegarth in Eskdale, on the edge of the Lake District. The trains run all the year round but with reduced service during the winter months. The miniature railway (known as La'al Ratty) takes forty-five minutes to make its journey. Brilliant scenery. Perfect for families. Timetables available from Tourist Information Centres or ring 0229 717171.

☆☆ **The Lakeside & Haverthwaite Railway**
Running on three and a half miles of track which was originally part of the Ulverston to Lakeside line, the railway connects with the southern steamer station on Windermere at Lakeside. Combined tickets are available for the railway and the boats, making it a useful way of getting up into the Lakes without taking the car north of Newby Bridge. Tel: 05395 31594.

☆ **South Tynedale Railway.** Trains run between Alston and Gilderdale, following part of the old Haltwhistle to Alston branch line (just like something out of a Rowland Emett cartoon). Trains are usually hauled by steam engines at weekends and bank hols., otherwise by diesel. There is also a cafe and souvenir shop at Alston station run as separate entities on the station platform. Shop is also Alston's TIC - spot the staff leaping nimbly between ticket sales for train, gift wrapping and leaflet dispensing. Incidentally this is the only TIC in Cumbria to have Net Curtains at its windows . . . . Tel: 0434 381696. (Alston, in case you were wondering, is in the extreme north-east of the county. In fact, British Telecom think it is in Northumberland.)

Coaches

Since deregulation, bus companies seem to be gobbling each other up at an alarming rate - which doesn't make for easy or cheap transport.

The main contender for popular routes in the whole of the county is the Cumberland Motor Services. Their HQ is Tanzier St., Whitehaven - 0946 63222. Enquiry Nos for local buses are:

Barrow 0229 821325; Carlisle 0228 48484; Kendal 0539 733221; Millom 0229 772257; Whitehaven 0946 63222 (also HQ); Workington 0900 603080.

One of their most useful services for the visitor is **The Borrowdale Bus**, which runs between Keswick and Seatoller. Information from tourist info centres, or ring CMS on their Whitehaven number.

In addition to the national bus companies, **Wright Brothers** offer a handy service from Keswick and Penrith to Newcastle, during the summer. Telephone Alston 0434 81200.

Worth ringing too is Cumbria County Council's "Travel Link" 0228 812812. They are making a good effort to link various bus companies into coherent routes. They will send timetables if you ring and ask.

Also worthy of mention are possible alternatives for short journeys - local taxi firms. They are some of the beneficiaries of the parlous state of local bus routes. In some instances, and for convenience and speed, they no longer seem so much of a luxury. In fact one large LD employer has considered taxi-ing staff to and from work.

Note also that CMS Minilink buses are individually named. How about travelling to Coniston aboard "Beatrix Potter", or up to Grasmere on "William Wordsworth"?

☆☆ Mountain Goat Minibuses

An enterprising minibus firm which sprang up in 1974 when Ribble started to cut down its rural services. They offer special day tours to various Lake District beauty spots, often with picnic included. Trips stop frequently for photographs and some include guided walks. The Goat and Boat trip, combines the minibus service with a trip on the Ullswater steamers.

They're spreading their wings as they grow older. Latest developments include group travel for anywhere in Britain, conference trips, and transport for disabled.

Hint: Theme days (trips to a number of visitor attractions linked by a common subject) are very popular but can get booked very quickly and don't operate every day. If you're only here for a week, check them out at the start of your holiday.

Mountain Goat, Victoria Street, Windermere (phone 05394 45161) and Market Square, Keswick (phone 07687 73962).

☆ Grass Routes

Operating a similar service to Mountain Goat, but with the emphasis on countryside and scenic routes. Enquiries to Windermere 05394 46760.

☆ Fellrunner

This is a small minibus company offering tours of the Eden Valley. A good way of seeing beautiful countryside without having to endure the traffic of the central Lakes. They are a registered charity - "The Fellrunner Community Minibus" run by volunteers. Proceeds of their guided tours go to support scheduled services. They do interesting tours in E. Cumbria. Some of them pick up at hotels if requested. Bookings through any TIC in the Eden Valley, or ring 0768 890063.

Coach Tours

There's been a considerable increase in "personalised tours" of late - tailoring trips to customers' requirements. A couple of interesting ones are:.
National Park Discovery Tours - Windermere 05394 88811.
Coast to Coast Packhorse - Kirkby Stephen 05396 23688. (They will act as people and baggage transporters in N. Lakes.)

Post Buses

This is a most ingenious scheme, hardly known elsewhere in England, whereby you can get a ride with the Postman. In various outlying districts, the GPO have made it possible for the mail vans to carry passengers as well as post. They use the familiar red coloured vehicles, though slightly bigger than normal, and with seats for a few passengers. They run scheduled services and are very handy.

Martindale Post Bus - enquiries P.O., Crown Square, Penrith. 0768 62708

Duddon Valley Post Bus - enquiries Broughton-in-Furness P.O. 0229 716220.

Grizedale Post Bus - enquiries Head Post Office, Ulverston 0229 552030.

The Duddon Post Bus, incidentally, gave John Cunliffe the idea for Postman Pat.

Motoring

First a word of warning. In the middle of the season, it can take an age to get through Bowness and Ambleside on the A592 and A591. If you *have* to go through them, set off early. Keswick should be easier these days, with all those new roads and flyovers round the town, but if you have to go *through* Keswick to get to Borrowdale, then that too can be hell. So start early. Similarly, in July and August don't expect to get along the A592 from Bowness to Newby Bridge in a hurry. You *always* end up behind someone travelling at 19 miles an hour looking at the view. (This is a good road for spotting locals - they are the ones with steam coming from their ears.)

And if you have not already secreted a spare key on your car, do it now, before you hit the Lakes. Those little magnet boxes are best, hidden under the car somehow. All tourist info centres moan that one of the most common enquiries is from people who have locked themselves out of their own car.

Beware theft from cars left in isolated car parks. The Police are now trying to be really helpful about this by sticking up huge fluorescent posters proclaiming: "Thieves operate in this area" - oh what a good idea, say all the vandals. So always hide or remove valuables.

Motoring organisations: **AA** 24-hour breakdown 0800 887766; info. service 0345 500600.
RAC 24 hour breakdown service Linkline 0800 828282.

Garages

The following petrol stations remain open late during the summer season.

Ambleside - Hill's Garage (05394 32144).
Kendal - Lound Road Garage (0539 723914).
Ings Service Station, Ings, Nr Kendal (0539 821375).
Southwaite - Granada Service, M6 N. & S. going (06974 73476), 24 hours.
Carlisle - Brunton Park Service Station (0228 28715).
Harraby Green (0228 20973).
Traveller's Check Hardwicke Green (0228 511213), 24 hours.
Bowness-on-Windermere - Rayrigg Motors, Rayrigg Road (05394 42716).

Newby Bridge - Newby Bridge Motors, A590 road (05395 31253).
Burton West Granada Services - N. going M6 (0524 781234).
Killington Lake Roadchef Services - S. going M6 (05396 20739).
Keswick - Fitz Park Service Station, Penrith Road. (07687 72386).

Car Parks

In the season all the Lakeland towns are murder for parking - and even popular villages get quickly overrun.

Carlisle Has disc parking. You get a cardboard clock for free from a garage, Tourist Information Centre or traffic warden and use it to show your time of arrival in the car windscreen. Free, but one hour maximum. Look out for the signs.

To park, try near the Civic Centre. Otherwise use the major car parks. There are several large ones, all very cheap compared with metropolitan car parks. The Viaduct one is usually busy, so try West Walls, which has a short cut to the city centre, or try the one beside the Castle.

Keswick Very poor. The central one, off Victoria Street, often has queues to get in during the summer, so try the one off Heads Road. Always best to get into Keswick as early as possible. Another possibility is the car park in Lake Road. Follow the signs for the Lake shore, park and then walk back into Keswick. Very cheeky visitors have been known to use the Pencil Museum's car park. Note well - Main Street is now pedestrians only on Saturdays.

Grasmere The police in Grasmere are very keen, so be warned. (A few summers ago one policeman even booked his own wife for parking on a yellow line.) There is a car park in Stock Lane just as you enter the village from the south - this is handy for Dove Cottage. If full, try the one behind the garden centre, opposite the church. Beware parking in the garden centre car park by mistake - their charges are huge, unless you go in and buy something. They're not very keen on giving change for the ticket machine in the other car park. Also try Broadgate - there's a nice riverside path from it which emerges by St Oswald's Church and misses the crowds.

Ambleside Parking in the street is limited to half-an-hour during the day. There are three main car parks in Ambleside. The one in the centre, by the library, is usually full and transforms itself into a market on Wednesdays, but there's often space in the other two and they are both quite good. If coming in the from north, use the car park opposite Charlotte Mason College. Handy for the town and it's a nice walk alongside the river and past the Bridge House. (Caution: do not be tempted at weekends by the College's large, empty, invitingly free car park, they now threaten clamps.) From the south, use the car park just past Hayes Garden World. It's a five-minute walk into town, or about ten minutes in the opposite direction to Waterhead and the Lake. Waterhead has two good car parks - and the walk into town is pleasant.

Hawkshead Rapidly becoming one large car park with a small village adjacent. The village itself is nearly all pedestrians only, so use the main car park and saunter about the village without fear of being run over.

Windermere Limited street parking (if you're lucky). Use the car park behind the Library. You could also try shopping at Booths' supermarket. They have a vast car park which you're allowed to use for 30 mins, providing your car is stuffed full of their goodies.

Bowness *The* place to avoid with a car in mid-season. There is limited street parking in Lake Road, coming down from Windermere, but you won't get in. (You will, however, get stuck behind someone else who is trying to get in and blocking the traffic.) There is also a small car park next to the cinema, usually full. The large car park in Rayrigg Road is good if you're early, but once past 11 o'clock there are often queues to get in. Far better are the two car parks down by the Bay. There's one behind the National Park information Centre and a large one along Glebe Road which often has spaces. Alternatively, if feeling like a nice stroll, use the car park at Ferry Nab (also useful for boat trailers - this is the SLDC launching site) and walk back into town along the lake shore and through Cockshott Point. Nearby Braithwaite Fold also opens as a car park in summer. Don't, whatever you do, just dump the car on the verge along Rayrigg Road. Bowness has a very efficient traffic warden these days, you know.

Coniston Use the main car park in the centre of the village. You have to pay, but it is by far the easiest.

Kendal Another horrid place to park. You always end up finding no spaces and having to go all round the one-way system to get back to the first car park you saw but decided to ignore in order to get closer to the shops. There is a good car park down by Abbot Hall, in Kirkland (the Council one – don't use the Museum car park, they will get cross, unless you're visiting the Museum). The best car parks are down on Blackhall Road, behind the new shopping centre. There's even a free car park by the river. It is always full. If you enter Kendal from the Kirkland end, you could turn up Gillingate and you might find a space by the road.

Car Tours

Several companies give tailor-made guided tours. Try Alistair's of Windermere 05394 88191 and Cumbrian Discoveries of Keswick 07687 78473.

Car Rentals

Ambleside: Young Motors Ltd., Knott Street (05394 32322)

Barrow: Low Road Garage (0229 822385)

Bowness: Brantfell Garage, Kendal Road (05394 42000)
Ansa International, Belsfield Hotel (05394 45910)

Carlisle: British Car Rentals, 2 The Church Viaduct Estate Road (0228 511760)

Grange-over-Sands: Grange garage now refers enquiries to Barrow (above).

Kendal: Avis Rentacar, Station Road (0539 733582)
Lakes and Dales, 97 Valley Drive (0539 729311)

Crooklands (near Kendal): Crooklands Self-Drive (05395 67414)

Keswick: Keswick Autocompany (07687 72064)

Penrith: Cumbrian Connection, Welsh's Yard (0768 67222)

Silloth: Coates Garage, Causeway Head (06973 31478)

Whitehaven: Autorent, 35 Central Road, Kells (0946 695078)

Taxis - no shortage of contenders. Are they all ex-bus drivers?

Carlisle: Border Cabs, 0228 48153/28849
City Taxis (24 hrs) 0228 20000

Kendal: Blue Star Taxis (24 hour), 0539 723670
Castle Taxis (24 hour), 0539 726233

Windermere: Blezard Taxis, 05394 42355
Lakes Taxis, 05394 46777/43692

Whitehaven: 5050 Taxis (24 hrs) 0946 695050

Keswick: Davies Radio Taxis, 07687 72676

Cockermouth: C & S Cars (24 hrs) 0900 828335

Penrith: Lakeland Taxis, 0768 65722

Ambleside: Busy B's Taxi Service 05394 31028
Rachael's Taxis 05394 33842

Grange: Reds Taxis (24 hrs) 05395 58527

Cycling

Cycle Hire is becoming more and more popular in the LD. Not just on the roads, either - they're increasing on the fells, thanks (if that's the word) to the advent of mountain bikes. Note that this is only permissible on bridle ways. If in doubt, ask at TIC to look at "Mountain Bike Code of Conduct" drawn up by Sports Council and Countryside Commission. Clearly identifies where bikes may legally be used and how to avoid antagonising others whilst doing so.

Cycle Tours

☆ **Cumbria Cycle Way** Good leaflet/map available from TICs. This is more a route, than a proper cycle way, despite its name, but it is an excellent ride. It directs you 280 miles (or 450k) along a circular route round coastal Cumbria from Furness up to the Solway plain, then through Carlisle (which is hell for cycling) and down the Eden Valley to Appleby and then to Kirkby Lonsdale. It is a carefully constructed route, through many miles of quiet minor roads, with an enormous amount of scenery - but none of it is in the Lake District.

There is also a **Forest Bicycle Route** in Grizedale Forest, using ten miles of signposted forest roads. No permission necessary and they can only be used by cyclists or pedestrians.

Cycling Guide

The best one is *Cycling in the Lake District*, by Richard Harries, Morland Publishing, 1984.

☆☆☆ Windermere Ferry

Four of the Lakes now have public transport of some sort on them - Windermere, Coniston, Ullswater and Derwentwater. (Details of the services are in Chapter 7.)

For road users it is worth pointing out at this stage that only Windermere has a car ferry. It runs all year round, except for Christmas and Boxing Day, from 0650 to 2150 (0950 to 2050 on Sundays and during the winter), crossing the Lake about once every twenty minutes.

1993 charges: 20p for pedestrians, £1.20p for cars (including occupants). The ferry runs from Ferry Nab, just south of Bowness, across to Ferry House at Far Sawrey and the service is run by the Highways Department of Cumbria County Council.

A Recommended Excursion by Public Transport

A good method of spending the day without a car is to use the A591, especially between Ambleside and Keswick. It is a brilliant route for public transport, with buses about every hour, and is the only route in Central Lakeland where you will see a double decker. Set off early from Ambleside and get on the top deck (when you go over Dunmail Raise on the top deck of a bus on a good day the view is tremendous). Travel up to Keswick, stopping off at Dove Cottage, Grasmere, and Castlerigg Stone Circle (just before Keswick). Time each visit so you don't have to wait too long for the next bus along to the next stage. Spend some time in Keswick, then catch the bus back to Ambleside, this time stopping off at Rydal Mount on the way. Coleridge and Wordsworth did this route all the time when visiting each other. On foot of course. They were tough in those days.

But do set off as early as possible (Dove Cottage is open at 9.30, Rydal Mount closes at 5.00, 4.00 Nov-Feb.), or very quickly your precious hours will disappear.

Two Excursions by Car

Half-Day

Head south from Bowness and cross Lake Windermere via the ferry. Drive towards Hawkshead, passing Hill Top and taking the west road round Esthwaite Water (prettier). Look round Hawkshead (good for teas) and perhaps visit the Grammar School. Then continue towards Coniston, turning off for Tarn Hows. Carry on into Coniston, then return via Ambleside.

Full Day

Leave Bowness via the A592. Go over the Kirkstone Pass to Ullswater. Wonderful views over the Lake. Turn left onto the A5091 through Dockray to join the A66 at Threlkeld and blast along to Keswick. From Keswick go down the Borrowdale Valley. Don't forget the Bowder Stone. Over Honister Pass. Stop at Buttermere and walk round the lake. Then continue to Lorton, back over the Whinlatter Pass to Keswick. Leave Keswick via the A591 (stop off at Castlerigg Stone Circle), turn off and go round the west side of Thirlmere (quieter and prettier with places to park and explore the shore), then continue through Grasmere and Rydal (where you have the temptations of the two Wordsworth homes) and back via Ambleside.

Chapter Four

Hotels

Where to stay - hotels, guest houses, farmhouses, caravans, camping, renting.

The choice is enormous, so all we intend to offer is a brief, personal selection, plus some broad general advice.

There are 1,000 hotels and guest houses in the Lakes, 550 bed and breakfast places, offering in all 26,000 beds. Then there are all those farms and caravan sites. So what do you do? Well, it's relatively easy to get a list of the local beds available, and most of the tourist information centres will help. Just turn up and ask. But no official is going to tell you what they're really like.

If you are booking from afar, and want it reasonable and clean, then fine, go ahead and get a copy of their latest list.

Cumbria - English Lake District is the official Guide published by the CTB and available, free, from the CTB at Ashleigh, Holly Road, Windermere. TICs will also probably have copies. It is intended as a general guide but incorporates all the CTB accommodation information. (NB: worth pointing out - CTB only ever list their own members.)

Prices This time we are not giving exact hotel prices. We did so first time, and oh the moans and groans from proprietors when they put their charges up and expected us to reprint immediately. Just think of our extra printing costs, every time they muck around with their details. So we are lumping them all into three broad bands, A, B and C, ranging from cheap to expensive. Pricing varies enormously at the posh end of the market. Some don't offer a price for singles, others do but put on such a heavy penalty that the price approaches that of a double.

Price Bands: For one person, for dinner, bed and breakfast.

> **A** £40 to £60
> **B** £60 to £80
> **C** £80 plus

De Luxe, De lightful Hotels

There are two hotels which stand head and shoulders above the rest for their high standards and attention to detail, for their food and service, for their furnishings and for their overall terribly good taste. Both are very expensive. The 1993 rates for Sharrow Bay, for dinner, bed and breakfast, ranged from £118 to £145 per person. Miller Howe went from £80-£125. Allow one week's notice in the summer to book dinner and around six weeks for a bedroom.

If you have the money, they are both well worth one night, if only for the experience. It will give you table talk for years wherever people of good taste are gathered together.

☆☆☆ Sharrow Bay Country House Hotel, Ullswater. 07684 86301. Price - C.

On Eastern shore of Ullswater, about two miles from Pooley Bridge.

Brian Sack and Francis Coulson still manage to keep it up, despite over 40 years at the top. Still regularly awarded the top accolades by all the best hotel and food guides in the world.

Pluses - Food sensational, setting equally sensational, 29 bedrooms, each bedroom a work of art, drawing rooms very posh, always quiet and discreet, no bar (what a blessing - you have drinks served in the drawing rooms as if in a private home).

Minuses - Very few, though there are those sour pusses who find the food too much, in quantity and richness, and say the bedrooms are over fancy. Drawing rooms are a bit fussy and formal, and you can feel equally on display. Try to book into the hotel proper, not the annexes.

☆☆☆ Miller Howe, Rayrigg Road, 05394 42536. Price - C. Overlooking Windermere, about 1 mile north of Bowness.

John Tovey is a much more extrovert character than the duo at Sharrow Bay. Look out for him, tripping round after dinner, unless he's off on tour, promoting his latest best seller, or appearing on TV. He's also more theatrical and dinner is like a stage performance. Starting from scratch 22 years ago, he has also built up his hotel - and himself - so that it now has an international reputation - yet like

46

Sharrow Bay it is totally English, using good Cumbrian materials and staff.

Pluses - Terrific food, very imaginative, sensational views, quiet but friendly atmosphere, handsome drawing rooms, 13 well equipped bedrooms.

Minuses - The lake views *are* brilliant, but the hotel is on a busy, boring road; some bedrooms are more flash than tasteful; despite Tovey's jovial personality, which makes his hotel not as intimidating as Sharrow Bay, some snotty people find it a trifle arriviste. Strict eating times, no choice. No lunch.

Classy Hotels

The success of the Big Two has had a great effect on the rest of the Lakes and standards of comfort and cuisine, taste and decor, have increased enormously in the last ten years. There are now several mini Sharrow Bays, less expensive, less publicised, but aiming for the same high standards and trying hard to avoid the mass produced, mass catering methods of the Trust House Forte type of hotels. They don't all succeed, but they are trying to stamp their individual personality and create hotels which they hope will appeal to the discerning.

☆☆ **Underscar Manor**, Applethwaite, near Keswick, tel: 07687 7500.

Always was classy, with its magnificent setting under Skiddaw, marvellous conservatory-dining room, 40 acres of gardens with deer and red squirrel, but suffered from endless changes. Now with the arrival of the Harrisons and chef Robert Thornton, fresh from Moss Nook Restaurant, Manchester, and a £1 million refit, it looks the Hotel most likely to zoom into the De Luxe class. Decor a bit flouncy, but bedrooms very comfortable, first class service, food excellent. Price - C.

☆☆ **Rothay Manor**, Rothay Bridge, Ambleside. 05394 33605.

Fine regency hotel, traditional fare and services. Price - B/C.

☆☆ **White Moss House**, Rydal Water, Grasmere. 05394 35295.

Well established quality hotel. Great views of Rydal Water and ideally situated for any number of walks, but road can be very busy during daytime. Price - C.

☆ **Leeming House Hotel,** Watermillock, Ulswater. 07684 86622.

Attempting in recent years to become very smart, but not quite yet in the Sharrow Bay class, though high quality service and comfort. Can arrange deer stalking and fishing. Price - C.

☆☆ **The Old Vicarage**, Witherslack, Grange-over-Sands. 05395 52381.

Small Georgian hotel, only seven bedrooms, in South Cumbria. Informal, quiet, but tasteful, good food. Price - B/C.

☆☆ **Michael's Nook Country House Hotel**, Grasmere. tel: 05394 35496.

Long established and ever so classy, just look at those antiques. Reg Gifford has kept up his high standards and still wins plaudits.

☆ **Langdale Chase**, Lake Windermere, near Ambleside. tel: 05394 32201.

Great lake side setting, lovely building, nicely old fashioned atmosphere, a hotel which has acquired a very loyal following over the years. Price - B.

☆ **Holbeck Ghyll Country House Hotel**, Holbeck Lane, Windermere. tel: 05394 32375.

Once Lord Lonsdale's Hunting Lodge, now a friendly, efficient and peaceful country hotel. Price - B.

☆ **Old Church Hotel**, Watermillock. tel: 07684 86204.

Brilliant setting on Ullswater, down a long private drive, very quiet and comfortable. Price - C.

☆ **Dale Head Hall**, Thirlmere. tel: 07687 72478.

With the arrival of the Lowes family, food and comfort has improved, so welcome to the classy section, folks. It should always have been there anyway, with its marvellous setting on Thirlmere, once the summer retreat of the Lord Mayor of Manchester. Dining room dates back to 1577. Nine bedrooms. Price - A-B.

☆ **Ivy House Hotel**, Braithwaite, Keswick. tel: 07687 78338.

Right inside the village, so easy to miss as you drive through, despite its vivid green façade. Bedrooms not quite up to the standard of the food, but Nick and Wendy Shill are trying very hard. Excellent base for climbers.

☆ **Crosby Lodge**, Crosby on Eden tel: 0228 573618.

The nicest place to stay in the Caslisle area. Beautiful setting in small stately home with excellent food. Personally run for 21 years by Michael and Patricia Sedgwick. Price - B.

☆ **Pickett Howe**, Buttermere Valley. tel: 0900 85444.

Newly converted 17th century farm house near Crummock. Only has four bedrooms, and not really a hotel, more a guest house, but it is definitely classy. David and Dani Edwards run it all on their own. She's an ex-teacher, he's ex-social worker. Excellent, imaginative food, artful bedrooms, utter peace and quiet. Price - A.

☆ **Kirkstone Foot Country House Hotel**, Kirkstone Pass Road, Ambleside. 05394 32232. Price - B.

☆ **Lindeth Fell Country House Hotel**, Bowness-on-Windermere. 05394 43286.

Run by Pat and Diana Kennedy. Small, friendly, high-class hotel set on the fells above town. Brilliant views and well away from the hordes. Strong emphasis on fresh food and local specialities (look out for the after dinner Kendal mintcake). Price - B.

☆ **Uplands Hotel**, Haggs Lane, Cartmel. 05395 36248.

Spawned by Miller Howe (subtitled 'In the Miller Howe Manner') and run by two of John Tovey's former right hand persons, Diana and Tom Peter. All the quality and comfort you would expect from Tovey training, but at around half the price of Miller Howe. Only four bedrooms. Price - B.

☆ **Appletree Holme**, Blawith, near Ulverston. tel: 0229 85618.

Another small - only four bedrooms - but bijou creation. Roy and Shirley Carlsen were really thinking of retiring when they sold Leeming House Hotel on Ullswater some 14 years ago and moved to this pretty but isolated 17th century farm house. Lo and behold, they have created another winner. (In 1993, the *Which Hotel Guide* named them Cumbria's Hotel of the Year). Basically an up market guest house, with luxury bathrooms, antiques, fine food cooked by Roy. Not cheap for a guest house - dinner is £21.50 - but certainly classy. Price - B.

Executive Hotels

First class hotels which have most of the accepted amenities, but often rather lacking in individual character or atmosphere. They are generally large, lots of bars, good for businessmen, large parties or, very important, good for children. Our top two De Luxe hotels actively discourage children under 13. Anyway, at those prices, who wants to take children. While the Classy Hotels are also rather wasted on children.

The following are not Executive in the Hilton, monster new building sense - and luckily nothing in the Lake District is like that - but in being large, functional and efficient. You might actually prefer them to some of the personal eccentricities and strange customs of the De Luxe and Classy hotels.

☆☆ **Tarn Hows Hotel**, Hawkshead. tel: 05394 36696.

Run by Alan and Karen Campbell, fresh from running King Hussein's palaces. This could be Classy, and might well be in the next edition, but at the moment it still feels

Executive. A lot of the £1 million face lift went into things like a leisure complex, complete with saunas and exercise thingies - who wants that in Lakeland when you have the fells - plus satellte TV in all bedrooms. Hotel still a bit stiff and formal, but excellent service, good food, and facilities. Price - B.

☆☆ Lodore Swiss Hotel, Keswick. 07687 77285.

Will still be saddened not to be classed as De Luxe, as they do try awfully hard, but somehow it's too big (72 rooms) and too functional to be hailed as an experience, but excellent at what it sets out to do. Now run by Stakis. Still good for families.

Fine setting on Derwentwater, with the Lodore Falls behind, good restaurant, two swimming pools, tennis, dancing, sauna, film shows, children's playground, colour TV and phones in all bedrooms. Price - C.

☆☆ Wordsworth Hotel, Grasmere. 05394 35592.

A skilful conversion of an old building with lots of luxury amenities like indoor swimming pool and sauna and phones and TV in all rooms and conference rooms. Prelude Restaurant smart, but not yet a taste thrill. 38 bedrooms. Price - C.

☆☆ Armathwaite Hall, 07687 76551.

This should be a *Classy* hotel, because of its outstanding views over Bass Lake, its imposing mansion building and its good service, but somehow it *looks* more individual and special than it is, despite lots of recent promotional gimmicks. Food can be very good, other times not so good. Bedrooms 37. Price - B.

☆ Belsfield Hotel, Bowness. 05394 42448.

Large Victorian house, 71 bedrooms, with lots of family amenities - swimming, clock golf, games, dancing. Price - C.

☆ Old England Hotel, Bowness. 05394 42444.

Old established mansion hotel with modern amenities - outdoor swimming pool, games room. 84 bedrooms. Price - C.

☆ The Crown, Wetheral, Nr Carlisle. 0228 561888.

Not in Lakeland proper, but one of the best of the county's executive hotels. Recently converted, at a vast expense, from old riverside hotel, with massive sports facilities, especially squash, very smart pine wood dining room and conference facilities. Handy for the Roman Wall and Borders as well as the Lakes. Price - B.

☆ Burn How Garden House Hotel, Bowness-on-Windermere. 05394 46226.

Unusual combination of nice Victorian house with

modern motel style chalets. Peaceful location, yet amongst all the Bowness action. Good for families. Well run by the effervescent Vicky Robinson. Price - A.

Keswick Hotel, Station Road, Keswick, tel: 07687 72020.

Keswick is surprisingly poor in classy or executive hotels, compared with Windermere. This should be up there with the stars, considering its spendid location, grounds and history, but has suffered from uncertainty and neglect in recent years. Too early to tell if it's now on its feet again. Reports, please.

Low Wood Hotel, Windermere. 05394 33338.

Lakeland's biggest hotel with 148 bedrooms, but for many years its fine Lakeside setting, with 3/4 mile of lake frontage, was ruined by its passion for the charabanc trade. In the post war years it became little more than a transit camp for coach parties. Now aiming for family and executive trade. Continually adding new bits, like the water-sports centre (much reviled by Friends of the Lakes), leisure and conference facilities. Price - B/C.

☆ North Lakes Gateway Hotel, 0768 68111.

Penrith's answer for all busy business people. Opened in October 1985. 85 rooms and a leisure club. Price - C.

☆ The Beech Hill, Bowness-on-Windermere. 05394 42137.

Modern hotel, right on lake shore, 3 miles south of Bowness. Conference rooms, plus own sauna, solarium and swimming pool. Price - B.

Hotels with Swimming Pools

Just in case that's really what you're after, here's a selection:

1 **Beech Hill Hotel**, Bowness-on-Windermere. 05394 42137.
  Pool (open to non-residents), sauna & solarium.
2 **Hillthwaite House Hotel**, Thornbarrow Road, Windermere.
  05394 43636. Pool (res. only), sauna & solarium.
3 **Old England Hotel**, Bowness. 05394 42488.
  Outdoor pool (res. only), sauna.
4 **Belsfield Hotel**, Bowness. 05394 42448.
  Pool (res. only), sauna.
5 **Burnside Hotel**, Bowness. 05394 42211.
  Pool and sports facilities (eg squash, badminton, gym, etc.) for residents, with a club for non-residents, daily m/shp available.
6 **Regent Hotel**, Waterhead, Ambleside. 05394 32254.
  Pool (res. only).
7 **Langdale Hotel & Country Club**, Elterwater. 05934 37302.
  Pool (club membership available), sauna & solarium.
8 **Whitewater Hotel**, The Lakeland Village, Backbarrow, Newby Bridge. 05395 31133. Pool (club memb.), sauna & solarium.
9 **Wordsworth Hotel**, Grasmere. 05394 35592.
  Pool (club membership), sauna, solarium, jacuzzi and gymnasium.

10 **Eccle Riggs Hotel**, Foxfield Road, Broughton-in-Furness.
0229 716398. Pool (open to non-res.), sauna & solarium.
11 **Lodore Swiss Hotel**, Keswick. 07687 77285.
Pool (res. only), sauna & solarium.
12 **Crown & Mitre Hotel**, English Street, Carlisle. 0228 25491.
Pool only (club for non-residents).
13 **Swallow Hilltop Hotel**, London Road, Carlisle. 0228 29255.
Pool (club for non-res.), sauna & solarium.
14 **The Appleby Manor Hotel**, Roman Road, Appleby. 07683 51571.
Pool (club for non-res.), sauna & solarium.
15 **North Lakes Gateway Hotel**, Ullswater Road, Penrith.
0768 68111. Pool, sauna, solarium (club for non-res.).

Small Hotels and Inns

A handful which have got individual character and one day might well jump up to be classed as Classy.

Sun Hotel, Coniston 05394 41248.

Regulars rave about the comfort and food. Beautiful setting. Price - B.

Pheasant Inn, Bassenthwaite Lake 07687 76234.

Old style inn, can be a bit like a road house in high summer with passing tourists, but very attractive. Price - C.

Three Shires Inn, Little Langdale. Langdale 05394 37215.

Despite several changes of ownership, still comfortable, simple, small hotel with friendly atmosphere. Price - A.

☆ Temple Sowerby House, Kirkby Thore 07683 61578.

Not in the LD proper, being six miles the other side of Penrith, on a main road, but a handsome Georgian house with a growing reputation for good imaginative food. Could eventually be in the Classy category. Price - B.

☆ Lupton Tower, Lupton, Nr. Kirkby Lonsdale. 05395 67400.

Another of Derek Hook's enterprising ventures (see chapter 5 for more about Mr Hook), this time in partnership with the Smith family. A nice, quiet, vegetarian hotel which opened in July 1987. Nine rooms. Price - A.

☆ Lancrigg Vegetarian Country House Hotel, Grasmere 05394 35317.

Pleasant hotel, hidden away from the crowds in Easedale. Ten rooms, some with whirlpool bath. (Veggies have fun too, you know . . . .) Price - A/B.

☆☆ Swinside Lodge, Newlands, Keswick. Tel: 07687 72948.

Famed for its excellent service and hospitality.

☆ **The Mill Hotel**, Mungrisdale. Tel: 07687 79659.

Not to be confused with the Mill pub next door. Good food, very reasonable accommodation.

Bower House Inn, Eskdale Green. 09467 23244.

Pretty Inn in a pretty valley. Bedrooms have TV and bathroom. Price - B.

Blue Bell at Heversham. 05395 62018.

Not really a small hotel - it has 26 rooms and a dining room which can take eighty people. It prefers to call itself a hostelry. The dining room is popular with locals. Price - B/C.

Bargain Places

☆☆ **High Greenrigg House**, 06974 78430.

Absolutely isolated, traditional Cumbrian farm house, out on the Caldbeck fells, away from all those nasty tourists, but handy for all the Northern Lakes. Very friendly, simple bedrooms, comfortable sitting room, bar, snooker, table tennis, first class home cooking, good packed lunches. Perfect for *real* open air lovers, especially families or parties. Personally run by Robin and Fran Jacobs. She's American. He's English. Price - such a bargain it doesn't even make our A level. They de-registered for VAT and in 1993 lowered the price even more - £26 for dinner, B & B. Incredible value.

☆ **Howtown Hotel**, Howtown, Ullswater.
07684 86514.

Complete opposite of High Greenrigg, being chintzy and rather old fashioned and not really very suitable for boisterous families (though they have separate cottage accommodation), but delightful, cosy and olde worlde, with brilliant views, right beside Howtown Pier. The Sharrow Bay bosses often drop in here to relax. Price - A.

☆ **Low Hall**, Brandlingill, Nr Cockermouth. Tel: 0900 826654.

17th century farmhouse near Lorton, handy for Loweswater, Crummock and Buttermere. Hard to find, so get exact details. New owners Enid and Hugh Davies. She's ex-teacher, yes one of the many, while he still works as a hospital consultant, but helps in the evenings. Very comfortable, relaxed, good food, great welcome. Price - A.

Guest Houses

There are hundreds of guest houses in the Lake District - here is a selection of good ones, recommended by our spies. Prices vary between £12.00 to £25.00 per person for B&B (1993 prices). The difference between a Guest House and a Hotel is that hotels have to offer lunch or dinner to non-residents.

Ambleside

Glenside, Old Lake Road. 05394 32635.

Holme Lea Guest House Church Street, Ambleside. Tel: 05394 32114.

Cartmel Fell

Lightwood Farm Guest House, nr. Bowland Bridge, Cartmel Fell. Tel: 05395 31454.
(NB this is not a working farm.)

Grange-over-Sands

Thornbank Guest House, 6 Thornfield Road, Grange-over-Sands. Tel: 05395 32664.

Grasmere

Banerigg Guest House, Lake Road, Grasmere. Tel: 05394 35204.

Keswick

Charnwood Guest House, 6 Eskin Street, Keswick. Tel: 07687 74111.

Linnett Hill Hotel, Penrith Road, Keswick. Tel: 07687 73109.

Rydal

Foxghyll Guest House, Under Loughrigg, Rydal. Tel: 05394 33292.

Rydal Holme Guest House, Rydal. Tel: 05394 33110.

Windermere

Brendan Chase Guest House, College Road, Windermere. Tel: 05394 45638.

Glenburn Hotel, New Road, W'mere.   Tel: 05394 42649.

Hawksmoor Hotel, Lake Road, Windermere Tel: 05394 42110.

Meadfoot Guest House, New Road, Windermere. Tel: 05394 42610.

Bargain Guest Houses

Highly recommended, nay award winning places.

Carlisle

The Beeches, Wood Street. Tel: 0228 511962.
Runner-up last year in an Excellence Award for England's B & B. Well done, Mrs. Kirpatrick.

Rosley

Causay Grange, Rosley, near Caldbeck. Tel: 06974 45358.
Ask for Mrs Falck.

Kendal

Holmfield, 41 Kendal Green. Tel: 0539 720790.
Very comfy. Thank you, Mrs. Kettle.

Farmhouses

They're always cheap, just look for the signs. You can
still find them for as low as £10 for bed and breakfast, but
are they any good? Hmm. You takes your chance. Here's
three good 'uns:

☆ **Bessiestown Farm**, Catlowdy, Penton, Longtown.
Tel: 0228 577219.

Not your actual Lakeland, though handy for the
Borders, but it's a real working farm with, you won't
believe it, a heated indoor swimming pool for guests. Even
gets RAC and AA acclaim. £21 B & B. Not cheap, but
think of the swimming.

☆ **Foldgate Farm**, Corney, Bootle. Tel: 0229 718660.

Run by Mary Hogg, great name for farming folk. Delightful cobbled courtyard, old stone barn, plenty of old
furniture and rag rugs, good cooking and what a bargain
- £12.50 B & B, or £19 with dinner.

☆ **Tarn House Farm**, Ravenstonedale, Nr. Kirkby
Stephen. Tel: 05396 23646.

Only two letting bedrooms but in seventeenth century
farmhouse on working farm. Has its own tarn (hence
name) where you can fish or just stroll around admiring
Howgill fells. House has tiny mullioned windows and
huge stone fireplaces. B & B £12, Dinner B & B £20.

Farmhouse Holidays

The more lively, clued-up farmers these days are band-
ing together to promote their varied attractions. So if for
example you want to stay on a farm in a particular area,
and enjoy some particular activity, they will fit you to the
right place, whether it's pony trekking you fancy or
fishing, rock climbing or fell walking, or perhaps you'd
like to see rare breeds, rare birds, buy farm produce, hire
mountain bikes, eat home made ice cream, watch sheep
shearing, watch the farmer milking, watch the farmer
counting his money, oops, that's private. Anyway, it's a
good idea, so start by sending off for a brochure for a
Cumbrian Farm Holiday:

Cumbria as a whole - Mike Powell, Cumbrian Farm Leisure Holidays, Oakbank Fisheries, Longtown, Cumbria,
CA6 5NA.

West Lakeland - Mrs. Morgan, High Dyonside, Distington, CA14 4QQ.

Border Country - Dorothy Downer, Bank End Farm, Road-head, Carlisle, CA6 NU.

Eden Valley - Mrs. Ivinson, Green View, Welton, Dalston, CA5 7ES.

South Lakeland - Mrs. Simpson, High Swinklebank Farm, Longsleddale, Kendal, LA8 9BD.

Camping Barns

A new Lakeland sleeping experience, unquote, which provides basic over night accommodation. Also known as Stone Tents. Lakeland farmers can now get grants to tart up their unused barns and provide clean, dry shelter - aimed at walkers or cyclists who don't want the drag of carrying a tent. Useful for families or parties up to 12, especially in winter or bad weather. Each barn offers a wooden sleeping platform, table, slate cooking bench, cold water tap and WC. No heating. Bring your own sleeping bag and stove. Unisex accommodation. Most of the farms also sell eggs and milk.

Centralised booking done from Blencathra NP Centre, Threlkeld, Keswick, CA12 4SG. Price - only £2.50 per night - which is cheaper than a Youth Hostel.

The aim is to have 12 Camping Barns, linked round the LD, so you can go from one to another. So far there are seven: Blake Beck Farm, near Saddleback; Bowber Head, near Ravenstonedale; Crag Farm, Buttermere; Fell End, near Broughton-in-Furness; Swallow Barn, Loweswater; Swirral Barn, Glenridding; Tarn Flatts, St. Bees.

Self-Catering

There are a number of private agencies operating in the Lake District, all of which have a selection of properties on their books:

Heart of the Lakes (6 mile radius, A/side 130 properties). Rydal Holme, Ambleside. Tel: 05394 32321.

Grey Abbey Properties (mainly North, 72 properties from caravans to cottages)
PO Box 23, Coach Road, Whitehaven. Tel: 0946 693346.

Holidays in Lakeland (All Lakes - 200 properties)
Stock Park Estate, Newby Bridge, Nr Ulverston.
Tel: 05395 31549.
Lakeland Cottage Holidays (Keswick area - 40 properties)
3, The Heads, Keswick. Tel: 07687 71071.

Lakelovers (mainly South - 90 properties)
The Toffee Loft, Ash Street, Bowness-on-Windermere.
Tel: 05394 88855.

Loweswater Holiday Cottages (9 units)
Scale Hill, Loweswater, Cockermouth. Tel: 0900 85232

Prices vary enormously, especially between central Lakes and the fringes. Big differences too between high and low season; a typical cottage sleeping six in Loweswater costing £220 in the winter will be £550 at the height of the summer. The rate often depends on the owner's reasons for needing the money (i.e. it might not be his full-time business), so you can get some good deals through the independent lists.

The Cumbria and Lakeland Self-Caterers' Association seeks to provide 'realistic minimum standards' for properties. They have a free leaflet which lists members, prices and details, available from the Secretary, CLSCA, Lesley Goodliffe, Monkhouse Hill Farm, Sedbergham, Carlisle. Tel: 06974 76254. CLSCA also has a vacancy advisory service, open all year - tel: 0229 57668.

Camping and Caravanning

Caravan Parks in the NP are licensed to be open from 1st March to 14th Nov. (newly extended from 31st Oct.). No fully residential sites. Caravans squatting on a site for more than 21 days are supposed to be painted with NPs environmental colours - sludge green and sludgier green.

There is a British Holiday Parks Grading Scheme in operation - a voluntary scheme and one in which participants are given a series of ticks (of the good well done variety) depending on the quality, standards and cleanliness of facilities. Six places have the maximum six ticks in Cumbria, three of them in NP:

The Quiet Site, Watermillock, Penrith. 07684 86337.

Cove Camping Site (tents only) Watermillock. 07684 86549.

Ings Caravan Park, Ings, Nr Kendal 0539 821426.

The English Tourist Board operates a "Rose Award" system for those parks which, on inspection, it thinks are the best of their kind. There are seven of these now in Cumbria: 4 on coastal sites, 3 in NP - all of these in Windermere area:

Fallbarrow Park, Rayrigg Road, Windermere. 05394 44428.

Ings Caravan Park, Ings, Nr. Kendal. 0539 821426.

Newby Bridge Caravan Park, Canny Hill, Newby Bridge. 05395 31030.

The National Trust have 3 very good camping sites:

Great Langdale. 05394 37668.

Low Wray Farm. 05394 32810.

Wasdale Head. 09467 26220.

The National Trust also have a caravan site (plus holiday cottages and chalets) at the S. end of Lake Windermere: Fell Foot Country Park. 05395 31273.

The best booklet available is produced by the NP "The Caravan and Tent Guide to Cumbria and the Lake District" - currently 95p and updated annually. They also deserve a commendation for listing camping only sites. Gives one a fair chance of escaping the ubiquitous white boxes.

And finally, campers are not encouraged to pitch tents where they fancy. NP Rangers have been known to come rattling on tent poles first thing in the morning to point out that one is illegally parked. Not conducive to sleep - or anything else.

Accommodation for the Disabled

As yet there is no specific guide to the LD for disabled people. There are moves afoot to do something, but ETB thinks this would be "discrimination".

However, the national charity "Holiday Care Service", which provides holiday information and support for disabled and others in need, has a leaflet on "Accessible Accommodation" in Cumbria (approx. 14 places in NP). These are places they have inspected with their "Accessible Standards". Their office is 0293 774535 or contact CTB for details 05394 44444.

Also Available is "Holidays in the British Isles" produced by RADAR - updated annually, and has a good section on Cumbrian accommodation, plus accessibility of various attractions.

TICs are usually very good at providing on-the-spot information about disabled loos, lots of steps, etc. - or will find out for you.

Two trusts exist to provide adventure holidays in the LD for disabled:

The Calvert Trust Adventure Centre
Little Crosthwaite, Under Skiddaw, Keswick.
Tel: 07687 72254.

The Calvert Trust has accommodation for 36 people (plus self-catering for 12) and run a number of activities, including archery, angling, bird watching, hill walking, nature trails, rock climbing, canoeing, pony trekking and sailing. They will take able-bodied people, but all their facilities are aimed at the disabled. For further details contact the warden.

Bendrigg Lodge
Old Hutton, Kendal.
Tel: 0539 723766.

Run by the Bendrigg Trust, this is another centre catering specifically for the disabled. It has accommodation for 35, plus self-catering for 20 (minimum booking of 10 for self-catering). They also provide a range of out-door activities.

General Hints on Accommodation

In the summer and school holidays, anything in a town like Bowness, Windermere, Ambleside and Keswick is bound to be busy, noisy and hectic. Unless you love that sort of thing, try a rural spot or a small village or head for the fringes, such as Furness, Cockermouth, Eden Valley. In those places, you will at least be able to park your car outside your digs.

At most of the hotels and larger guest houses, it is worth asking about winter prices and bargain breaks. There are all sorts of price incentives to get people into the area out of season.

Accommodation Registers

There are four of these available for the LD produced by local councils. Each covers a specific area and gives around 80% of the accommodation available. They give loads of addresses, prices and facilities. They have started to go all fancy and glossy - and that's just the titles. Available from local TICs or from the following:

South Lakeland
Where To Stay in S. Lakeland.
Available from Kendal Tourist Information Centre. Tel: 0539 725758. £1 incl. p & p., 75p for callers.

Keswick
"Keswick on Derwentwater and N. Lakes - where to stay and what to do".
Price 75p including postage, 60p for callers.
Available from The Moot Hall TIC. Tel: 07687 72645.

Eden Valley
"Where to stay in Eden". Free but enclose a large SAE. Available from: Penrith TIC, Robinson's School, Middlegate, Penrith. Tel: 0768 67466.

Copeland (W Coast, Eskdale, Ennerdale & Wasdale)
Where To Stay In Western Lakes and Coast. Free.
Whitehaven TIC, Civic Hall, Lowther Street, Whitehaven. Tel: 0946 695678.

Cockermouth and District; Carlisle; Furness
all produce their own accommodation guides. Carlisle's is *very* glossy, Furness covers Barrow and Dalton as they aren't considered to be in S. Lakes. Ahh. . . . Shame. Ring TICs for details.

Complaints?

It's no use letting off steam at the first tourist information assistant you see, as TICs cannot handle your complaints for you, so if you want to air a legitimate gripe about accommodation, write to:

Senior Accommodation Officer,
Cumbria Tourist Board,
Ashleigh,
Holly Road,
Windermere. Tel: 05394 44444.

Personal Choice Even with money to burn, I would not spend the whole of a week's holiday at either of the Big Two posh hotels, Sharrow Bay and Miller Howe. Despite a picnic lunch and trying to be sensible at dinner, it is hard not to feel bloated and soporific after just three days. You can have too much of a good thing. So even if you have the money, save them to the end of the hols as a treat, perhaps booking in for one or two nights, with dinner of course, as that's the highlight. Before that, book into a cheap Inn or Guest House in a completely different part of the Lakes for the first part of the week, such as our Bargain Places, and have some active days and hearty simple meals, then finish off with a guzzle. If of course you are on a very tight budget, or you have teenagers you want rid of, then the best accommodation bargain by far is . . .

Youth Hostels

There are 30 youth hostels in Cumbria, 22 of them inside the National Park:

Alston, Ambleside, Arnside, Black Sail, Buttermere, Carrock Fell, Cockermouth, Coniston - Coppermines, Coniston - Holly How, Derwentwater, Dufton, Elterwater, Ennerdale, Eskdale, Grasmere - Butharlyp How, Grasmere - Thorney How, Hawkshead, Helvellyn, High Close, Honister, Kendal, Keswick, Kirkby Stephen, Longthwaite, Patterdale, Skiddaw House, Slaidburn, Thirlmere, Wasdale and Windermere.

They all vary in standard and scale. Some, like Ambleside, have all mod cons, look right over the lake, with 240 beds, while Black Sail is little more than a remote mountain hut with only 18 beds. In general, though, the standard of them is getting better all the time.

Here are the three nicest Youth Hostels, in our opinion:

☆☆ **Black Sail Hut,** Ennerdale (OS Ref: 194124). No telephone.

☆☆☆ **Patterdale Youth Hostel**, Goldrill House, Patterdale, Nr Penrith. Tel: 07684 82394. (OS Ref: 399156).

☆☆ **Carrock Fell Youth Hostel**, High Row Cottages, Haltcliffe, Hesket Newmarket, Wigton. Tel: 06974 78325. (OS Ref: 358355).

Which are best often depends largely upon the warden, but these three were considered excellent in recent years. Black Sail is rightly renowned for people wanting to get away from it all; tucked away at the head of Ennerdale it is very simple and completely inaccessible by motor vehicle.

Membership Apply to YHA, Trevelyan House, St Albans, Herts, or any hostel. Adult Membership in 1993 is £9.00 per year. Don't forget you don't have to be a Youth - any age is welcome - and these days Hostels have car parks, many cater for families and they are still incredibly cheap, from £3.00 per night. A neat way of using them, if the adults prefer more comfort in their old or middle age, is to book into a good hotel - but put the children in the nearest YHA.

Regional Office YHA, Milburn House, Dean Street, Newcastle, NE1 1LF. Tel: 091 221 2101.

Chapter Five

Eating

A selection of the top Lakeland restaurants, plus some good lunch and tea places in the various towns and some nice pubs.

Restaurants

In London and Manchester and the big towns, it's a general rule that hotel meals are poor and that it's best to look for a proper restaurant. In the Lakes, the opposite often applies. A good hotel in the Lakes usually offers the best food in that area, while most of the street restaurants are little more than caffs, producing fry-ups for the tourists. But there are exceptions, and they are increasing all the time. There is not the huge selection of good and cheap ethnic restaurants, which London and most large British towns now offer these days, but if you go slightly up market for the more ambitious restaurants, some with definite pretensions and others boasting top class home fare, then there is quite a choice.

We have whittled down our own tastings, and taken expert soundings, and offer what we think are the top Lakeland restaurants. There are so many good ones that we have continued to split it up into two lists - the Top Five, plus The Others. Recommended Vegetarian and Ethnic Eating are listed separately.

Prices The range is A, B and C, from cheapish to expensive, according to the average price for one person having dinner, without wine or service.

> **A** under £15
> **B** £15-£25
> **C** over £25

Top Five Lakeland Restaurants

☆☆☆ **Sharrow Bay Country House Hotel**,
Howtown Road, Ullswater. Tel: 07684 86301.
   See Hotel listing for details. Price - C.

☆☆☆ **Miller Howe**, Rayrigg Road, Windermere.
Tel: 05394 42536.
   See Hotel listing for details. Price - C.

☆☆ **Underscar Manor**, Applethwaite.
Tel: 07687 7500.
   See also Hotel listing. Eating wise, this is the one to watch, the one most likely to get up there with Sharrow and Miller How. Robert Thornton has managed to combine delicate, balanced, imaginative French cuisine with decent helpings. Taste thrills all the way. And look out for the synchronised service, almost up to Olympics standard. Pity about the pianist. The staff are entertaining enough on their own. Price - C.

☆☆ **Porthole Eating House,** 3 Ash Street,
Bowness-on-Windermere. Tel: 05394 42793.
   Italian-French, run by an Italian-Cumbrian, Gianni Berton, and his Manchester-Cumbrian wife, Judy, since 1972. The mixture works, brilliantly. Always very popular, efficient yet informal, with great care taken over everything, from the yummy treacle bread to start with, to the Windermere char, if it's on. Don't forget to take coffee or pre-drinks upstairs. Easy not to realise they have a large lounge bar, hidden away. Price - B.

☆☆ **Quince and Medlar**, 13 Castlegate, Cockermouth. Tel: 0900 823579.
   Change of ownership since the last edition, but guess what, it's even better. Colin Le Voi, who cooks, and wife Louisa, who waits, fresh from Sharrow Bay, who both look about 13, have now made this the nation's top Veggie restaurant - with Numero Uno awards to prove it. Really, we should give them three stars, because of their enormous success, but as a dedicated meat eater, I'm keeping them in their place. Ingenious menu, using vegetarian and ethnic dishes from all over the world. Do try their roulades and cheese beignet. Good wine list. No smoking. New sitting room, but still a small restaurant, so essential to book. Closed Mondays. Price - B.

Other Top Restaurants

☆☆ **La Primavera**, Greta Bridge, Keswick.
Tel: 07687 74621.
   Opened in 1986 but didn't make it into our last edition. On our first test visit, the electicity was off and everything

a shambles. Now Guiseppe (from Sorrento) and wife Pamela (from Maryport) are into their stride - food excellent, service terrific. Perhaps not quite yet the atmosphere of the Porthole, run by that other Italian-Cumbrian duo, but it will come. The Victorian building, once full of arts and crafts, makes a fine setting. Good parking, which is unusual for Keswick. Also does bar snacks, if you just want to check the ambience and save pennies. Closed Mondays. Price - B.

☆ **Michael's Nook**, Grasmere. Tel: 05394 35496.
See also Hotel listings.

☆☆ **Jackson's Bistro**, St Martin's Square, Bowness. Tel: 05394 46264.
Frank and Christine Jackson ran Greenriggs at Underbarrow for ten years and have now gone urban with this smart, cheerful bistro. Two floors, attractive decor, excellent value for money. Price - A.

☆☆ **Merewood Country House Hotel**, Ecclerigg, Windermere. Tel: 05394 46484.
Windermere's newest restaurant and hotel. Aiming for the same market as Sharrow Bay and Miller Howe but trying to do something a little different from the other two. Lovely old house in a superb setting, good atmosphere and excellent food. Price - C.

☆☆ **The Old Vicarage**, Witherslack, Grange-over-Sands. Tel: 05395 52381.
See also Hotel listing. A Lakeland dream come true - how two couples, absolute amateurs, gave up London commuter living after 25 years, fled to the Lakes, started a little guest house, doing B&B at first, now blossomed into one of the best small, select hotels in South Lakes. Five course dinners, all works of art. Price - B.

☆☆ **Roger's Restaurant**, 4 High Street, Windermere. Tel: 05394 44954.
Owned and run by Roger Pergl-Wilson. A smart, modern French restaurant offering some of the best quality cooking in the district. Menus change daily and home-grown herbs play an important part. Price - A/B.

☆☆ **Rothay Manor Hotel and Restaurant**, Rothay Bridge, Ambleside. Tel: 05394 33605.
See also Hotel listing. A Regency hotel, built up by the late and greatly missed Bronwen Nixon and her two sons, famed for its soups and starters. Five-course dinners are good value, usually traditional French or English. Lamb a speciality, along with game when in season. Sweets are excellent . Price - B.

☆☆ **Kirkstone Foot Country House Hotel,**
Kirkstone Pass. Tel: 05394 32232.

A 17th century manor which has been converted into a luxury hotel with self-catering apartments. All fresh food with a traditional English main course and imaginative sweets and starters. One sitting at 8 o'clock prompt - set menu but specialities can be catered for if you give plenty of warning. Elegant and very good value for money. Annabel and Andrew Bedford run it. Price - B.

☆ **Leeming Country House Hotel,** Watermillock, Ullswater. Tel: 07684 86622.

See also Hotel listing. Classically-designed restaurant. In the evening there is a fixed price menu based on excellent local supplies, ranging from roast beef to guinea fowl with celery and walnut stuffing. Delicious, beautifully presented sweets. Price - B.

☆☆ **Uplands Country House Hotel,**
Haggs Lane, Cartmel. Tel: 05395 36248.

See also Hotel listing. A Miller Howe offshoot, but less pretentious. Excellent evening meals at reasonable prices. Price - B.

☆ **Passepartout,** 51 Castlegate, Penrith.
Tel: 0768 65852.

Still a pleasant eating place in an arid eating area. (Strange that with all those aristocratic families around Penrith there should be so few high class places for them to eat. Perhaps it's always visitors who are prepared to spend their dosh, not locals.) So well done the Robinsons, she an ex-French teacher and he a former senior lecturer in catering. (Hmm.) Efficient French-English cuisine. Very popular at week-ends. Price - A.

☆ **Rampsbeck Country House Hotel,** Watermillock, Ullswater. Tel: 07684 86442.

A sensational situation right on the shore, with a reputation for first class cuisine nouvelle which is well worth trying, though on our test lunch we were the only ones in the dining room. A delightful surprise, though, when you consider how boring the bar meals are. Price - B.

☆ **Chez Collette,** Queen Street, Whitehaven.
Tel: 0946 590661.

John Leak, ex-London, and Collette, ex-Manchester, have come from India to Whitehaven to open a French restaurant. You what? Well, it works. Simple but stylish decor, good food, ambitious menu, service a bit slow. With Bruno's round the corner, Whitehaven is fast becoming a foodie town. Must be the middle management from Sellafield, throwing their money around. Price A.

☆ **Bruno's,** Church Street, Whitehaven.
Tel: 0946 65270.

Well established and very popular Italian restaurant. Can get busy and noisy, especially when Bruno himself is around. One of those stage Italians with a Central Casting accent - but he is the real thing, from Livorno. Ask for the leaflet, "Who is Bruno" and admire his English punctuation. Now has six bedrooms. Price - A.

☆ **The Retreat,** Birkby, Maryport.
Tel: 0900 814056.

Such a shame Maryport has nowhere decent to eat, but at least *The Retreat*, just out of the town, is still going strong. Handsome building, elegant rooms, first class food, personally run by Rudi and Alison. A German-Cumbrian partnership this time. Price - B.

☆ **The Village Restaurant,** Victoria Street, Windermere. Tel: 05394 43429.

Pizza and Steak restaurant, but don't be put off by that. Good range, friendly service, reasonable prices, especially their two course fixed meals. Closed Thursdays. Evenings from 6. Price - A.

☆ **Cheers,** Main Street, Cockermouth.
Tel: 0900 822109.

Awful title, but best home made pizzas and pastas in Cumbria, so they boast. Well, perhaps the best in Cockermouth. But it is cheerful. Good value, hearty eating. Closed Mondays. Evenings only. Price - A.

☆ **Fantails,** Wetheral, near Carlisle.
Tel: 0228 560239.

Classy food, arty situation, but no good for anyone with poorly legs as it's all upstairs. Well worth it, though, as the Carlisle area is still thin on elegant eating. Price - B.

☆ **The Bay Horse,** Canal Foot, Ulverston.
Tel: 0229 53972.

Formerly a simple hostelry overlooking Morecambe Bay for cross sands travellers; then a bistro was attached; now there's a six bedroom extension. Part of the Miller Howe empire, from whence chef Robert Lyons came, but not as theatrical or expensive. Nice touches in the dining room such as binoculars so you can watch the bird life between courses. Don't be put off by the horrible road approach past the Glaxo works. Also does bar meals and afternoon teas. Price - B.

Skinburness Hotel, Silloth. Tel: 06973 32332.

Not a lot of eating choice, on this isolated part of the Solway coast, so let's hope the Skinburness continues to flourish. Hearty bar meals, classier stuff in the smart dining room. Price - B.

☆ **Tullythwaite House**, Crosthwaite, Nr Bowland Bridge. 05395 68397.

A small farmhouse at the back of Cartmel Fell, between Kendal and Lake Windermere. Owners Mr and Mrs Greenwood have been there 7 years now, producing excellent evening meals (Wednesday to Saturday only and lunches on Sundays). Small, personal service, using local produce. Price (evening meals) - B.

☆ **Aynsome Manor**, Cartmel, Nr Grange-over-Sands. Tel: 05395 36653.

Pleasant manor house set in parklands just outside Cartmel village. Price - A.

☆ **Belmont Manor Hotel**, Holbeck, Windermere. Tel: 05394 33316.

Works hard to produce pleasant atmosphere and agreeable food.

☆ **Stampers Restaurant**, Church Street, Ambleside. Tel: 05394 32775.

Below Wordsworth's old stamp house. Setting a bit cramped and cafeish, but food excellent with local specialities such as Herdwick and pigeon. Friendly, personal service.

Smaller Restaurants, Good Teas and Light Lunches

A speciality of Lakeland is the small tea or coffee shop, where you can get home-baked cakes and light lunches. Often these are combined with some other attraction, such as a historic house (eg, Brantwood, Dalemain and Hutton-in-the-Forest). They tend to be popular with locals as well as tourists. The cafe at the Kirkstone Slate Gallery was so popular that there was a public campaign which got it reopened after a year. Here are some recommendations for good teas and lunches throughout the Lakes, town by town.

This list also includes some of the smaller, less pretentious eating places which haven't quite made it into our Top Restaurants. Some of these also do teas and lunches, but not all the cafes do evening meals. We have indicated which of them do. Closing times can vary enormously, compared to the cities, often as early as 7.30 pm.

This time we've also indicated those places where food has priority over the dreaded weed. These are either completely 'no smoking' or have banished smokers to a separate room (merely putting them on separate tables never works.)

Ambleside

☆☆ **Sheila's Cottage**, The Slack. Tel: 05394 33079. No smoking.

One of the best tea shops around Ambleside. Evening meals but it *does* suffer from the holier than the riff-raff malaise.

☆ **Zeffirelli's Wholefood Pizzeria**, Compston Road. Tel: 05394 33845. No smoking.

No pre-booking except meal+cinema seat. It's part of a cinema, shops, coffee lounge, all very arty and stylish. There's no Mr Zeffirelli by the way, so don't ask for him. The owner is Derek Hook from Blackpool. It's a cinematic joke, gerrit. **Pizzeria** does evening meals; during the day go to the **Garden Room Cafe** downstairs. **Pizzeria** has the plastic-wipe-clean-menu syndrome - where has its spontaneity gone?

Stock Ghyll Snacks and Grills, Central Buildings. Tel: 05394 33334.

Still the best sausage, egg and chips in the Lake District? All day breakfasts.

Kirkstone Slate Galleries, Skelwith Bridge. Tel: 05394 33296. No smoking.

Lovely soup. Enormous portions of home made cakes and puds.

Apple Pie Eating House and Bakery, Rydal Road. Tel: 05394 33679.

Instantly recognisable by queues spilling into street, so maybe it doesn't need our support, but it's a busy cheerful cafe and bakery with excellent soups, cakes, pastries, baked on premises.

Wilf's

Wilf is still recovering from the shock of losing his premises - a sad loss to the stomachs of Ambleside, but take every opportunity to catch him as "Wilf on Wheels" 05394 88271. Outside catering, frequently seen at sporting events and shows, now about to launch into a 'ring and bring' facility for groups too exhausted to venture out for a meal.

Appleby

The Copper Kettle, 17 Boroughgate. Tel: 07683 51605.

Bowness-on-Windermere

The Alpine, Crag Brow. Tel: 05394 42884.

Looks unprepossessing but good value coffee and home cooking. A good budget cafe.

Tom Brosters, Queens Square. Tel: 05394 43535.

After being the Chameleon of Bowness (every time you looked it seemed to be a different name and decor). TB seems to be getting well established and well regarded for providing nice food. Just a small gripe: it's a bit like eating in a goldfish bowl - lots of glass, minimal curtaining.

Rastelli's Pizzeria, Lake Road. Tel: 05394 44227.

Broughton-in-Furness

Beswick's Restaurant, The Square.
Tel: 0229 716285. No smoking.

Open during the day in summer, evenings all year.

Caldbeck

Priests Mill, Caldbeck. Tel: 06974 78369.

Converted watermill, very tastefully done. Modest but healthy lunches and teas. Also craft shops, with persons crafting away, and enthusiastic mining museum.

Parkend Restaurant, Tel: 06974 78494.

Yet another change of ownership. If only they'd stay, this pretty country restaurant might get back to its former glory. They're trying hard, with hearty fare.

Carlisle

Hudson's, Treasury Court, Fisher Street.
Tel: 0228 47733. No smoking.

Lordy's, 10 Lonsdale Street. Tel: 0228 42014.

More of a restaurant but very reasonable.

☆ **Cafe Carlyle**, Carlyle Court, Fisher Street.
Tel: 0228 818583.

New wine bar, in new precinct, but it thinks it's in olde France. Good coffee, good light meals.

Cartmel

St Mary's Lodge. Tel: 05395 36379.

A pleasant and homely tea room near the Priory.

Egg-Pudding Stone Licensed Restaurant, Cartmel Craft Centre, Broughton Lodge Farm, Field Broughton.
Tel: 05395 36009.

Healthy and very tasty meals and snacks in crafty atmosphere. No smoking.

Cockermouth

☆☆ **Over The Top**, Kirkgate . Tel: 0900 827016.

Healthy, home cooking. Best cappuccino in Cockermouth. Now expanded downstairs.

☆ **Norham Restaurant**, Main Street, Cockermouth.
Tel: 0900 824330.

Good home made light meals, country atmosphere.

(And don't forget **Wordsworth House** does very good teas; worth the entrance fee.)

Coniston

Blue Bird Cafe, Coniston Boating Centre, Lake Road.
Tel: 05394 41649.

A neat little cafe just by the lake.

Jumping Jenny, Brantwood. Tel: 05394 41396.

Yes, Ruskin's House - now does good teas and lunches. Open to non-visitors to the house. Welcoming wood-burning stove in winter. Don't expect to be served in a hurry . . . .

Dent

Stone Close, Main Street, Dent. Tel: 05396 25231.

Excellent lunches, teas and evening meals (latter by booking only), all in a 17th century cottage, complete with flagged floors and cast iron range. (They also do bed and breakfast at very reasonable rates.)

Embleton

☆ **Wythop Mill**, Tel: 07687 76394.

New restaurant been added. Good light meals. Week-end dinners more ambitious, but not cheap.

Grasmere

Baldry's, Red Lion Square . Tel: 05394 35301.

A nice cafe in an area which is otherwise starting to slip a bit. Good home-made fare, especially the apple pie, or in my case the lemon meringue.

Greystoke

☆ **How Mill**, Johnby. Tel: 08534 216.

Now this is unusual, a working farmer and his wife doing week-end high teas, dinners and Sunday lunch. Hard to find, but a real experience

Hawkshead

Minstrel's Gallery, The Square.
Tel: 05394 36423. No smoking.

Grandy Nook Coffee Shop, Vicarage Lane.
Tel: 05394 36404. No smoking.

Excellent coffee shop, which also does evening meals in summer.

Kendal

Brewery Arts Centre, 122 Highgate. Tel: 0539 725133.

Pizza Plus serves from 5.30-7.00pm so good to eat before going into their new cinema. Coffee shop open all day in exhibition area - nice to have somethng to look at while guzzling.

☆☆ **Farrers Coffee Shop**, Stricklandgate.
Tel: 0539 731707. No smoking.

A real, old fashioned, excellent value coffee shop. The coffee comes in one of those plunger thingies. You can also buy packets of coffee and tea in the shop, along with various arcane implements for brewing same.

☆ **The Moon Restaurant**, 129 Highgate. Tel: 0539 729254.
No smoking.

With that name it would be tempting to say it lacks atmosphere, but it wouldn't be true. Evening meals only.

Union Jack Cafe, Kirkland. 0539 722458.

Kirkland has lacked a nice, family cafe to encourage shoppers down to this part of town. Welcome the Union Jack, now less of a transport cafe than formerly. They even do vegetarian snacks (though usually with chips).

Pizza Margherita, Highgate. Tel: 0539 731303.

Keswick

☆☆ **Maysons**, 33 Lake Road. Tel: 07687 74104.

My favourite Lakeland place for a light meal - something tasty and unusual available almost any time of day.

☆ **Abraham's Tearoom**, Borrowdale. Tel: 07687 72178.

New coversion at the top of George Fisher's outdoor shop, so get those climbing boots on as it's 38 steps to get a cup of tea, but worth it. Views marvellous, the building fascinating - once the home of the famous photographers. Good light meals available all day, every day. No evenings. Extra marks if you can find the lavatory.

☆ **Wild Strawberry**, Main Street. Tel: 07687 74399.

Was all gifts at one time, but now practically all teas and light meals, traditionally done. Closed Wednesdays and evenings.

Great Little Tea Shop, Lake Road. Tel: 07687 73545.

Tea shop with a green conscience.

Old Sawmill, Dodd Wood, Underskiddaw.
Tel: 07687 74317.

Part of the Mirehouse estate, but there is no charge to get in. The cafe makes the best fruit cake in Cumbria.

Kirkby Lonsdale

Nutter's Food and Fun, 1 Market Square.
Tel: 05242 72130.

Simon of the late-lamented Nutter's Eating House in Kendal, is doing missionary work in K.L. Stuffiness not permitted, children actively welcomed.

Melmerby

☆☆ **The Village Bakery**. Tel: 0768 881515.

A tiny village, 10 miles north east of Penrith, so not exactly on the usual tourist round but a wonderful stopping off point if you're making the trek to Newcastle. Excellent cafe in a converted eighteenth-century barn. Home produce using locally ground flours, much it available to take away. Definately worth a detours. Baking in wood fired ovens, craft exhibitions, sales upstairs.

Newby Bridge

Fell Foot Cafe, Fell Foot Park. Tel: 05395 31274.

N.T.s access point to S. end of Lake - cafe has more importance when approached from Lake . . . .

Penrith

In Clover, Wholefood Restaurant, Poet's Walk.
Tel: 0768 67474. No smoking.

Ravenstonedale

☆ **The Fat Lamb Hotel and Restaurant,** Crossbank, Fell End, Ravenstonedale. Tel: 05396 23242.

An old coaching inn set high on remote moorland. You can't miss it. In the field there is the only remaining member of a rare breed of Long Necked Sheep (it's actually a Llama, very confusing for late-night revellers).

Seatoller

☆ **Yew Tree Restaurant**, Seatoller. Tel: 07687 77634.

Sedbergh

The Copper Kettle Tearooms, 43 Main Street.
Tel: 05396 20995.

Change of name and owners. Very good food. A little known gem.

Staveley

Wedge Hall Gallery & Tea Room, Windermere Road.
Tel: 0539 821130.

Just what Staveley needs to divert people from thundering past on the new bypass. Locally made goodies - both food and crafts.

Ulverston

Peppermill, Market Street. Tel: 0229 57564.

Corny red tables and chianti bottles with candles, but good food at reasonable prices. 'Best omlettes in Furness', so one fan says.

Whinlatter

☆ **Hampers**. Whinlatter Visitor Centre. Tel: 07687 78068.
Part of the centre, but run separately. Great setting, great teas and light meals, with wine or beer. Perfect place after a hard climb. Closed January.

Windermere

Lakeland Plastics, Alexandra Buildings (right behind the Railway Station). Tel: 05394 2255. No smoking.

Renoir's, Main Road. Tel: 05394 44863.
Slightly continental atmosphere, home baking.

Vegetarian Eating

There has always been a tradition of veggie eating in the Lakes, but usually of the faintly eccentric kind, popular with Wizened Wonders with hairy knees clutching Fabian pamphlets. The point was to make it politically veggie, not artistically tasty, so non-veggies scoffed or laughed at the very idea of nut cutlets, and never ventured in.

Now the world and his wife, or at least their children, have gone veggie mad. (My three children are all veggie, but I am allowed meat on Wednesdays.) It's part of the healthy living, healthy eating kick, and let's not be horrible to the poor animals. Interesting that it should have taken off so much in Lakeland, where the main sport for centuries has been doing horrible things to animals, such as foxes.

This new breed of veggie restaurants and hotels are ever so homely and artistic, and welcome the unconverted. They've had a good effect on ordinary, meaty places, who more and more publicly offer the choice of a veggie dish or menu. (In the old days, you had to force it out of them.) You also now get many places which offer the meat dish as the eccentric alternative, such as Sheila's Cottage in Ambleside or Over The Top in Cockermouth, both of which are keenest to see you guzzling their healthy stuff or the fruity cordials.

Here's a selection of specialist veggie places, some of which are also mentioned above.

Vegetarian Restaurants and Cafes

☆☆ **Quince and Medlar**, Cockermouth. Tel: 0900 823579.
The best in Cumbria, if not all Britain. (See **Top Restaurants** for details.)
☆ **Harvest Vegetarian Restaurant**, Compston Road, Ambleside. Tel: 05394 33151. No smoking. Evenings only.

☆ **Zeffirelli's Wholefood Pizzeria**, Ambleside. Tel: 05394 33845
(See **Smaller Restaurants** for details.)

☆ **Lupton Tower**, Lupton, Nr. Kirkby Lonsdale.
Tel: 05395 67400.

Nice, quiet vegetarian hotel and restaurant. (See Chapter Four for details.)

Rowan Tree, Langdale Road, Grasmere. Tel: 05394 35528

Waterside Wholefoods, Waterside. Tel: 0539 729743.

Zeffirelli's Garden Room Cafe, Ambleside. Tel: 05394 33845.

(See **Smaller Restaurants** for details.)

Vegetarian Hotels and Guest Houses

☆ **Lancrigg House**, Easedale, Grasmere. Tel: 05394 35317.

Set in 27 acres, in an area loved by the Wordsworths. The Whittinghams used to run the Rowan Tree, so they can be trusted to provide high class veggie cuisine, but now in their small hotel they are also offering such wicked things as a sauna and whirlpool baths. Price - B.

Crosthwaite Mill, Crosthwaite, Kendal. Tel: 05395 68314.

Orchard House, Borrowdale Road, Keswick.
Tel: 07687 72830.

Long established veggie guest house, going back 30 years. They still talk about the veggie lasagna. Price - A.

Fair Place, Watermillock on Ullswater.
Tel: 07684 86235.

Small guest house with classic overtones. (The owners were in a string quartet, so the music is always high class – they also sell upmarket hi-fi equipment.) Price - A.

There is now a little booklet, the *Vegetarian Directory*, planned to come out annually, which lists vegetarian and vegan restaurants, hotels, whole food shops and even veggie pub meals in Cumbria. Modest, but useful. Only 25p. Available at most TICs or contact Secretary of the Kendal Vegetarians. Tel: 0539 725219.

Ethnic Eating

Do you come all the way to the Lakes to eat foreign? They seem to think so in Bowness where you can't move for all the Greek, Italian, Swiss, Chinese and Indian restaurants. The hard bit is finding good English nosh.

Here's our recommended selection of Chinese and Indian restaurants:

The China Boat, Church Street, Bowness.
Tel: 05394 46326.

Good value - also take-aways.

☆ **Jade Fountain Chinese Restaurant**, Ulverston.
Tel: 0229 555047.

Universal rave reports from our spies.

Rajah Tandoori and Curry Restaurant, Ash Street, Bowness. Tel: 05394 45852.
Lakeland's only Tandoori? We shall see.

The Magic Wok, 2 Crescent Road, Windermere.
Tel: 05394 88668.
Cantonese menu, interesting tasty dishes, good take-away service.

Pub Meals

Pubs are becoming increasingly popular eating places for tourists in the Lake District and some of them are very good indeed. Here are twenty-five of the best, ordered roughly north to south:

Pheasant Inn, Cumwhitton, nr Carlisle. Tel: 0228 560102
Nicest decor of any Cumbrian pub.

The Sun Inn, Ireby. Tel: 06973 71346.

The Old Crown, Hesket Newmarket. Tel: 06974 78288.
Real beer, brewed on the premises.

Shepherd's Inn Melmerby. Tel: 0768 881217.

The Sun Inn, Bassenthwaite Village. Tel: 07687 76439.

Kirkstile Inn, Loweswater. Tel: 0900 85219.

Pheasant Inn, Wythop Village, Bassenthwaite Lake.
Tel: 07687 76234 (also see Hotels).

Dog and Gun, Lake Road, Keswick. Tel: 07687 73463.

Borrowdale Hotel, Borrowdale, nr Keswick.
Tel: 07687 77224.

Bridge Hotel, Buttermere Village. Tel: 07687 70252.

Queen's Head, Tirril, nr Penrith. Tel: 0768 63219.

The Outgate Inn, Outgate, Hawkshead.
Tel: 05394 36413.

Drunken Duck, Barn Gates, nr Hawkshead.
Tel: 05394 36347.

Britannia Inn, Elterwater. Tel: 05394 37210.

Queen's Head Hotel, Hawkshead. Tel: 05394 36271.

Tower Bank Arms, Near Sawrey. Tel: 05394 36334.
The Mortal Man, Troutbeck, Windermere.
Tel: 05394 33193.

Brown Horse Inn, Winster. Tel: 05394 43443.

Hare and Hounds, Bowland Bridge. Tel: 05395 68333.

Angler's Arms, Haverthwaite. Tel: 05395 31216.

Farmer's Arms, Lowick Green. Tel: 0229 861376.

Hare and Hounds, Levens Bridge. Tel: 05395 60783.

Royal Oak Inn, Bongate, Appleby. Tel: 07683 51463.

Mason's Arms, Strawberry Bank, Cartmel Fell.
Tel: 05395 68486.
Famed for its selection of exotic beers, now including its own, brewed on the premises. Food also very good.

Lindale Inn, Lindale, Grange-o'-Sands. Tel: 05395 32416.

In addition, **The Punch Bowl,** Crosthwaite (tel: 05395 68237) gets a mention for its ever improving menu.

Best Pub Meals
Best in the North: Still the Sun Inn, Bassenthwaite Village.
Best in South: Queen's Head, Hawkshead - heading upmarket at a rate of knots but still good value for money.

Good Beer
So much for the food, now for the liquid stuff, the real stuff of course, which real ale drinkers drool over while making skitty comments about that fizzy beer which the Big Breweries pump out everywhere. John Ogden, a terribly keen amateur drinker of northern brews, recommends four which can be found in most parts of Lakeland, plus two he is not so keen on. (The comments are all his.)

Best Brews
Jennings Very popular with enthusiasts. The brewery sits majestically on the banks of the Cocker in Cockermouth and from it come beers of distinction. A local trad brewery, as much a part of the Lakes as Herdwick sheep. Jennings Mild is superb, rich and creamy. Their Marathon Bitter also excellent.

Matthew Brown Well done Blackburn, for giving us Wainwright and Matthew Brown. Much of it is sold in the Lakes and perhaps in recognition of this they have a nice John Peel bitter. The beer was named after him, not the other way round.

Not Best Brews
Hartley's Brewed in Ulverston. Seems weak and characterless. Could explain Stan Laurel's early departure to the USA. They drink Hartley's in Barrow. Enough said.

Specialist Food Products
Yes, Cumbria does have them. Some export all over the country. Here are three of the most famous plus some interesting small enterprises.

Alston Cheeses, The Butts, Alston. Tel: 0434 81913.
Specialise in local and North Country cheeses (including Smoked Tynedale and North Pennine).

Ashdown Smokers, Skelleragh Farm, Corney, Nr. Bootle. Tel: 0229 718324.

Dry curing and smoking, wild game and Herdwick Macon (macon is mutton bacon).

Bar Woodall Cumberland Hams, Lane End, Waberthwaite, Nr. Millom. Tel: 0229 717237.

Makers of the famous Waberthwaite Cumberland sausage (probably the county's best). They use traditional ingredients - ale, molasses - and no artificial preservatives. Has a postal service (and currently supplies the London Hilton Hotel) and various outlets throughout the county.

Tynedale Spa Cheese, Holme View, Gilsland. Tel: 06977 47481.

Cumberland Cheese, Thornby Moor Dairy, Aikton, Wigton. Tel: 06973 43160.

Cumbria Honey, 36 Clifford Road, Penrith. Tel: 0768 62489.

Ancient Receipes, Longtown, Carlisle. Tel: 0228 792062 (Pickles and Preserves).

1915 Anglers Hotel
Ennerdale
(Abrahams Series)

Chapter Six

Towns and Villages

Details and descriptions of the main towns and larger villages in the Lake District, plus their history and main amenities.

☆☆ **Bowness and Windermere**   Population 8,500

The largest town in the National Park. And it can certainly seem it on a bank holiday when it becomes the number one tourist attraction of the Lake District - especially for day trippers as it is the only central LD town to have a railway station. Has the feeling of a seaside resort, rather than an inland town, with most of the usual seaside amenities, but manages, if only just at times, to avoid the worst of seaside squalor and things like amusement arcades and tries hard to remain dignified, despite the hordes.

History Technically, it is two towns, but they are virtually joined together and always considered as one. Bowness is an ancient village, right on the lakeside, centred round the 15th century St Martin's Church. (Martin was a Roman Officer who divided his cloak in half to help a beggar. Jolly kind of him.) The name Bowness comes from Bulness, meaning a promontory which looks like a bull's head, and it does, if you study the map, jutting out into the lake beside Bowness Bay.

Windermere was originally a little village called Birthwaite, about a mile away inland. It only became known as Windermere after the arrival of the Railway in 1848. Wordsworth, fearing that the horrid Lancashire hordes would soon be rushing round the lake to gape at him at Rydal and so ruin his tranquility, tried to stop the railway. He predicted that the little village would be inundated by 'The Advance of the Ten Thousand'. He was right. A veritable explosion took place and Bowness and Windermere changed almost overnight. It wasn't just the hordes but the

New Wealthy from Lancashire who built splendid mansions, many of them Italianate or Gothic fantasies, grand holiday homes to show off their own grandness. There still is a lot of money around Windermere, and quite a few palatial homes and private yacht harbours, but many of the bigger Victorian mansions are no longer private homes. Brockhole, the National Park Centre, used to be one, and so was Belsfield, now a hotel. Belsfield was built by H W Schneider, who used to commute each day to his industrial empire in Barrow, going on his own launch down Windermere to Lakeside, then by a special carriage on the Furness Railway to Barrow. Ah, those were the days.

Amenities Railway station; cruisers on the lake; regular ferry across the lake from Bowness; bus station; masses of hotels and boarding houses; shops; boats; TIC in Victoria Road and at Bowness Bay; Mountain Goat Minibus HQ; Windermere Steamboat Museum; aquarium; cinema; Old Laundry theatre and exhibition; de luxe hotel, Miller Howe, on Rayrigg Road; good food at Porthole Restaurant and Jackson's Bistro; brilliant view of Lake from Orrest Head, just outside Windermere, where on a very clear day you might glimpse Morecambe Bay and Blackpool Tower.

Handy for Beatrix Potter countryside across the ferry; National Park Centre at Brockhole. But oh, those summer crowds.

☆☆ **Keswick** Population 4,762

'The full perfection of Keswick consists of three circumstances, beauty, horror and immensity united' - that was said by an earlier guide book, some two hundred years ago. Also sometimes regally referred to as 'The Queen of Lakeland'. Keswick has a fantastic setting, sandwiched between Derwentwater and Blencathra and Skiddaw. In fact, it is most impressive when seen from a distance as bits of it nowadays scarcely live up to its promise. It is now a major tourist centre and has more bed and breakfast and guest houses per head of population than anywhere else in the country. It is the favourite centre for Lakeland climbers and serious fell walkers. Always busy in the summer and only really attractive to walk round in the winter.

The lakeshore walk, along Lake Road, is becoming spoilt too with a rather unpleasant tea garden and the collection of portacabins housing the Blue Box Theatre. The theatre itself is first class and a commendable venture, but its setting is tatty. It is soon to have a permanent building, in the same place, when they get all the money. Meanwhile, the latest attraction in Keswick is the Cars of the Stars museum which you can get to along the new shopping precinct, Pack Horse Court, near the Moot Hall.

History The oldest building is Crosthwaite Church at the north west corner of town. The foundations date from 1181, but most of the fabric of the building dates from the 14th century and later. Inside is a memorial to Robert Southey, with an inscription written by his friend William Wordsworth. Canon Rawnsley, co-founder of the National Trust, is buried in the churchyard. Brandlehow, on Derwentwater, was the first property acquired by the Trust in 1902.

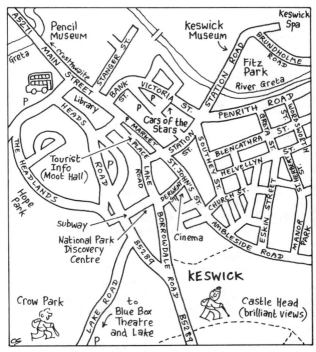

Originally a small market town, Keswick became prosperous with the arrival of the mining industry in the 16th century. Mining engineers were imported from Germany to look for copper, lead, silver and iron. They were treated with suspicion by the locals and forced to make their homes on Derwent Island, but they must have overcome the hostility as German surnames can still be found amongst the local population. The town also became famous for the black-lead mined in Borrowdale and so the Cumberland Pencil Company was born. Southey and Coleridge lived in Keswick at Greta Hall (now part of Keswick school) and overlooking the town is Windebrowe, where William and Dorothy Wordsworth lived for a short time before moving to Dove Cottage.

In 1865 the Cockermouth-Penrith railway line opened and put Keswick on the tourist map. Most of the town's central buildings are Victorian. The Moot Hall, in the market square, was built in 1813. Look out for an unusual one-handed clock. One visitor described it as a cross between an art gallery and a public lavatory, but it actually contains a very good tourist information centre and a small gallery.

The railway line no longer exists, unfortunately, and it has been replaced by the horrid and unloved A66. One of the Special Planning Board's notable failures - they fought hard to stop it but were overruled by central government.

Amenities Bus Station; Derwent Launch Company; Mountain Goat Coach Station. Loads of small hotels - the Station Hotel is the oldest in Keswick; Fitz Park Museum; Pencil Museum; Cars of the Stars; Leisure Pool. Very good information centre in the Moot Hall; cinema; Blue Box Theatre in Lake Road.

Handy for Derwentwater and Bassenthwaite, Thirlmere, Skiddaw, Blencathra, Borrowdale (and the famous Bowder Stone), Castlerigg Stone Circle. Access to the western lakes - Loweswater, Crummock, Buttermere and Ennerdale.

☆☆ **Ambleside** Population 2,671

Beautifully situated in the Rothay valley, one mile north of the head of Lake Windermere. Ambleside is more centrally situated than Bowness and is one of the major centres for the climbing and walking fraternity. It is good, too, for the general visitor and has more escape routes to the surrounding fells and lakes than anywhere else in the Lake District. It gets very, very busy in the summer but, unlike some (eg, Grasmere), it doesn't die in winter and can still be quite lively and interesting when the winter fell walking enthusiasts start arriving.

History The name itself comes from the old Norse for riverside pastures and the town has a long history due to its position at the crossing of many old pack-horse routes. The Romans had a fort at Waterhead, one mile south of the town. Probably built around AD79, Galava fort protected the road which ran from Brougham over Hardknott to Ravenglass. Few stones remain, but the layout is still visible from the surrounding fells - especially Todd Crag on Loughrigg. Recent excavations have revealed more.

The town's most famous building is the Bridge House, which stands in Rydal Road *over* Stock Beck. Local legend says that it was built by a Scotsman to avoid Land Tax, but it was actually the apple-storing house belonging to Ambleside Hall, when this part of the town was all orchard. It is now a National Trust Information Centre but has also been a weaver's shop, family home, cobbler's and a tea shop.

The oldest part of the town dates from the 15th century and is on the Kirkstone side of the river. This was once a centre for corn and bobbin mills and a restored waterwheel can be seen just below the bridge on North Road.

Originally, the railway was to have come right through to Ambleside (there were plans to carry it on up to Keswick and put a tunnel through Dunmail Raise) but it was shelved and 19th century tourists had to come up from Windermere by steam launch and charabanc. An enterprising gentleman by the name of Mr Parsons reinstated the horse and carriage and offers trips from the steamer pier at Waterhead into the centre of Ambleside. Browns coaches also run a quicker but less ethnic minibus service (summer only).

The teacher-training college in the centre of town is named after its founder Charlotte Mason, one of Ambleside's famous residents, and now has the additional title "Lancaster University Lake District Campus". Others included the diarist and close friend of Wordsworth, Harriet Martineau, Dr Arnold of Rugby and W E Forster.

Amenities Bus station; Tourist Information Centre in Church Street; cinema; Armitt Collection; good waterfall and walk (much loved by the Victorians) beside Stock Ghyll, behind the Salutation Hotel. At Waterhead there is another Tourist Information Centre, plus the Windermere cruisers, launches and rowing boat hire.

Handy for Rydal Mount, Windermere steamers, Tarn Hows, Elterwater, Townend at Troutbeck, Loughrigg Fell, the Langdales, Skelwith Force . . . virtually anywhere in the South Lakes. Good small food shops, e.g. Lucy's Specialist Grocers in Chuch Street.

☆☆ **Grasmere** Population 841

Grasmere is everyone's idea of a picturesque Lakeland village and now forever associated with William and Dorothy Wordsworth. Grasmere looks very pretty, especially if seen from Loughrigg Terrace, looking down over the lake with the village against the background of Helm Crag and Dunmail Raise, but the surrounding fells can give it a damp, claustrophobic air, especially in winter. The village is almost wholly orientated towards tourists with cafes and tourist shops. In winter it used to die completely - even the two banks still close down for most of the week - though the presence of sweaters/jumpers shops now encourages the village to stay open out of season. In the summer, it is overrun - the sports field becomes an unsightly mass of caravans and the roads into the village become blocked with coaches disgorging hordes of Japanese in search of Dove Cottage. For all this, Grasmere thinks rather a lot of itself - disdaining what it sees as the commercialism of Dove Cottage and the Museum whilst continuing to feed off the visitors they bring to the area.

In 1979 a member of Grasmere WI compiled a short history of the village which contained the following notable sentence on the subject of 'off-comers':

"Grasmere is the poorer for the losses it has sustained during the last 25 years, losses of people who are not matched by the newer people who have come into the village, many of whom may be good and nice people but are not of the same calibre as their predecessors". So, please don't spit or swear, especially near a resident.

History An ancient road ran through the valley. The village itself is really a string of hamlets along the old pack-horse route to Whitehaven. The road used to come over White Moss and past Dove Cottage, which was originally an inn. The present main road was built in the 1830's. Coming from Ambleside you encounter a rather nasty bend, just before coming into view of the lake; this is known locally as Penny Rock because blasting the rocks to put the road through added a penny to the rates. There is a corpse track over White Moss from Rydal. Coffins were once carried along here to Grasmere church. Up the hill, past Dove Cottage, there is a large, flat stone known as a coffin stone, where the bearers used to rest.

Most of the village buildings are 19th or early 20th century, though the surrounding farms are far older. Grasmere Church, dedicated to St Oswald, dates from the 13th century and is the scene of one of Lakeland's rush-bearing ceremonies. The Wordsworth family graves are in the churchyard and the poet's great-great-great grandson now lives in the valley.

Grasmere Sports Day is one of the oldest and most popular traditional events in the Lake District (probably dating back to Viking times) and involves people from all over the North. At one time even Dove Cottage would close down on Sports Day, so that the staff could go along. Now they have to keep at it, catering for the hordes.

Amenities Tourist Information Centre; boat hire on the Lake; Dove Cottage and the Wordsworth Museum; used to have a good garden centre, now more of a hunt the plants place. During the summer months the Grasmere Players put on amateur theatrical productions for visitors.

Handy for Helvellyn, Fairfield, Thirlmere, Rydal, Loughrigg and Easedale Tarn. Grasmere is at the traditional dividing line between North and South Lakeland - Dunmail Raise - now the main transport artery, the A591. If going south, a nicer route is over Red Bank to Elterwater and back into Ambleside through Clappersgate. This route is also handy for Coniston and Hawkshead and the Langdales.

☆ **Coniston** Population 868

Probably the most disappointing of the major Lakeland villages. It has a magnificent setting but the grey, stone-built village has little character of its own and almost wholly given over to the tourist industry. Its best feature is the way the Old Man rises dramatically behind the houses when seen from the village centre. The road from the south can be rather dreary, apart from Blawith Common. Still, a good centre for walkers, though climbers now seem to prefer the Langdales and Borrowdale.

History

Coniston grew up in the 18th century as a mining village, though copper was mined locally as far back as the Norman times. In the 16th century, Keswick's resident German miners were brought in and the ore extracted was sent up to Keswick for smelting. The area around Church Beck is still referred to as Coppermines Valley.

Coniston was once served by a railway line which came up from Furness. The closure of the line rendered the village rather inaccessible compared to the central Lakeland villages. Its most famous resident was John Ruskin and the 16th century St Andrew's church in the centre of the village contains his tomb. On the village green, just opposite the car park, a large, green-slate seat acts as a memorial to Donald Campbell, who died attempting the world water speed record on the lake in 1967. The name Coniston means 'the king's farm'.

Coniston's oldest building is Coniston Old Hall, a 15th century building once associated with the area's largest landowners, the Flemings. It is now owned by the National Trust and is being restored to its 17th century condition.

Amenities

A good Tourist Information Centre and bookshop in Yewdale Road; Ruskin Museum; launches and boat hire on the lake, plus Gondola.

Handy for

Coniston Old Man, the Furness Fells, Hawkshead, Brantwood.

☆☆ Broughton-in-Furness Population 478

An old market town, built largely in the 18th century. Broughton has a quiet character and the market square has hardly changed in the last two centuries. You can still see the old stone fish slabs. The market itself is on Tuesdays. Because it has been largely missed by the tourist hordes, Broughton is a nice little village, unspoilt and a friendly place to shop. The obelisk in the square was erected to commemorate the jubilee of George III.

Nearby is Broughton Tower (now a select retirement emporium and not open to the public) which was once an old pele tower. The Broughton family are associated with this area back to before the Norman conquest. The name 'Broughton' means 'the hamlet by the stream' - the '-in-Furness' bit was added later to distinguish it from the innumerable other Broughtons dotted about the north-west.

Amenities Broughton is a good base from which to explore the Duddon Valley, Furness Fells and Swinside Stone Circle.

☆☆☆ Hawkshead Population 530

In lowland countryside near the head of Esthwaite Water, Hawkshead is generally reckoned to be the quaintest and prettiest village in the Lake District. Consequently it gets very crowded in mid-summer. Cars are banned from the village itself, which is a good idea, but gives the village something of the air of an open-air museum. It has an attractive muddle of squares and cobbled streets, overhung by timber-framed 17th century buildings. It isn't *too* difficult to imagine what it must have been like when Wordsworth went to school here.

History An important wool town in the Middle Ages. It once contained seven inns. St Michael's Church, up on the hill overlooking the village, is one of the most interesting Lakeland churches. There has been a chapel or church on this site since the 12th century but the present building dates from about the 15th. Inside are decorations and painted texts dating from around 1680.

Ann Tyson's Cottage is in the centre of the village, in Vicarage Lane. It is identified by a plaque, but when William Wordsworth lodged with her, Ann Tyson lived at Colthouse, just outside the village.

In 1548, William Sawrey, the Vicar of Urswick, stayed at what is now the Old Courthouse. Local records say that he was besieged for two days by a 'tumult of insurrection', men armed to the teeth with swords, clubs and daggers. They demanded that he should come out "for they would have one of his arms or legs before going away". Eventually, they were dispersed by neighbours. Why, or what it was all about, no one knows. The name of the village is Old Norse and means' Hauk's summer pasture'.

Amenities Best reached via Windermere Ferry if you are in a hurry. Tourist Information Centre in the main car park. Hawkshead Old Courthouse; Grammar School; Beatrix Potter Gallery. Good pubs, reasonable tea shops.

Handy for Rusland Valley, Grizedale, Beatrix Potter country, Esthwaite Water, Tarn Hows.

☆ Patterdale and Glenridding Population 444

Two rather shapeless villages at the southern end of Ullswater, separated by less than a mile. Patterdale is the prettier and more of a real village. But the setting is spectacular, surrounded on almost all sides by mountains with the only open view over towards the lake. It is a superb centre for walking. The name is a corruption of

'Patrick's Dale'. The patron saint of Ireland is supposed to have preached and baptised here once and along the road towards the boat landing at Glenridding there is St Patrick's Well, which was once thought to have healing properties. Glenridding was a mining village until the mines closed in 1962. Lead was discovered in the area in the 17th century and mining was at its height in the early 19th century with Greenside being one of the best lead mines in the country. Glenridding is best used as a walking centre and as an access to the lake.

Amenities Tourist Information Centre. The two hotels opposite sell reasonable bar lunches. Lake steamers; boat hire and a yachting and windsurfing school available at Glenridding.

Handy for Ullswater, Aira Force, Seldom Seen (a small row of mining cottages hidden up the valley from Glenridding), Brotherswater, Fairfield, Striding Edge - Patterdale is the best place from which to approach Helvellyn - Place Fell. As a centre for walking, Patterdale is excellent.

☆ **Caldbeck** Population 600

As Grasmere is to Wordsworth, so Caldbeck, in its own little way, is to John Peel, the famous huntsman and hero of the song. Set near open fells to the 'back o' Skidda', on the Northern boundary of the National Park, it has a traditional village green, duck pond, a 12th century church and an amazing river gorge called the Howk. Look out for the signs. Behind the church is St Mungo's Well. The churchyard has the bodies of two famous Lakeland characters - John Peel and Mary Robinson, the Beauty of Buttermere. Caldbeck is a real, working village, not yet overrun by tourists, despite a gift shop in a barn. Home of Chris Bonington the mountaineer.

Amenities No hotels, but one pub, Odd Fellows Arms; good village shop; Priests Mill contains craft shops, books and light meals, mining museum. On a busy bank holiday, the Caldbeck Fells will still be quiet and uncrowded. Promise.

Handy for Caldbeck Fells, Skiddaw, Mungrisdale, Bassenthwaite, the Solway Coast.

Cumbrian Towns

The above towns and villages are all in the National Park, but there are many towns and villages on the fringes of the Park which you are likely to visit. Places like Kendal and Cockermouth are assumed to be in the National Park because they are so Lake Districty. These are the main ones you might visit.

☆☆ **Carlisle** Population 70,000

A bustling market and industrial town. Carlisle is Cumbria's capital city, the home of the County Council, Radio Cumbria, Border Television, Cumbria's only Football League team and a host of industries. Not a huge place by southern standards, but it makes up for it with an exciting and confusing one-way system. The city has a long history, much of it reflected in the architecture. It also has a castle and Cumbria's only cathedral.

History It became an administrative centre during the Roman invasion, much of its subsequent history revolving around its proximity to the border (which was not always north of the city - there were times when Carlisle itself was part of Scotland). The Romans called it Luguvalium and placed a fort at Stanwix, on Hadrian's Wall which ran along the northern outskirts of the city.

There has been a castle at Carlisle since 1092 (the first was probably built of wood), occupying a good strategic position which was easily defended. Throughout the Middle Ages it was continually plundered, attacked and generally demolished by marauding Scots. The castle became more and more important and walls were built around the city. In 1568, Mary Queen of Scots fled her own country and was imprisoned at the Castle.

Amenities The castle still stands and today houses the Border Regiment Museum. Carlisle has an excellent museum at Tullie House, a fascinating town trail and a neat cathedral. It has a good main-line railway link with Newcastle, Scotland and the south. Carlisle has its own airfield (with a rather limited range of services). Leisure centre at the Sands. Very good new shopping precinct in The Lanes, flashy yet tasteful. Excellent Victorian covered market. Guildhall Museum. Best bits are round the Old Town Hall (TIC), Fisher Street and Castle Street, now mainly pedestrianised. Hurrah.

☆☆ **Penrith** Population 12,000

A friendly, sandstone-built market town on the eastern fringes of the Lake District. Its character is rather muted, spoilt by traffic during the week. A little overlooked and forgotten, compared with Carlisle, but a nice, friendly place for shopping - especially during the week. One of its best attractions is the view from Penrith Beacon, which stands on a hill overlooking the town. It gives a superb view west across the plain to the Lakeland Fells.

History Dates back to Roman times and was beloved by the marauding Scots once the Romans had gone. An unusual castle, originally merely a defensive tower, was built around 1400 and enlarged in subsequent years, falling into disuse during the 16th century and providing a stock of building material for the local houses. The oldest and most interesting buildings are to be found around the church, most of which date from the 1700's. William and Dorothy Wordsworth went to school in Penrith, for a time, and in later life William wrote of the town's famous Beacon. This structure was once a link in a communication chain which ran the length of the country and was a useful early warning system when the Scots were on the rampage again.

Amenities Penrith makes a reasonable base for a Lakeland or Eden Valley holiday and is improving all the time. Railway station (though trains from Carlisle to Oxenholme don't always bother to stop). The castle - now in ruins - is open to the public and lies in the public park. St Andrew's Church area is very attractive. There is a cinema (which is nothing special and lags behind those in Bowness and Ambleside) but no theatre. Interesting Steam Museum. Very nice bookshop, The Bluebell, in Angel Square, an attractive new shopping area. There are also two olde worlde shops at either end of Market Square which have somehow survived for over 200 years. Graham's, the posh grocers, is Penrith's answer to Fortnum and Mason. Very county. Arnison, the drapers, established 1740, once the home of Wordsworth's grandparents, is in a magnificent time warp. A sticker on the front door announces 'We stock nylons'.

☆☆ **Kendal** Population 23,000

Kendal has suffered in the last few years. Whereas we rated it highly in the first edition, nowadays Penrith seems the friendlier, more attractive place to shop in. Kendal is being spoilt by the traffic and building societies springing up all over the place. The one-way system is diabolical. Take a navigator to make notes of likely parking places as you are swept past them, then aim for them on the second time around.

It is a shame, because Kendal is a busy market town and is quite lively culturally, largely thanks to the Brewery Arts Centre. The best part of Kendal, right at the southern end of the main shopping street, is Kirkland (often referred

KENDAL

to as Kirkland Village). If you're coming in from the south, park at the parish church, then walk along the riverside and go up into the town centre via Kent Street and Market Place. In the town centre is a shopping development, the Westmorland Shopping Centre, with much use made of local stone and natural lighting. It has suffered from high rents/low take-up, but hopefully with chains such as Body Shop showing faith, other will follow.

History It used to be the largest town in the old county of Westmorland, now the administrative centre for the Lake District Special Planning Board (despite being outside the National Park). There was once a Roman fort just south of the town, called Alauna. Suffered from the Scots (like everywhere else) but settled down a little during the 14th century and became famous for Kendal Green, a heavy cloth advertised by Shakespeare in 'Henry IV'.

The castle, which stands on the hill to the east of the River Kent, was built by William Rufus and once belonged to Thomas Parr. His daughter, Katherine, later achieved fame as one of the wives of Henry VIII. Today it is a ruin, but commands a fine view over the town.

Amenities It has one of the best art galleries and museums in the region, Abbot Hall, along with a fascinating Arts Centre at the old Brewery in Highgate. Also has a cinema, now at Brewery Arts, and a good leisure centre. Not too brilliant an area for restaurants, however, but good tea places. Kendal itself has a railway station in the town, plus the main-line station at Oxenholme, hidden miles from anywhere to the east of the town. The town is still reasonable for shopping of all kinds - including some unusual little shops tucked away from the shopping centre. The town also has a thriving insurance industry. Has recently succumbed to out-of-town mega-store mania. (Don't confuse Asda with the new hospital next door . . .).

☆☆ **Cockermouth** Population 7,000

For some reason, the National Park boundary line does a rather vicious loop around Cockermouth, excluding it from the Park. A pity, as it well deserves to be inside. Cockermouth is a fine little town, far easier for everyday shopping than Keswick and distinctly on the way up. Main Street, Market Place and Kirkgate are very attractive and the area around All Saints Church, beside the River Cocker, is pretty. The church too is good, although the wall-to-wall carpet looks a bit odd. Cockermouth has a nice community air about it, the worst aspect of the tourist industry being notably restrained. Perhaps there are advantages in being outside the National Park, after all.

History Cockermouth's most famous building today is undoubtedly Wordsworth House, a fine, Georgian building which dominates the main street. Cockermouth's other notable building is the castle, built originally in the 13th century, though most of what remains dates from 100 years later. Much of it is in ruins, though part is still lived in, by Lady Egremont. It is rarely open to the public, but if you ask nicely, you might be let in. The best time to try is during Cockermouth Festival. The town was subject to the usual Scottish raids and the castle was besieged by Royalists during the Civil War.

Amenities Of all the towns lying just outside the Lake District, Cockermouth is probably the quietest and most interesting to escape to when the crowds of the central Lakes begin to annoy. No cinema or theatre (although Rosehill is within striking distance) and no rail links. Wordsworth House remains the town's main tourist

WAKEFIELD RD.

Wordsworth House

River Derwent

GOTE RD.

CASTLEGATE

MARKET PLACE

CROWN ST.

MAIN STREET

P

STATION ST.

Tourist Info

All Saints Church

KIRKGATE

P

SOUTH STREET

COCKER LANE

BULLART ST.

P

KITTSON LANE

STATION ROAD

LORTON ST.

B5292

RIVERSIDE

River Cocker

VICTORIA RD.

N.B. Parking in Main Street is often hopeless, so try Walter Willsons...

NEW ROAD

TWEED MILL LANE

ROAD

LAMPLUGH RD.

A5086

FERN BANK

Hope Park

RUBBYBANKS RD.

PARKSIDE AVE.

COCKERMOUTH

attraction, but don't miss Market Place and Kirkgate. Cockermouth is good for provision shopping, especially since the new Walter Willson opened - not so hot for gifts and Lake District souvenirs. Good teas, antiques, excellent veggie dinners at Quince and Medlar, three nice little museums (toys, crystals, printing), good art gallery.

☆☆ Whitehaven Population 26,000

While Cockermouth and Penrith have crept into Lakeland, and been accepted as one of us, the West Coast towns have long been considered out of sight, if not off the map. Few tourists will linger long in Barrow, unless they love industrial history, or are trying the find Furness Abbey or Piel Island, or will find much to detain them in Workington, apart from Portland Square, but hurry hurry to Whitehaven, before everyone else discovers it. At the moment, it's a tourist free zone. There you will mingle with ethnic Cumbrians. 'Coom on, Tracey'.

History In the 18th century, Whitehaven was the nation's third port, after London and Bristol, rich on coal exports and tobacco imports. The Georgian town had been laid out on a grid pattern by the Lowther family, still big in Cumbria, the first planned town in Britain. George Washington's granny lived in Whitehaven. John Paul Jones, founder of the American Navy, raided the town in 1778, the last occasion on which Britain was invaded from the sea.

Amenities After some dismal decades of decline in the shipping and coal industries, Whitehaven is coming to life again. You can see it in the spruced up Georgian streets and squares. It's not all hand-outs and guilt money from Sellafield - but civic pride and a new if gentler affluence. The Georgian bit is towards the harbour - Lowther Street, King Street, Roper Street. Once you've worked out the one way streets, and managed to park, you can explore all the delights on foot. Pause a while to read the monster mosaic poem in the Market Place, then you can go to Michael Moon's amazing book shop and compliment him. (He wrote the verse). The entire harbour is now a conservation area. Walk out on Sir John Rennie's West Pier, till you're almost half way to America, touch the sand-stone blocks, then look back and think of England. Don't forget St Bees just down the coast. Excellent eating at Chez Collette and Bruno's. Museum in the Civic Hall. Culture at Rosehill Theatre.

☆ **Maryport** Population 11,000

Was originally a village called Ellenfoot, till Humphrey Senhouse developed the port and called it after his wife Mary. Sweet, huh. Birthplace of Thomas Ismay, founder of the White Star Line, who built the Titanic, and Joseph Lister, the surgeon. Today, it's a smaller, but somehow sadder version of Whitehaven, despite all that development in the Harbour. The plans are exciting, the new buildings architecturally interesting, the new Marina attractive, the Flying Buzzard amusing, but much of the harbour still looks like a waste land. In the town itself, don't miss the quaint little maritime museum. Find the cobbled Fleming Square, walk on to the Senhouse Roman Museum, down the cliff, and back along the promenade. You'll probably meet no one.

☆ **Ulverston** Population 11,000

Ulverston is a typical, friendly, northern market town (great on Thursdays) with a market cross, a nice old cobbled street and a nearby canal. Overlooking the town is the monument to Sir John Barrow - a 90 foot high imitation of the Eddystone Lighthouse which is a feature of the landscape that can be seen for miles. There is a public path up

Hoad Hill leading to the monument and from this vantage there are good views of the town and surrounding countryside. Ulverston is largely unspoilt, but shows signs of decay, which is a great pity. It holds the world's largest collection of Laural and Hardy memorabilia, in the Laurel and Hardy Museum. It is also good for teas and lunches - try the Renaissance Centre in Fountain Street.

☆☆ Grange-over-Sands Population 4,000

Cumbria's riviera, according to the Tourist Board people, who cunningly photograph it to include Grange's solitary palm tree swaying in the breeze. It is a Victorian town, genteel and once a popular holiday resort. If the beach was better, it might have become another Blackpool. As it is, it tends to be popular mostly as a retirement town (known locally as 'the waiting room'), though the choice may seem an odd one as Grange is famous for its hills. The town is largely unspoilt and seems to be made entirely of grey limestone. Behind the town, on Hampsfell, is a spectacular limestone escarpment, now protected but once quarried extensively for building houses and walls. On the escarpment is a peculiar limestone structure known as Hampsfell Hospice, built for the 'shelter and entertainment' of wanderers over the fell. The 'entertainment' largely consists of a direction indicator on the roof (there is a metal stairway leading up to it) which enables the visitor to 'sight' various features of the landscape. The view from here on a clear day is fantastic - from Blackpool Tower to Skiddaw.

The sands across to Morecambe Bay are very dangerous, although there is a highway - if you know where to look for it - and the official guide takes across parties. The beach is unsuitable for swimming (although there is the occasional windsurfer) and rather spoilt by the railway line which cuts across between the beach and the town. A good promenade, though, leading along to the open-air, salt-water swimming pool.

Villages

In alphabetical order, nine villages we think worth a detour.

☆☆ Askham

An ancient and pretty village a few miles south of Penrith. Many houses dated between 1650 and 1750. Askham Hall is 14th century in parts and was developed on the site of a pele tower. It is now the home of the Earl of Lonsdale. Lowther Castle is only a facade, now mostly ruins. It was not a genuine castle but a Gothic mansion built in the 19th century. Nearby is Lowther Park. The village is handy for Haweswater, Penrith, Ullswater and the Eden Valley. Good pubs.

☆☆☆ Cartmel

A lovely little village, just west of Grange-over-Sands, with a beautiful square, an old village pump still standing and a nice river running through it. Very picturesque and popular on Sunday lunchtimes as it contains a number of good pubs (the King's Arms is probably the best). Most famous for the Priory, which dates back to 1188, though only the Priory Church and Gatehouse remains, now owned by the National Trust and usually houses exhibitions of paintings by the Lake Artists Society. The square is often spoilt by parked cars - the best place to park is through the village, by the race course. The village is becoming a bit picture-book, but is still less of an open museum than Hawkshead.

☆☆ Grange-in-Borrowdale

Once a grange of Furness Abbey. Only a small hamlet but beautifully situated alongside the River Derwent. One of Lakeland's prettiest villages.

☆☆ Hesket Newmarket

A northern hamlet, well out of the tourist beat. Once an important market, now it is just a pleasant village built around a long green. Dickens stayed in the village in 1857 whilst on a Lake District tour. Hesket Hall is a dull but odd building with a peculiar roof and twelve, angular projections forming the walls. The corners of these projections are supposed to make an effective sundial. Good pub, with its own real ale.

☆ Ireby

On the northern edge of the Lakes. It gained a market charter in the 13th century but in time Wigton and Cockermouth proved too much competition for it. Look out for the original church, a simple Norman affair, stuck in a field 1 1/2 miles outside the village on the Torpenhow road. Ireby is good as a base for the Solway Coast, Bassenthwaite and Skiddaw.

☆☆☆ Maulds Meaburn

Not in the LD proper, as it's across the M6, towards Appleby, but many discriminating Cumbrians consider it the county's prettiest village. Fascinating stone houses, each one different, on either bank of the River Lyvennet. No pub.

☆ Rosthwaite

A little hamlet in the Borrowdale Valley, useful as a base for setting off for Watendlath, Seatoller, Langstrath and Sty Head. The footpath up to Watendlath used to be quite attractive but now appears on the landscape as a mini-motorway.

☆☆☆ **Troutbeck**

One of the Lakes' most famous villages. Strung along a hillside just north of Windermere, it is really a series of hamlets grouped about a series of wells. The cottages and barns date from the 17th to 19th century - the finest of all being Townend, built in 1626 and now looked after by the National Trust and open to the public. There are two old, restored inns, the sign to the Mortal Man being quite famous for its rhyme:

> *O mortal man that lives by bread,*
> *What is it makes thy nose so red?*
> *Thou silly fool that looks so pale,*
> *'Tis drinking Sally Birkett's ale.'*

Note that there is another Lakeland Troutbeck, just off the A66 near Threlkeld. Even Pevsner got the two muddled.

☆☆☆ **Watendlath**

A moorland hamlet of farms, set artistically beside a large tarn. It is situated to the east of Rosthwaite and was the remote, isolated setting for Hugh Walpole's 'Judith Paris'. Now it is a magnet for tourists and is to be avoided on summer bank holidays. It can be reached by leaving the main Borrowdale road and crossing Ashness Bridge. This road is a menace in the high season and it is better to leave the car and walk. Good teas.

Best Kept Cumbrian Villages

For those who like their villages terribly clean. The Best Kept Village Competition has been run by Voluntary Action Cumbria for the past twenty-five years, awarding large and small villages that have been kept neat and tidy. It covers the whole county, not just the NP. For the past ten years, these have been the award-winners:

Best Kept Large Village   Best Kept Small Village

	Best Kept Large Village		Best Kept Small Village
1983	Braithwaite	1983	Warcop
1984	Lazonby	1984	Bassenthwaite
1985	Grasmere	1985	Bouth
1986	Dalston	1986	Great Salkeld
1987	Natland	1987	Wreay (Carlisle)
1988	Thursby	1988	Bassenthwaite
1989	Dalston	1989	Great Orton
1990	Levens	1990	West Newton
1991	Lazonby	1991	West Newton
1992	Caldbeck	1992	Great Strickland

Chapter Seven

Lakes

Facts and facilities of the Major Lakes, including steamers, sailing, fishing and other amenities. Plus a look at some rather interesting Tarns.

There are sixteen lakes in the Lake District, so most experts agree. The other bits of water are tarns. A few tarns, despite their second division status, are in fact bigger than one of the so-called lakes, but most tarns are small, in fact very small, and some have not even the dignity of being named. It's the Sixteen Lakes which are the glamorous attractions, the crowd pullers.

Only one of the Sixteen Lakes should technically ever have the word 'Lake' attached to its name. All the Lakes, you see, have either the word 'mere' or 'water' already in their name, so there is no need for the word 'Lake'. Except one. Which is it? Read on . . .

Lakes	Length (miles)	Width (miles)	Height above sea level (feet)	Depth (max. feet)
Windermere	10 1/2	1	130	219
Ullswater	7 1/2	3/4	476	205
Coniston	5 1/4	1/2	143	184
Bassenthwaite	4	3/4	223	70
Haweswater	4	1/2	790	198
Thirlmere	3 5/8	1/2	583	158
Derwent Water	3	1 1/4	244	72
Wastwater	3	1/2	200	258
Crummock	2 1/2	5/8	321	144
Ennerdale	2 1/2	3/4	368	148
Esthwaite	1 1/2	3/8	217	80
Buttermere	1 1/4	3/8	329	94
Loweswater	1 1/4	3/8	429	60
Grasmere	1	1/2	208	75
Rydal Water	3/4	1/4	181	55
Elterwater	1/2	1/4	187	50

☆☆☆ **Windermere**

Windermere is not just Cumbria's, but England's largest lake - 10 1/2 miles long and one mile wide with a maximum depth of 219 feet. It is named after a Norse hero, Winand or Vinandr, and until this century it was a busy highway, probably used by the Romans for ferrying troops and then later used for transporting iron ore and charcoal and passengers. Now, for the last 80 years, the boats are purely pleasure bound - but there are still hundreds and hundreds of them. In the season, they glisten from afar like tadpoles with hardly enough water to go round, or so it often appears.

Windermere in summer is not a place for peace and quiet. It is still a beautiful lake, with well wooded shores and some dramatic mountain views looking east and north across and up the lake, but it is essentially a playground, with more aquatic diversions than any other English lake.

To escape the crowds, yet still savour the lake, get across quickly from Bowness on the ferry and walk the western side. There is no road nor any towns or villages along the western shore. You can walk a lakeside public path, most of the way, then gaze across at the mansions, and the masses, on the other side and try to pretend you can't hear the motor boats.

Amenities

Windermere Cruisers   The cruiser operations on Windermere has now reverted to its original, 1848, name of the Windermere Iron Steamboat Company. (After the trading standards people looked long and hard at the word 'steamboat', but they've let it go.) They run three boats, Swan, Teal and Tern. There is a regular service up and down the lake, from Lakeside in the south up to Bowness and then to Ambleside, a one way trip of approximately 1 1/4 hours. First boat from Lakeside is usually about nine o'clock in the morning.

Services run from Good Friday to early November, seven days a week, with evening cruises on Wednesdays and Saturdays during the summer season. All boats are fully licensed. They also do "The Lakeland Link" in summer season - Ambleside/Bowness by boat to Lakeside, train to Haverthwaite, bus to Holker Hall. Admission price to HH and afternoon tea at Lakeside included in price £16.75 return.

Special Fares   Lots of permutations, such as all day sails between any of the piers, family tickets, seven day tickets, special pensioner rates.

Best Bargain   Rail-Sail tickets; you can start on the little private steam railway line at Haverthwaite, go by train to Lakeside, then into a cruiser and up the lake and back. The Rail-Sail ticket is a good way to get a feeling of the lake and surrounding area - and it is also good for parking as there's ample car parking near Lakeside and at Haverthwaite. Parking in Bowness or Ambleside can be hell in the season.

Further details Timetables from any TIC, hotel foyers, or the Manager, Windermere Iron Steamboat Co, Lakeside, Ulverston. Tel: 05395 31188.

Bowness Bay Boating Company and Ambleside Motor Launch Co.
Regular launch services from Bowness and Waterhead all year round, except Christmas Day. They call in at the Windermere Steamboat Museum and Brockhole on selected trips. Special winter services, including Winter Wonderland cruises. Evening cruises with wine and trips round the islands. Guided commentary on all trips. Also motor and rowing boats for hire.

    Bowness - telephone 05394 43360
    Waterhead - telephone 05394 33187.

Windermere Ferry Regular, all round the year, all day long, public service from Bowness Nab across the lake, for cars and pedestrians. Queues form in the height of the summer, so heed the notices about any delays. Takes only seven minutes.

    The ferry is a vital link for holiday makers and for those who live on the western shores of the lake as by road, round the lake, can put up to an hour and at least ten miles on the journey.

    There has been some sort of ferry using this exact crossing for about 500 years. Wordsworth went across it as a school boy, on his way to Hawkshead. Today, it's a motorised service, but if you look carefully you'll see the boat pulls itself across the lake on two chains. Very ingenious.

Windermere Boat Registration Scheme All power-driven boats must be registered for use on Windermere - this means power-driven vessels of any kind, even seaplanes. Once registered, the vessel has to display a registration number of a certain size and type. LDSPB's address in Kendal deals with paperwork/computer work. The place to get details and apply for registration of boats is now Lake Adminstration Office, Ferry Nab, Windermere 05394 42753. This makes sense since this is also the public slipway. Also deals with moorings and has the Lake Warden's base. There is a yearly charge to register.

Navigation Rules There are currently 10,000 boats registered. The slight drop in numbers of sportsboats is considered to be because some people already assume the 10 mph speed limit is in force. Could also be The Recession. Increase in number of jet skis - now 300 - reflects their extreme mobility, not their extreme nuisance factor. Just a thought - was the flying boat that landed on the lake in 1990 registered? When you register, one of the details you have to give is the length of boat. If all the boats currently registered were placed bow to stern and strung along the length of the lake, they would more than cover the distance from Fell Foot to Waterhead.

Lake Rules The only lake at present with no maximum speed limit, but there are 10mph and 6mph speed zones. Look out for speed cops. Yes, they do exist.

Lake Windermere Collision Rules Copies available from Lake Administration Office, Ferry Nab - will send by post, or from TICs.

Sailing Boat Hire, Canoe Hire both available on Lake: Windermere Sailing Centre at Millerground 05394 88107.

Rowing Boat Hire very popular on Windermere - boats available from Bowness Bay Boating Co./Ambleside Motor Launch Co.

Sailing Clubs Royal Windermere Yacht Club - tel. 05394 43106; Lake District Boat Club - tel. 05394 43595.

Sailing Holidays Windermere Lake Holidays Afloat, Bowness Bay - telephone 05394 43415. Hire sailing cruisers by the weekend or week.

Water Skiing The 6mph restriction applies to all boats in the speed limit areas - anyone exceeding the limit is liable to prosecution. Water skiing can become dangerous on summer weekends, the lake gets so crowded. A good club exists - Low Wood Water Sports Centre, Low Wood Hotel. Telephone 05394 34004. They offer "come and try . . ." facilities.

Lake Warden Public slipway, Ferry Nab, Bowness-on-Windermere - telephone 05394 42753. Summer - open daily between 0800-2200 hrs, winter - 0900 - 1700. Closed Christmas Day.

Moorings Contact Lake Administration Office for residential moorings and holiday moorings.

Marina Yes, Windermere does have one, near Storrs Hall. Usually thought of by road bound landlubbbers as a holiday village. It is, but it does have boating facilities. Passing craft can go in and tie up. 05394 46551.

Launch Sites

1. Public slipway, Ferry Nab (1/4 mile south of Bowness). Two launch facilities with car parking and room for trailers. Lake Administration Office. Fee payable (but usually the cheapest). 05394 42753.

2. Windermere Aquatic, Glebe Road, Bowness - telephone 05394 42121. Fee payable.

3. Waterhead Marine, Waterhead, Ambleside - telephone 05394 32424. Fee payable.

4. Low Wood Sports Centre, Low Wood Hotel, Ambleside - telephone 05394 34004. Fee payable - higher than the others but includes use of all facilities and is for a day, not per launch.

These sites are all for powered craft and dinghies. Launching for small (under 5hp) craft and dinghies available at Waterhead and Fell Foot (latter owned by the N.T. and only open from March to October). 05395 31273. Charge made at Waterhead by Bowness Bay Boating Co, who lease the beach.

Launching for non-powered craft only - dinghies, canoes, windsurfers available from NT land along the western shore between Ferry House and Wray Castle - contact The Warden,, Harrowslack House, Far Sawrey. 05394 44746. Fee payable. N.T. very particular about beaching power boats on their shoreline - basically you can't.

Other Attractions

Belle Isle Well - it's still attractive to sail round - pity there's no landing.

Windermere Steamboat Museum. Rayrigg Road, Windermere - telephone 05394 45565. (see chapter 10).

Brockhole National Park Visitor Centre
(see chapter 2).

Wray Castle On the western shore, just north of the Ferry landing stage. Owned by the National Trust. Grounds open to the public. (See chapter 12).

Lake Windermere Festival runs for 10 days in early July. Lots of events and attractions, mostly centring on Bowness and Waterhead. Also helicopter flights, water ski displays, power boat races. Contact Bowness Bay TIC for dates.

Windermere Power Boat Week based at the Low Wood Water Sports Centre. A week of attempts on various world records. Usually held the beginning of October. Contact the School on 05394 34004 for further details.

Swimming You can swim almost anywhere, if you can escape the private gardens and private launching sites. And if you can stand the cold. But it is very cold, even at the height of the season, and can be dangerous, with all the power boats zooming about. Best place is Fell Foot Park, the National Trust place at the southern end of the lake.

First man to swim the entire length of Windermere was Joseph Foster of Oldham in September 1911. An annual Windermere swim is held every spring.

Motor Boat Racing takes place regularly at Windermere Motor Boat Club, Broad Leys, Ghyll Head (tel: 05394 43284). First races were held in 1918. In 1930, Sir Henry Seagrave was drowned while speeding on Windermere.

☆☆☆ Ullswater

Windermere is bigger and has more going on, Derwentwater is more compact, but Ullswater has variety and grandeur and is bordered by some of the best walks in the Lake District. If we had to choose just one lake, for amenities and for beauty, it would be Ullswater.

At the Pooley Bridge end it is gentle, flat, almost boring, but as you work your way along its length, the landscape around becomes more picturesque and then, finally, you get the grandeur and magnificence of the southern end at Glenridding. A good view is also to be had from Kirkstone Pass, looking down with Brothers Water in the foreground.

Ullswater is a serpentine lake, snaking its way through the landscape for seven and a half miles. It is three-quarters of a mile wide and 205 feet deep. It is best explored from the southern end, where the lake is dominated by St Sunday Crag, Place Fell, Fairfield and Helvellyn. Walk along the path on the eastern shore from Howtown to Patterdale and you'll appreciate the lake at its best. The opposite side, where the main road is, is usually crowded in summer and best avoided by walkers.

During the 1960's, Ullswater was the scene of a battle between the National Park Authority and Manchester Corporation, who wanted to extract water to feed the reservoir at Haweswater. As a compromise, the pumping station was hidden completely underground at the northern end and now the average visitor is not even aware of its existence.

Ullswater is probably the best lake for sailing. The peace used to be spoilt somewhat by large numbers of water-skiers, until the effective ban in 1983 when the speed limit over the whole lake was dropped to 10mph. Someone has actually managed it at that speed, so water-skiers haven't been outlawed (which would have been unfair). It just isn't very exciting any more.

The name comes from the first Lord of Ullswater, a Norse settler named L'Ulf. Ullswater is a public highway and was once used for transporting miners and ore from Glenridding. At the lake foot is a hill called Dunmallet which was once the site of an Iron Age fortification.

Amenities

Anyone can launch a boat on Ullswater, either sail or motorised, and there is no registration scheme like Windermere. There is, however, a speed restriction which covers the whole lake.

Steamers Two 'steamers' run up and down the lake. They resemble the cruisers on Windermere (and like them, 'steamer' is a courtesy title since they all run on diesel). These are run by the delightfully named Ullswater Navigation and Transit Company Limited and both are over a hundred years old. 'Lady of the Lake' was first launched in 1877 and 'Raven' twelve years later. They run from the pier at Glenridding to Pooley Bridge, stopping off at Howtown. The main service runs from the Sunday before Easter until the 30th September. During October, a reduced service runs from Glenridding to Howtown, which takes 35 minutes. Going the whole length of the lake takes about an hour.

Ullswater Navigation and Transit Company Ltd
13 Maude Street   The Pier
Kendal   Glenridding
0539 721626   07684 82229.

Boat Hire Rowing and motor boats from Glenridding and Pooley Bridge. Also from Ullswater Caravan, Camping and Marina Park, Watermillock. Tel: 07684 86666. Sailing craft from Glenridding Sailing School (see below).

Sailing Ullswater is excellent for sailing (especially now the water-skiers have gone). Launching can take place at Willow Trees, just north of the Glenridding steamer pier, or at Glencoyne Bay or Howtown.

The Glenridding Sailing School is based at The Spit, Glenridding; contact Tony or Kate Longworth 07684 86601 (home) or 07684 82541 (Sailing school). Sailing craft can be launched for a small charge and a rescue service operates, rescuing "everything in sight".

Warning - there is a 10mph speed restriction over the whole lake and as at Windermere, the National Park people have a patrol boat. (Incidentally, one of our researchers, putting in time, analysed the Ullswater steamers' timetable - and found they must be averaging 12mph . . .)

Launch Sites

1. Howtown - access from the B5320, 3 miles south of Pooley Bridge, at a public launch site. All craft, max. length 20'.

2. Glencoyne Bay - 1 mile north of Glenridding on the A592. Light powered craft only.

3. National Trust land - north of steamer pier by the Willow Trees, or on the adjoining beach at Glenridding. No powered craft.

4. Ullswater Yacht Club, Howtown. 07684 86333.

5. Park Foot Caravan Site. 07684 86309.

Also from Ullswater Caravan, Camping and Marina Park and Glenridding Sailing School.

Other Attractions Gowbarrow Park, now a National Trust property, open to the public and the site of Wordsworth's daffodils. Aira Force; Askham; Dacre.

☆☆ Coniston Water

If you travel along the busy road near the western shore, Coniston can be a little disappointing. You can see the lake, but it is against a background of low fells and forest plantations. This is also the most 'touristy' route, with ice cream vans in every layby. It is quieter and more satisfying along the narrow road on the east and from here you can see Coniston Water at its best, with the Old Man and its neighbours rearing up magnificently in the background. (This can often happen with the lakes - you get there, wonder what all the fuss is about, trundle about a bit - then suddenly it hits you.)

The lake is 5 1/4 miles long, half-a-mile wide and 184 feet deep. It has three small islands, all owned by the National Trust. Peel Island featured in Arthur Ransome's *Swallows and Amazons* as Wild Cat Island. On some very old maps, Coniston appears as Thurston's Mere. It has been a public highway for centuries. Ore mined at the head of the lake used to be carried down to the foot and then transported to the quay at Greenodd (yes, that jumble of roads and bypasses - which cunningly conceals one or two nice houses - was once a busy port).

The lake is famous as the scene of Donald Campbell's attempts at the world water speed record. In 1959 he established a record of 260.35mph in Bluebird. He was killed trying to break the record in 1967 and his body has never been recovered. There is a memorial in the village. Photographs of his attempts can be seen in the Ruskin Museum.

Amenities

Coniston has a lake transport service, but it seems a shame to classify it mundanely as an 'amenity' as it is really one of the lake's star attractions . . .

☆☆☆ Gondola

In 1859, a steam yacht, Gondola, was launched from Coniston Hall and ran a regular service up and down the lake for nearly 80 years. Eventually it was taken out of service, its engine sold to power a saw mill and the hull became a house boat. It was washed ashore in 1963 and lay derelict until the National Trust started taking an interest in the mid-70's. With some daring, they decided to try to restore her. Now owned and operated by the Trust, this unique and beautiful craft has been back in service since 1980. It takes over 80 passengers, is decked out with luxurious upholstery and fittings and is the only silent method of powered transport anywhere in the Lake District. It is uncanny. Highly recommended, just for the experience. Best to sit at the front - there can be specks of soot at the back.

Gondola runs from April to the beginning of October, daily except for Saturdays, that's when the amazing Mr Spragg cleans all the miles of pipe. . . . It travels the 25 minute route between Coniston pier and Park-A-Moor, on the south-east shore, and stops off at Brantwood on the eastern shore.

Note: If the weather is bad, Gondola sometimes cannot run. To check, ring The Booking Secretary, Coniston, on 05394 41288, or the Tourist Information Centre, 05394 41533.

Boats Coniston is still a public highway, but launching is restricted due to land access. The best place - also for boat hire - Coniston Boating Centre at the north of the lake (telephone 05394 41366). It is run by the National Park people. They hire rowing and motor boats, and very quiet electric launches, sailing dinghies and Canadian canoes and can offer assistance with launching and recovery, for a small charge.

Rowing boats can be launched from the two car parks at either end of the lake - Monk Coniston and Brown Howe. At Coniston Hall there is a sailing club and RYA members are welcome - apply to Coniston Old Hall, Coniston, Cumbria. 05394 41580.

There is a speed restriction of 10mph over the whole lake.

Launching Sites

1. Coniston Boating Centre, telephone 05394 41366. All craft. Fee payable.

2. Access from Monk Coniston car park at north end of the lake (not power).

3. Access from Brown Howe car park at south-west end of the lake. No power craft.

Other attractions The star of Coniston's shoreline is Brantwood, Ruskin's home, which stands on the eastern bank. (See chapter 11.) There are nature trails available for this part of the shore. The road down the east side has several nice little car parks tucked amongst the trees.

☆ Bassenthwaite Lake

This is it - the only true 'lake' in the Lake District; the others are all 'meres' or 'waters'. However, just to confuse matters, Wordsworth called it Broadwater. It is one of the largest lakes but also one of the shallowest - 4 miles long, 3/4 mile wide, but just 70 feet deep. It is the most northerly of the lakes and has no real settlement on its shores. Apart from the hideous A66, which blasts its way up the west side, the shores are relatively unspoilt and as the lake is now owned by the Lake District Special Planning Board, it should be kept that way. It is a good lake for bird life, although there are no recognised hides.

Towering over the lake at the Thornthwaite corner is a craggy white rock which looks down over the A66. This is known as 'The Bishop'. Legend has it that a bishop once tried to ride up the screes at this point to demonstrate his faith in God. His horse, however, must have been less pious because it fell and they were both killed. By tradition, the rock is kept whitewashed by the landlord of the nearby hotel. (Volunteers welcome.) On the day of the Silver Jubilee in 1977, the stone appeared red, white and blue - painted by hands unknown.

An excellent view of the lake and the surrounding countryside is available from Dodd, on the east side.

Bassenthwaite can look very mysterious - which is how Tennyson saw it when he stayed by its shores and wrote *Idylls of the King*.

Amenities No public right of navigation.

Very few. Because of attempts to conserve wildlife in the area, shore access is limited and all powered craft are banned. There are few public launch sites. LDSPB controls access. Permits to launch dinghies, canoes, windsurfers and rowing boats can be obtained from their National Park Blencathra Centre, Threlkeld 07687 79633 and also from various outlets around the lake. Priority is given to wildlife so some areas of lake are permanently no-go zones.

Bassenthwaite Sailing Club, 07687 76341, is at the north end of Lake. Members of other sailing clubs can launch here.

There is a shore path which runs the length of the west shore, though this isn't the best point from which to view the lake. The only access to the east shore is at Mirehouse, which has a wooded walk in the grounds. The house is now open to the public.

Car park near south end of Lake - Woodend - also good for Whinlatter forest.

Launching Sites Piel Wyke, Beck Wythop.

☆ Haweswater

One long reservoir - 4 miles long, half-a-mile wide and 198 feet deep. It *used* to be only 2 1/2 miles long and 3/8 of a mile wide and the water level was 96 feet lower. At its head stood the attractive village of Mardale, whose farms in the middle of the last century used to send 3000lb of butter a week to Manchester. There was also the Dun Bull, a renowned inn. Then, in 1940, the Manchester Water Corporation stepped in, spent £5,000,000 on building a 120 foot high dam and Haweswater became a reservoir. Mardale is now under the water.

Haweswater is one of the most isolated and difficult lakes to reach. From the central lakes you have to make a long detour by road and travel out towards Penrith. It is only accessible from the north-east and south-east sides and is in wild and unspoilt countryside. Rather lonely and if you're only in the area for a short time you might not think it is worth it, but loved by Lakeland experts. The best way to discover Haweswater is to park at the head of the Kentmere Valley (turn up from Staveley) and walk over the Nan Bield Pass. Haweswater remains the largest reservoir in the north-west. The National Park people and the North West Water Authority are plotting better access for the future, but its very wildness has attracted nature conservation proposals, so the public may end up no better off. In very dry weather, when the water is low, the shore line goes bleached and looks very strange and moon-like. In very, very dry weather, look out for signs of the sunken village.

Amenities None, except for the scenery.

☆☆ Thirlmere

Another reservoir. Thirlmere was once two much-smaller lakes, called Leatheswater and Brackmere, with a footbridge across their narrow middle. In 1879, the area was purchased by Manchester Corporation Water Works, a dam was built at the north end and the water level raised by 54 feet. It is now called Thirlmere, which means the lake with the hollow (the hollow presumably being where the two earlier lakes joined). It is now just over 5 1/2 miles long and half-a-mile wide. At its deepest it is 160 feet.

Thirlmere is in fact quite a pretty lake, very clear and pure and the woods along the west shore have a wild look about them, despite being conifers. It is best appreciated from the lovely little road which threads its way along the west shore line, through the trees. From the A591, it can look rather barren, especially in mid summer when the water level drops, leaving a ragged, white scar round the 'rim' of the lake. One of the best and most peculiar viewpoints is at Hause Point, about half-way along the west road. You have to climb some metals steps and find yourself on top of a rock along with a garden seat. The view to Dunmail Raise is good although Helvellyn is uninspiring from this angle.

The lake has now been opened up to the public by the NWWA. There is access at most of the laybys along the west road and from the Station Coppice car park, half-way along the east side. There is a forest trail on each side of the lake, although the Launchy Gill and Swirls nature trails have suffered from tree felling recently and are very difficult to negotiate. On the west side is a new footpath, constructed by the British Trust for Conservation Volunteers, which leads to Raven Crag, an excellent viewpoint.

Unspoilt lakeshore footpath and access for boating at Armboth, on the west shore. Strictly no powered craft, but sailing dinghies, canoes and sailboards permitted. No permission necessary and no fee payable. The lake is open to fishing to holders of NWWA rod licences. No permit necessary.

☆☆☆ Derwentwater

Now we enter an area of raging controversy; which is best, Ullswater or Derwentwater? We think Ullswater just makes it, thanks to its magnificent scenery and variety, but Derwentwater has been called 'the Queen of the Lakes' and it is nicely compact and very pretty. Friars Crag, which is along Lake Road, less than a mile from the centre of Keswick, has one of the finest views in the country, looking across the lake and down into Borrowdale. Derwentwater is great for walking, but don't bother with the road. For a really spectacular excursion use the launch service - there are piers all round the lake and good walks are available from any of them.

The name means the 'lake of the river which abounds in oak trees'. The shores are still heavily-wooded and largely in the care of the National Trust. It is 1 1/4 miles wide and therefore the widest of the lakes. (Most of them have a superlative of one sort, if you search hard enough.) It's three miles long but its maximum depth is only 72 feet. The average depth is 18 feet, which means that this is one of the first lakes to *freeze* over. Famous for skating.

It has five islands - Derwent, Lord's, Rampsholme and St Herbert's. Lord's Island used to be the site of the house of the Earl of Derwentwater, hence the name. St Herbert's is reputed to have once been the home of St Herbert or Hubert, a disciple of St Cuthbert. It became a place of pilgrimage and the spot where the monks and friars used to wait for the boat to take them across is now called Friars Crag.

The fifth island is a real oddity. Marked on the maps as Floating Island, it is down in the south-west corner and only appears once every three years or so. No, it isn't a ghost - it's a mass of weeds and rotting vegetation which pops to the surface now and then, buoyed up by marsh gases. More of an event than an island.

Derwentwater is a public highway and was used for transporting charcoal, graphite and ore. Keswick's miners used to live on Derwent Island.

Amenities

The Derwentwater Launch Company operates a launch service which runs from Lake Side, just outside Keswick. The launches are unlike those on Ullswater and Windermere, being a lot smaller and with no pretensions to being called steamers. The launches leave every half-hour (every 15 minutes during July and August); the first goes round the lake clockwise, then anti-clockwise. The clockwise route takes you to the piers at Ashness Bridge, Lodore Falls, High Brandlehow, Low Brandlehow, Hawse End, Nichol End and back to Keswick. The round trip takes 50 minutes and the time between piers is about 10 minutes each. The service runs from a week before Easter to the last Sunday in November. It is a good way of getting to a number of walks, but the launches themselves can be noisy and uncomfortable.

Keswick Launch Co
Boat Landing, Lakeside
Keswick
07687 72263.

Boat Hire Nichol End Marine offer all types of boats, sailing craft and canoes - 07687 73082. Platty Plus Canoes and Kyaks at Derwentwater Marine do craft hire - 07687 71447.

Launching Sites

1. Derwentwater Marina, Portinscale, Keswick, telephone 07687 72912. Daily charge.

2. Keswick Launch Co, telephone 07687 72263. Facilities for launching between March and November. Any size but no power above 10hp. Small charge.

3. Nichol End Marine, Portinscale, telephone 07687 73082. Charge according to length of craft.

4. NT land near the B5289, opposite Barrow House Lodge. Not power craft, and only if can be manhandled - no trailers.

5. LDSPB car park at Kettlewell, half-a-mile north of Lodore. No power craft.

Walks Roads runs along either side of Derwentwater, but the one on the western side is narrow and can become quickly congested, especially during Bank Holiday weekends. Typically, it has the best views. You can walk around most of the lake and the surrounding fells give some fantastic views. Travelling on the lake is the best way of getting to Lodore Falls and Ashness Bridge, if you can stand those noisy launches.

☆☆☆ Wastwater

Wasdale was the original name, meaning the valley with the lake, so the 'water' part is redundant, strictly-speaking. It doesn't matter - this is the deepest, most dramatic and most haunting of all the lakes. It is well over towards the coast and the only way to it by car is over Wrynose and Hardknott, or from the West Coast. Approach through Greendale and you suddenly come within sight of a view which is in almost every book on the Lake District - the famous Wastwater screes. Nearly two thousand feet high, they plunge into the lake, presenting a sheer wall which goes down to the maximum depth of the lake, 258 feet. Although it looks vertical, it's not, as you can see if you manage the walk along the shore. There is a path along the foot of the screes, but it is exceptionally tough going. Best seen on a still, sunny day when the screes are reflected in the lake and can look frightening. Look up the lake and you see a view which is also familiar - Great Gable flanked by Kirkfell and Lingmell. Recognise it? It is the emblem on the National Park badge.

Wastwater is three miles long, a quiet, unspoilt lake, a favourite starting point for walkers and mountaineers. No boating. There is a good walk along the entire length of the west shore - the road is usually pretty quiet. At the head of the lake there is a very small village and the Wasdale Head Inn, which has good bar meals and a smart climbing shop. The hotel is famed among the mountaineering fraternity.

Don't miss St Olaf's Church, hidden in a field behind a clump of fir trees, said to be the smallest church in England. In the little graveyard are memorials to dead climbers, killed on Scafell, Gable and the Himalayas.

After Ullswater, this is our second choice lake. If you have only time for two lakes, Wastwater gives you the perfect antidote to those bigger, over-populated busy lakes. Although there are no amenities on the lake itself, the valley offers you England's deepest lake, highest mountain and smallest church. And the attractive Wasdale Head Inn (telephone 09467 229) was once run by Will Ritson, the biggest liar in England . . .

Shush . . . Wastwater is now becoming a sailboarder's paradise, despite the fact that it is strictly illegal. Hands up all those who saw the Countryside Commission's National Parks campaign poster a few years back? This featured a picture of Wastwater - complete with sailboard! (Thereby completing a hat-trick of errors - not only is the lake a reservoir and therefore administered by the NWWA, but the fell in the background - the screes - is owned by the NT. Nothing to do with the NP appeared in the picture.)

☆☆ Crummock Water

The name is Celtic, hence its Scottish sound, meaning a crooked or bent lake. It is curved, 2 1/2 miles long by 5/8 mile wide and 144 feet deep. It is separated from Buttermere by a narrow, half-mile strip of land and they were probably both one lake, back in the ancient, geological past. It is bigger than Buttermere, very attractive, but nowhere

115.ª Crummock and Buttermere. Early Morning.

as busy. The approach from Loweswater, going along the east shore is a very pretty road with the lake in the foreground against Mellbreak and Ling Crags. There is a footpath along the west shore, going from Buttermere village to Loweswater and this gives some excellent views up the valley. The lake is now owned by the National Trust. There is no public launch site, but small dinghies, boards and canoes can be launched from access land at various points. Permission has to be obtained and paid for from Mrs Beard at Rannerdale Farm, Buttermere. 07687 70232. Mrs Beard has asked us to point out that access is only possible for small craft that can be person-handled over the field and down a steep bank - she says people come with big boats and trailers and find themselves disappointed.

The inns at Loweswater and Buttermere offer reasonable accommodation and good bar meals.

☆☆ Ennerdale Water

Like Wastwater, it is on the western flanks of the Lake District and is one of the wildest and remotest lakes. It has a good name for solitude and quiet, with the result that you might meet lots of other people who've also gone there to be alone. The Forestry Commission have recently rather drawn people's attention to it by making noises about their valley forest trails. The valley is dominated by their plantations, but at least they have kept out the cars and allow free access. You can walk all around the lake, although things get a little scree-y on the southern shoreline. Park at Bowness Point, where the road ends and there's a good car park with toilets. Walk along the shore to the lake foot - good place for picnics - then back by the other side.

The lake is owned by the North West Water Authority and no private boating is allowed. It is actually a reservoir, but the dam is hardly noticeable.

Amenities are few, apart from car park and picnic points. No hotels, pubs or village. Access from the central lakes is difficult and means either coming down via Cockermouth or heading towards the coast from Buttermere, leaving the fells and then turning back in again.

The big thing about Ennerdale is that it is the only completely road-free lake in the whole of the Lake District. Every other lake, even Wastwater, has a road along at least part of its shore. So it makes a perfect, peaceful circular walk. Easy going most of the way, even with children. Allow about four hours.

☆ Esthwaite Water

Wordsworth knew this lake well as a boy, but nowadays it can be easily missed if you're rushing up to Hawkshead. Not a very spectacular location, but conventionally pretty, surrounded by low fells and minor roads. In some ways similar to Rydal or Grasmere, but without the crowds and cars. A public footpath runs from near the village to the shore at the north-west and down in the south-west is a good car park and access point. This gives a good view across the lake and is the only public launch point for rowing boats (the only form of craft allowed on the lake.) Permits necessary to launch rowing boats obtainable from Hawkshead P.O. 05394 36201 or from Hawkshead Trout Farm, telephone 05394 36541. Rowing boats can also be hired from the trout farm.

☆☆☆ Buttermere

The name is a dead giveaway and means 'the lake by the dairy pastures'. It is a perfect little lake. You can walk right round it, with only a few yards on the road, and the views are superb. The early tourists used to rave about it being "the quintessence of natural beauty" and if you're based in the north and have time for only one low-level, easy, family walk, do this one. Park in the village, follow the footpath across farmland to the lakeshore. Go round anti-clockwise and along the north shore you'll enter a short tunnel, cut through the rock. The story goes that the local landowner had it blasted through because he was annoyed at not being able to walk all round the lake. The lake is only 1 1/4 miles long and 3/8 wide, so the entire walk won't take you much more than two hours.

If you're feeling too lazy, you can park at the southern end and look across the water to High Stile. You can also launch small boats, canoes and windsurfers from here, but you have to get permission, either from Mrs Richardson, Gatesgarth Farm 07687 70256 in the village, or the Kirkstile Inn, Loweswater. The lake is now owned by the National Trust. Buttermere village has two reasonable inns, with good beers, but they can get very busy.

☆☆ Loweswater

Probably the most forgotten of the sixteen lakes, which is a great shame as it is very pretty. Its uniqueness lies in the fact that it is the only one whose waters flow in towards the centre of the Lake District. There, that's one for the record books.

Loweswater is a nice, gentle lake, though looking east over it there are some rather grand views. There is a small car park at the southern end and from here you can follow a footpath right round the lake. If you prefer something more gentle, go into the woods along the west side, owned by the National Trust and provided with variously-placed seats. It is popular with locals as a Sunday afternoon sort of a place. The car park at the foot has room for only about 20 cars, which gives you an idea of how remote it is. Loweswater means 'the leafy lake', referring to the woods which flank one side. It is about 1 1/4 miles long, 3/8 wide and about 60 feet deep, which makes it another early lake to freeze over in winter. Very good pub meals at Kirkstile Inn, Loweswater.

When doing Loweswater, make sure to take in the Lorton Valley, which has some of the most attractive, lushest scenery in the Northern Lakes, and don't forget that Crummock Water and Buttermere are round the corner. The three lakes go together, making a perfect string of pearls. With clever car parking arrangements, you could walk them all in a day, sticking each time to the road-less shores, taking in refreshments at the Loweswater and Buttermere pubs. What bliss.

☆☆☆ Grasmere

Everyone likes Grasmere. And with all that fame and literary name, how could we begrudge it three stars. It is a 'delightful' little lake, completely surrounded by fells, nice to look at from every angle. It has one island, centrally-placed, no piers or steamers, and on the west side the fields come right down to the water's edge. The only thing which spoils it is the 'beach' at the foot of the lake, under Loughrigg Terrace, which can get quite busy in summer. The other drawbacks are the crowds in Grasmere Village and the A591, which runs along the lake's east side. Lots of people stop along this road to take photographs. Don't. If you want to be different, go back and park at White Moss, then walk over the old road towards Dove Cottage. About half-way you'll see a seat in some woods on your right. A little farther along there is a gate. From this seat you get a good, if less panoramic, view of the lake with Silver How as its backdrop. When the lake is still and the sun is shining in the early morning, the island seems to be sitting on a mirror and the view is absolutely magic. Another classic view is from the top of Loughrigg Terrace, with Dunmail Raise in the background.

You can walk right round the lake, although you are on that horrid road a lot of the way. There is a nice little wood at the southern end. The island belongs to the National

Trust. William and Dorothy Wordsworth used to picnic there and the stone barn was used to shelter sheep, which were taken across in flat-bottomed boats. Arguably the best place from which to see Grasmere vale is from a rowing boat in the middle of the lake and the island is great for picnics (but no camping).

No powered craft allowed, although sailing is permitted and you'll see the occasional windsurfer. The only public launch site is at Well Foot Boat Landing, Bank Road. They also hire rowing boats and provide teas.

The name, by the way, simply means 'the lake with the grassy shore'.

☆☆☆ Rydal Water

A reedy little lake, usually mentioned in the same breath as Grasmere - the advantage of both for the passing rubber necks is that you can get a good view of them from the road as you whizz past in your car.

The river which flows out of Grasmere enters Rydal, then flows out at the foot down to Waterhead. If you are keen, you could canoe all the way from Grasmere to Lakeside, although the walk back wouldn't be much fun. It used to be called Routhermere or Rothaymere (after the river which flows 'through' it). It gets its name from Rydal village, though it isn't actually in Rydal 'dale' at all.

There's a lovely old bridge just to the south, called Pelter Bridge, where you can turn off the A591 onto the Under Loughrigg road. Park here and walk up the lane back to the lake. The view from the bench as you come into sight of the lake is a classic and especially lovely in winter. Carry on and walk right round the lake up to White Moss, then follow the road back. The 'beach' on the south shore is good for swimming. No public launching or boats allowed, although you may see the odd canoeist. Rydal isn't very large - just 3/4 mile long by 1/4 mile wide, but it can be absolutely superb first thing in the morning or in the winter when there is no one else about. In summer it gets very busy and for all its charm it is best avoided on busy days for the more remote lakes - unless you get up very early in the morning.

Elterwater

This is a peculiar little lake, with a funny shape, the smallest of the sixteen - in fact, it sometimes gets omitted altogether and Brothers Water often gets included instead. Tucked away at the foot of the Langdales, you get glimpses of it as you travel along the B5343. It is only half-a-mile long and has not got much to offer in the way of walks or boating. It is best reached by parking in the car park at the eastern end, crossing the road and entering the wood. A footpath runs along the side of the lake and up to the little village. Its chief distinction is the good view this path gives you, looking over the lake to the Langdales. Nice for a quiet stroll - that one view apart - but not really typical Lake District. The name is rather nice, though - Elter is the old Norse for 'swan', so this is - 'swan lake' - presumably because of the Whooper swans which call in when migrating from their Siberian winter.

Tarns

So much for the lakes. Now for their less famous, less popular little brothers, the tarns. It's impossible to tell how many there are as the smallest have no names and are therefore rather difficult to count, but the Lakeland artist, W. Heaton Cooper names and paints or draws 103 of them in his classic study, *The Tarns of Lakeland* (reprinted by Frank Peters, Kendal, 1983, price £15.95).

One of them (Tarn Hows) is in fact more visited than any of the lakes and two of them (Brothers Water and Devoke Water) are as large as the smaller so called lakes. One of the 'un-named' tarns has been given a name to show it hasn't got one - Innominate Tarn. That's on the top of Haystacks, one of the most beautifully situated tarns in the entire Lake District. Its claim to fame is that this is the spot where the Blessed Wainwright has had his ashes scattered. "Wainwright's Tarn" would be nice, but the O.S. aren't keen.

Meanwhile, here is a brief selection of the bigger, better known tarns which are worth considering for a visit, if you want to see a tarn.

☆☆ Tarn Hows

One of the most popular places in the entire Lake District. You see it on postcards all over the area. Very heavily visited during the summer. It's free and open and so impossible to count but in 1974 it was estimated that 3/4 million people came to Tarn Hows.

It lies between Hawkshead and Coniston and is signposted simply as 'The Tarns'. There are two car parks, some public toilets and one of the most delightful views in Lakeland. It is a beautiful tarn, lush and very chocolate box, only 1/2 mile long, surrounded by woods and with a path all the way round. To the west, the immense bulk of Wetherlam looms. Walk a little way and you get a good view down over Coniston Water.

It is usually referred to as a man-made tarn, but there used to be several much smaller tarns here, originally called Monk Coniston Tarns. Then, about 70 years ago, the local landowner built a dam and converted the marshy ground into one tarn, with two little islands. The present name really refers to the farm to the south west. It has been in the hands of the National Trust since 1930 who do much to control the level of erosion, but with the number of footbridges, paths and fences springing up, it is becoming more artificial every year. Avoid it on bank holiday weekends and during the school holidays. Or go very, very early. It is really only at its best during the winter, when it can be very beautiful - and good for skating.

Brothers Water

Sometimes classed as the sixteenth lake - an idea which seems to come in and out of fashion - which means down-grading Elterwater into a tarn. It lies just to the south of Ullswater, forming a well-known view from Kirkstone Pass. it may once have been part of Ullswater. A footpath skirts its shores on the west and the road on the east. Not really worth stopping for, not with Ullswater beckoning.

It used to be called Broadwater and is said to have got its present name when two brothers drowned in it, whilst skating, in 1785.

☆ Devoke Water

As large as Rydal, but still reckoned to be a tarn. It is rather out of the way and in a rather austere moorland setting, due east of Ravenglass. Only approachable by foot. From the central lakes it involves a long drag over Wrynose. Hardly worth going specially all that way, unless you're into Bronze Age settlements - there are about 400 ancient cairns and 'hutments' in evidence around the tarn, dating from around the time when the area was first cleared of forest. Much loved by Norman Nicholson for its desolate feeling. The name says it all, really - 'the dark one'.

Overwater Tarn

Just north of Bassenthwaite, on the very edge of the Lake District. Named after another Norseman. (One begins to suspect they only really came to Britain to make names for themselves in the Lake District.) It has been enlarged by damming at the north end to turn it into a reservoir for Wigton. Handed over to the National Trust in 1992. Could be open to the public, one day.

Alcock Tarn

A small, part-artificial tarn on the fell to the east of Grasmere. There's a good path to it on the road to White Moss, above Town End. A good objective for an afternoon stroll. Not spectacular (quite the reverse, in fact, you tend to think it's something else until you read the sign board) but there are some good views from round about, taking in Coniston, Langdale and Helvellyn mountain ranges. It used to be called Buttercrags until a man named Alcock dammed it and stocked it with trout.

☆☆ Grisedale Tarn

One of the largest, deepest and set in splendid scenery.

It is on the Grisedale route to Dollywaggon Pike and Helvellyn, so it is for dedicated fell-walkers only. The pass was once a packhorse route through to Penrith. The tarn is over 100 feet deep. Nearby is a rock bearing an inscription to commemorate the parting of Wordsworth and his brother John, who died five years later - without William ever seeing him again - when his ship, the Abergavenny, sank in 1805. The inscription was put there at the insistence of the energetic Canon Rawnsley.

☆☆☆ Easedale Tarn

As tarns go, it deserved three stars as it is one of the nicest and easiest to get to and it has one of the best approach marches, right alongside Sour Milk Ghyll, with its beautiful tumbling waterfalls and small ponds. (Great for a' hot, summer day.) The tarn lies north west of Grasmere village; just opposite the green is a road which leads to Easedale car park. The walk is up the Easedale Valley. The tarn itself has a rather sombre setting, though there are repeatedly good views back down the valley. The mass of stones on the left as you come within sight of the tarn are the remains of an old refreshment hut. A painting, showing what it was once like, is hanging in Dove Cottage. William and Dorothy Wordsworth knew and loved this little hidden tarn.

☆☆ Red Tarn

On Helvellyn and one of the highest and most magnifi-cently-sited of all the tarns in the Lake District. It lies in the depths of an immense bowl, formed by Helvellyn, Striding Edge and Swirrel Edge. Not as deep as it appears, it is only 85 feet. In the last century, a dam was built to supply the mines at Glenridding.

Loughrigg Tarn

On the west side of Loughrigg Fell, passed by the road from Grasmere over Red Bank. Wordsworth said it had "a margin of smooth green meadows, of rocks, and rocky woods, a few reeds here, a few waterlilies there", which just about sums it up. No public access to it. Nice to come across, not worth going to a lot of trouble to seek out.

☆☆☆ Blea Tarn

Say that you have been to Blea Tarn and the response is likely to be: "which one?" So we'll start with the prettiest and most accessible. It is in the Langdales, between Little and Great Langdale.

The easiest way to find it is to follow the B5343 along Great Langdale, until it becomes a minor road and begins to climb. At the top, there's a car park on the left and one of the best tarns in Lakeland on your right. You can walk right round it and it has some of the best views in the area.

☆ Blea Tarn II

Above Boot in Eskdale and accessible only to those on foot. Rather a long way to get to it, but worth it because it is very pretty.

Blea Tarn III

Just south east of Watendlath, high up to the west of Thirlmere. Set in a bog and very boring. Only worth mentioning because it is higher than the other two.

Final Warnings - Lest You Forget.

Private powered craft are only allowed on the following lakes - at 10 mph and under - except Windermere - at the moment . . .

Windermere	Coniston
Derwent Water	Ullswater

Note: These are the only four lakes with regular steamers or launch services.

No private craft, either powered motors or sailing dinghies, are allowed on the following, however tempting it may look -

Ennerdale	Wastwater	Loweswater
Rydal Water	Haweswater	Tarn Howes
Bea Tarn	Overwater	Yew Tree Tarn
Lrigg Tarn	Little Langdale Tarn	

Chapter Eight

Mountains

Mountains and other Natural Features, including Fells and Dales, Passes and Waterfalls, with brief descriptions and recommended routes.

Mountains

There are four mountains in the Lake District over 3,000 feet, or three if you count Scafell Pike and Scafell as one, which they're not, as they have separate summits, but most visitors and many natives refer to having climbed 'Scafell' and mean in fact they've climbed Scafell Pike, ignoring or forgetting the twin peak of Scafell which is assumed to be part of the same, but is fifty feet lower.

Such a pity about metres. There was something satisfying and rather grand and important about getting above the magical 3,000 feet mark. Getting above 920 metres not only seems lower but not nearly as impressive. However, if only to give the printers more work, we will use both measurements in our Mountains guide.

The four big ones are:

Scafell Pike	3,210 feet, 978 metres
Scafell	3,162 feet, 964 metres
Helvellyn	3,118 feet, 950 metres
Skiddaw	3,053 feet, 931 metres.

Scafell Pike, Helvellyn and Skiddaw also happen to be the most popular mountains, climbed the most often, though figures are naturally non-existent. They haven't quite yet got to a turnstile on the top, though on busy days it could ease congestion as there is very often a queue to stand on the final cairn.

Note well: our routes are purely rough guides, to be used with a good map.

Top Three Mountains

☆☆☆ **Scafell Pike** 3,210 feet, 978m

England's highest, the hardest to get to of all the popular Lake District mountains, the one which has seen terrible accidents, but the one which you can boast most about - if you honestly get to the top. It's not really very difficult, but a long slow climb which means the weather is more likely to be different on top, usually worse, so be well prepared with stout footwear, some extra warmth and good rainwear.

Part of a range of peaks known as the Scafell Pikes which you have to work your way over or round before you finally start climbing the big one, hence the relatively long time needed to get up, compared with some other mountains which happen to be much nearer civilisation or parking. That's what makes Scafell all the more special. Samuel Taylor Coleridge did it in 1802, all on his own, without a guide or companion, carrying a pen and a bottle of ink with him. He wrote a letter on top, so his is the first *recorded* climb of Scafell, then he hurried down any old way, ignoring all the easy paths, which is not to be recommended.

A ravine called Piers Gill is about the most dangerous part. In 1921, someone fell down it, breaking both ankles, and lay at the bottom for eighteen days. He was finally found, having landed near a pool of water, which had kept him alive.

Routes The shortest and quickest but steepest route is from Wasdale Head, going up Lingmell Gill, but you have to get round and into Wasdale in the first place, which is a long drive for anyone in Central Lakeland.

From Seathwaite walk straight up the valley till you hit Stockley Bridge, then cut right up Sty Head Gill for Sty Head Tarn. You'll probably see hordes of walkers by the tarn, socks and boots off, resting or guzzling. Once over Sty Head Pass, you hit a long, open walk which takes you along the western flank of Scafell Pike, a route known as the Guides' Walk or the Corridor. It finally takes you straight up to the summit, over rougher, rockier ground, but still not too difficult.

The actual summit is not very exciting or pretty, being rather bleak and barren. But on a clear day the views are sensational.

On the way back, if the day is clear and you feel confident, try varying the route into Borrowdale by coming down via Sprinkling Tarn. The round trip should take about six hours. On a hot day, celebrate with a dip in the ice green, marvellous marble water at Stockley Bridge.

☆☆☆ **Skiddaw** 3,053 feet, 931m

There are clever folks, the real climbing types, who are rather scornful about Skiddaw, dismissing it as easy peasy, nowt more than a stroll, with no hairy or horrible bits where real men can break their legs. All true. It is rather a cuddly, rounded, modest sort of mountain, but it makes an excellent mountain walk all the same. How nice not to walk in fear and dread. How reassuring to think that even if the mist comes down or it grows dark, you should be perfectly safe. Just follow the crowds.

Skiddaw was the first popular mountain climb in Lakeland and that lovely open path from the Keswick side has been used by millions for over 150 years. You could probably take a pram up it. In the last war, motor bikes and army vehicles went up it. No bother.

In 1815, Wordsworth and Southey took their respective families for a bonfire party to celebrate Waterloo, with the servants carrying up roast beef and plum pudding. It's that sort of friendly, accessible mountain. Terribly handy for parking.

Skiddaw dominates the Northern Fells, Big Brother over its surrounding mountain mass, a landmark for miles around and people who live beyond it describe themselves as living Back O' Skiddaw.

Routes Several ways up. From the Bass Lake side, coming from Bassenthwaite village, you can get up it from Millbeck or from High Side.

Or you can approach it from the rear, the eastern side which is hidden from Keswick. It's an excellent approach, hardly used, though it means a long, but exciting walk from Dash Falls. If you do this route, look out for Skiddaw House, an amazing building, stuck literally in the middle of nowhere, once used by shepherds, and now recently converted into a youth hostel. Provides good shelter in bad weather.

Best route The famous one, from Keswick. By far the most popular and probably the most dramatic, as you rise very quickly and can get good views over your shoulder, looking over Keswick and Derwentwater, and pat yourself on the back for doing so well. Come out of Keswick and turn right just past the big roundabout, following the sign saying Skiddaw, heading up the little road towards Underscar. You eventually hit a rather rough road, Gale Road. Go right along it to the very end and you'll find car parking space probably already full, so come back and find some space on the road. This drive is a bit of a cheat, as you've saved almost 1,000 feet already. Real climbers start from Keswick and climb Latrigg first. But it means that you can come straight out of the car and can start climbing. You actually see children *running* to get up. That beautiful grassy slope, right in front of you, looks so attractive and tantalising almost like a grass ski slope. This takes you up Jenkin Hill, the first slope of Skiddaw, and it is in fact the steepest. After that, it's a long but easier walk to the summit. The top can be freezing, so take warm clothes. Can all be done in three hours, even with the children or a family dog.

☆☆☆ Helvellyn 3,118 feet, 950m

Often considered the finest of the Big Four by Lakeland experts, for its brilliant views and exciting summit. In some ways the most dangerous, at least it seems to have more accidents than any other Lakeland mountain. But Wordsworth climbed it safely aged seventy. Makes you sick.

Routes From the King's Head Inn, Thirlspot, follow the whitewashed stones, crossing over Helvellyn Gill to join the route up from Swirls car park, gaining Helvellyn via Lower Man.

Or from Grasmere follow the old packhorse road up Great Tongue to Grisedale Tarn. Fairfield is on the right and Seat Sandal on the left, in front Dollywaggon Pike. Climb up Dollywaggon Pike to Helvellyn. Steep at first but a good expedition, with fine views all round.

Or from the little church at Wythburn follow the path through the forestry plantation, up the side of Combe Gill onto Swallow Scarth and Helvellyn on your left.

Best routes From Glenridding car park, follow the lane on the other side of the beck until you reach a fork in the path. Take the left fork indicating Lanty Tarn. Follow the zig-zag path to Lanty Tarn, which is set amidst trees and is very pretty. Go down the hill, through a small plantation and up onto the ridge taking the right hand path up the fellside. Grisedale valley is on your left. Once on the ridge cross over the stile and take the left hand path onto Striding Edge. The edge is narrow and involves a bit of scrambling but this can be avoided by using the path a little lower down (approx 20 feet). Red Tarn is on the right. It gets its name because when the sun rises the tarn appears dark red in colour. Traditional to watch the sunrise from the summit on Midsummer's Day - always a lot of people there, but worth the trip.

Getting off the Edge and onto Helvellyn is interesting (more scrambling) and the path up Helvellyn is steep. Once on the summit you can rest on the seats in the shelter. Fantastic all round views.

Way down is by Swirral Edge and path down to Red Tarn. Follow the path back to the stile and take the left path down to Mires Beck, keeping the wall on your right. Good views down on to Ullswater and peaceful on a nice summer's day. When you reach the bottom keep right of the beck and follow it back to the car park.

Note: Only experienced walkers should take this route in poor weather conditions.

Other Recommended Mountains

Eight other Big mountains, all worth attempting sometime.

☆☆ **Great Gable** 2,949 feet, 899m

Paths up from Wasdale, Seathwaite and Honister, the latter being the easiest over Brandreth and Green Gable.

Park at Seathwaite (parking neatly, nose to the wall) and walk up Sour Milk Ghyll onto Green Gable, across Windy Gap and onto Gable - quite steep. Good views into Wasdale Valley and of the Scafells. Westmorland Cairn is well worth a visit - probably the most spectacular view of the Lakeland crags, down into Great Hell Gate and to Tophet Bastion.

☆☆ **Bow Fell** 2,960 feet, 902m

Park in the National Trust car park in Langdale and walk up Mickleden, which is nice and flat, passing under Pike O'Stickle. Take the left path when you reach the guide stone, and up Rossett Ghyll. Go beyond Angle Tarn and turn left up Ore Gap which takes you onto Bow Fell.

On a clear day the views are fantastic, seeing as far as Ingleborough in the Pennines and even Snaefell on the Isle of Man.

For the return, head for the Three Tarns and take the left path down the Band back into Langdale.

☆☆ **Pillar** 2,927 feet, 892m

Possible from Ennerdale following a long path through the forestry plantations.

From Wasdale follow the bridleway up Mosedale and over Black Sail Pass and an easy walk up onto Pillar, noticing Robinson's Cairn on the right, which marks the climbers' traverse to Pillar Rock.

Pillar is part of the famous Mosedale Horseshoe walk which takes in Steeple and Yewbarrow. From Pillar it is recommended that you take the same route down as others are very steep and only for the sure footed.

☆☆ **Blencathra** 2,847 feet, 868m

Or Saddleback, as it's also known. For the more adventurous, follow the footpath along Sharp Edge - the best ridge walk in the Lake District (best not to undertake this route in the wet). Scales Tarn is down to the left and the path leads onto the summit. Return by Hallsfell which is quite steep.

An easier route is from the Blencathra Centre (may be marked as Blencathra Hospital on maps) which can be reached by taking Blease Road in Threlkeld. There is a public car park behind the Centre. Follow the footpath over Knowe Crag. Return the same way. This is really only a half day walk.

☆☆ Crinkle Crags 2,816 feet, 858m

The quickest and easiest route onto Crinkle Crags is from the Three Shire Stone at the top of Wrynose Pass, going over Cold Pike.

For a day's outing the best route is: Park in Langdale and follow the track to Stool End Farm, turning left up Oxendale. Go up Brown Gill and over Great Knott. An interesting walk providing easy scrambling. There is one difficult steep section which may be climbed if competent, otherwise take the footpath west (left) of this. Continue along the top of the crags, to Shelter Crags and down to the Three Tarns. Here take the path back down to Langdale, taking the right fork down Hell Gill, into Oxendale.

An interesting and varied route, providing excellent views all round.

Note: In misty weather it is easy to inadvertently descend Long Top (this is the next top after the awkward section) thereby losing several hundred feet and going towards the Eskdale Valley.

☆ High Street 2,718 feet, 829m

From Hartsop, park in the car park and walk up Hayeswater Gill to Hayeswater, onto the Knott and along the ridge to High Street. The cairn on Thornthwaite Crag is about 14 foot high, which must be one of the most remarkable in the Lake District. Only a short distance from the summit of High Street. Walk beyond here and down in Threshthwaite Cove, quite steep and a bit tricky, back to the car park.

From Kentmere - up the Nan Bield Pass, over Mardale Ill Bell.

From Troutbeck - up the Garburn road; a long walk.

Best route: Park at the head of Haweswater Reservoir, walk up the Gatesgarth Pass onto Harter Fell and along the ridge, crossing over the Nan Bield Pass. Small Water is the tarn down on the right. Over Mardale Ill Bell, onto summit. Descend by walking north a short distance and down Long Stile and Heron Crag, and a short walk by the lakeshore back to the car park. A fairly long but not difficult walk, providing views into the Longsleddale, Kentmere and Haweswater valleys. Good views over Lakeland fells, varying from where you stand on High Street.

☆☆ Fairfield 2,863 feet, 873m

Various ways to the summit.

From Grasmere take the path near Swan Hotel up Stone Arthur and onto Greatrigg Man and then across a short distance to Fairfield. Steep at first.

From Patterdale follow the bridleway up Grisedale to Grisedale tarn. Here take the very steep and not very pleasant path to the summit.

From Ambleside: The Fairfield Horseshoe is a long but easy mountain walk. After completing it there is a real sense of accomplishment. From the central car park go up the Kirkstone Road a little way, turn left up Nook Lane, right to the end, passing through a farm to Low Sweden Bridge. Follow the path onto Low Pike and then High Pike, Dove Crag and onto summit, which is a bit disappointing as it's a massive boulder-strewn area. Return by Greatrigg Man and Heron Pike, down to Rydal Mount. The footpath then leads through Rydal Hall back into Ambleside.

Best route: Park in Patterdale and walk up the road by Patterdale Hall. A few hundred yards on the left take the path eventually leading up onto St Sunday Crag. Return by the ridge off Hart Crag, over Hoggil Brow. This superb walk is only slightly spoiled by the short road walk back into Patterdale.

☆ **Coniston Old Man** 2,635 feet, 803m

Park in Coniston village and go across the old railway bridge up the steep metalled road onto the Walna Scar Road (not a highway). Bear right and follow the path to Goats Water. Dow Crag is the impressive rock face on the left. Follow the path past the tarn and out of the hollow and right onto the summit of the Old Man. An easy, very pleasant walk and the best way onto the summit.

Go down by the steep footpath down to Low Water and through the jumble of relics from the coppermines, down into Coppermines Valley. There are a few houses, mostly climbing club huts, and a YHA. Follow the track back into the village, finishing by the Sun Hotel.

Fells

Fells are mountains which didn't grow, but they can provide just as much pleasure, and even danger, as their big brothers. Here are eight, around 1,000 to 2,000 feet high, which are recommended.

☆☆ **Castle Crag** 980 feet, 299m

A small crag with old slate quarries, north of Rosthwaite, Borrowdale.

Park in Rosthwaite car park. (Travelling south, turn right just before Scafell Hotel, car park is on right a few hundred yards up the road.) Walk to the end of the road, passing through a farmyard and follow the track right of river, eventually crossing to the left. Follow the riverbank path through the wood to the campsite at Hollows Farm. Beautiful walk when river is full and on a sunny day. Turn left through a gate and up the track by side of Broadslack Gill to the old slate workings. Turn left up the track over the spoil heaps, up a steep path onto Castle Crag. Marvellous views all round, probably one of the best viewpoints in Borrowdale area.

☆☆ **Cat Bells** 1,481 feet, 451m

Off the road leading south from Portinscale to Grange-in-Borrowdale.

Park at Gutherscale car park on western side of Derwentwater, and follow the erosion control signs up the steep fellside to the summit. Very good views in all directions, especially into Newlands Valley. Descent by dropping down to Hause Gate and turn left down to the road at Manesty. Walk south a short distance and turn off left and take the path leading through the woods and beside Derwentwater, back to Hawes End. Very attractive walk beside the lakeshore. Good fun for a family walk.

☆☆ **Harter Fell** 2,129 feet, 649m

In the Dunnerdale Valley. Routes from Eskdale and Hardknott Pass

Best route: Park in the Forestry Commission car park at Birks Bridge, follow the track through the plantation to an old farm, turn right up the gill which eventually leads onto the summit. A fairly short trip (1/2 day) steep but fairly easy. The summit is quite craggy and provides a good playground for children. Good views to the Scafells and Dow Crag range.

☆☆ **Haystacks** 1,959 feet, 597m

On south west side of Buttermere.

Easiest approach is from Honister. Park in car park at YHA, follow the track towards the quarries but turn left after a few yards, up the steep fell path. Follow this to Blackbeck Tarn and onto Haystacks.

Park at Gatesgarth, Buttermere, follow the Scarth Gap Pass, turn left at top and onto Haystacks. Nice gentle walk, with good views over Buttermere and Crummock Water and across to Gable and Ennerdale Valley. Several tarns, Blackbeck being the largest. Descend by Warnscale Beck.

☆☆ **Helm Crag** 1,299 feet, 396m

Park in the car park up Easedale Road on the north side of Grasmere village. Walk beyond Easedale House and up the steep path onto Helm Crag and climb both pillars on the summit before continuing along the ridge over Moment Crag (pausing here) to the old boundary fence. The fence itself is no longer there but the posts remain and one stile. Cross over the stile (everyone does) and turn south to Codale Head, and down to Codale tarn and Easedale Tarn. Finish off by going down Sour Milk Ghyll. A nice walk with varying scenery and views.

☆☆ **Lingmoor** (Brown Howe), Little Langdale 1,530 feet, 466m

Park in the car park opposite Blea Tarn. Walk down the hill towards Langdale a short distance and follow the path onto Side Pike. Walk up the hill and onto Brown Howe. Good all round views of Langdale Valley and across the Coniston range. Lingmoor is a bit of a surprise, once you have gained height it can be seen that it opens out into a moorland type plateau, complete with tarn. Only a short walk from the car but interesting and well worth the trip.

☆☆ **Loughrigg Fell** 1,101 feet, 336m

Park in the car park on the A591 between Rydal Water and Grasmere. Cross over the River Rothay through the wood onto the Terrace. An easy plod with lots of seats. Good views over Grasmere and area. Follow the Terrace to the gate and turn left up some steep steps of strange proportions. Impossible to get a good walking rhythm on these. The real summit is the one with the trig point. Spectacular views.

☆ **Walla Crag**, Borrowdale 1,234 feet, 376m

Above the B5289 south of Keswick, the first craggy outcrop high on the left as you drive down the valley. Easy family walk.

Park in Great Wood car park south of Keswick; from the car park follow the signs, turning left through the woods towards the TV aerial, heading towards Rakefoot Farm onto the fellside. Pass through a gate keeping the boundary wall on your right hand side. Fine views over the Borrowdale Valley and higher fells; Grisedale Pike, Skiddaw, etc. Descend the same way or by Cat Gill, which is very steep and loose and should only be undertaken by the sure-footed.

Dales

And now eight dales to explore, by foot or car, which are attractive and interesting in their own right but which also offer fairly easy walks and explorations for those sensible people who want to leave their cars and strike out on their own.

☆☆☆ **Langdale**

The most popular valley in the Lake District. It consists of two dales, joining at Elterwater and separated by Lingmoor Fell, called Great Langdale and Little Langdale. Great Langdale is the more popular and the little, winding road which runs its length is sometimes crammed with cars in mid-summer. It has dramatic scenery, especially during the drive up the valley, the Langdale Pikes suddenly rearing up in front of you. Many walks onto the higher fells, with lower fells at the Elterwater end of the valley. Good walks in Little Langdale, which is charming, though not as spectacular.

For low level walks in Great Langdale, try Oxendale and Mickleden, both of which give a sense of being amongst the mountains. At the head of the valley, the Old Dungeon Ghyll hotel is a famous meeting place for climbers and walkers and the nearby Stickle Barn provides a good cafe and bar. Make an early start, if you want a decent parking spot. Avoid the new houses at Chapel Stile. Ugh.

☆☆☆ Borrowdale

One of the prettiest valleys in the Lakes with spectacular views, but gets very crowded. A southern extension of the Vale of Derwentwater with a variety of scenery and contrasts. A good area from which to walk, low-lying and higher fells are easily accessible and so are many valley walks. The drive around the west side of Derwentwater provides good views of the lake. Good low-level walks up the Langstrath Valley (visit Black Moss Pot) and Greenup Ghyll. Borrowdale seems to come to an end just beyond Grange, where the slopes of Grange Fell and Castle Crag come together to give barely enough room for the river and road to pass through. These are the famous 'Jaws of Borrowdale'. Don't be put off - the valley opens up beyond and continues a long way down to the village of Seatoller and then up to Seathwaite. Gets very busy in the summer.

☆☆ Duddon Valley

Also known as Dunnerdale, this is the valley of the River Duddon. Wordsworth wrote thirty-five sonnets on this charming river. The whole valley is lovely, with plenty of car parking and pleasant walks on the surrounding fells. Ideal for picnicking and swimming. At the northern end is Birks Bridge, a little packhorse bridge in a renowned beauty spot.

☆☆☆ Wasdale

The most inaccessible valley in the area, therefore one of the quietest, even at the height of the season. The Wasdale Head Hotel is famous for its association with the development of rock climbing at the turn of the century. Good bar meals. Wast Water is the most foreboding of the lakes. The whole valley, though spectacular, has a brooding air about it. Just read the tombstones at the little church at the head of Wasdale.

Good climbing and walking base for Gable and the Scafell range.

☆☆ Eskdale

Very popular with tourists, though only the lower-half - from Boot - is really well known to visitors. A beautiful valley, its head lies at Esk Hause in wild and dramatic scenery, the foot is amongst the plains and sand dunes at Newbiggin. The road only traverses about four miles of the dale itself. To explore the foot of the valley at its best, leave the car at Ravenglass and take the miniature railway to the Dalegarth terminus and walk back, detouring to follow the River Esk through lovely woods and pastures.

☆ Ennerdale

One of the few Lakeland valleys not properly accessible by road. Wild and isolated (or it used to be - becoming increasingly popular of late), the head of the dale is spectacular with Steeple and Pillar rising above the dark conifer plantations. The road goes along the north shore of the lake as far as Bowness Point (a good viewpoint). Thereafter it is for walkers only. There are Forestry Commission trails amongst the woods. It helps if you like conifers.

☆ Swindale

Reached from Bampton or Shap, a lovely, long valley, usually forgotten by the hordes. Rolling fells provide plenty of interest with low-level and higher walks, especially onto the ridges, with good views down into the neighbouring valleys. No proper road up it; this is a walker's valley.

☆☆ Vale of Lorton

Not technically a dale, more a sequence of valleys, but the lushest, prettiest part of the Northern Lakes. It's best to explore it from Cockermouth to get the full shape and extent. Coming from Keswick, you can get into it over the Whinlatter Pass, hitting the village of Lorton, where you turn left and follow the River Cocker upstream, and very gently and subtly, three marvellous lakes carefully unfold themselves for your inspection. First there's Loweswater, then bigger Crummock Water and finally the most popular of the three, Buttermere. Go right to the end of the valley and you can get back towards Keswick, over Honister Pass this time. Excellent walks all the way, either round lakes or up the surrounding fells, with some nice hamlets and pubs to explore along the way.

Passes

Lakeland has several, dramatic mountain passes suitable for motor traffic. Some are famous. Two are notorious. All of them are exciting as for those lazy motorists who never leave the wheel but want to go home and boast that they have scaled the Lakeland heights . . .

☆☆ Hardknott Pass 1,291 feet, 394m

The Lake District's most exciting road. Hair-raising in places, with 1-in-3 gradients, sharp bends and a delightful sheer drop on the west hand side. It can also get very busy in summer, with numerous hold-ups as motorists shuffle about on the steep bits to get past each other. Cyclists are advised by a sign at the top to dismount and walk the descent (but you're allowed to cycle up it, if you've the stamina and the gears). At one time, you could regularly watch the 2CVs being pushed up by groups of students.

Just below the summit, on the Eskdale side, there are parking places and Hardknott Fort, which guards over this once Roman road, should not be missed.

Worth trying for the dramatic views alone, but only if your nerves, brakes and engine are in good shape.

☆ Wrynose Pass 1,281 feet, 391m

The second of the Big Two and probably the more famous, though staff at Tourist Information Centres frequently get asked the way to Rhino Pass or even Buffalo Pass. Goes from Little Langdale and heads west towards Eskdale. Notoriously steep and narrow (although the best is yet to come). There are places where it is impossible for two cars to pass. Special passing places provided. These are *not* laybys and anyone parking in them deserves to have their handbrake released. At the summit is a pillar of rock called Three Shires Stone which used to mark the meeting point of the boundaries of Lancashire, Westmorland and Cumberland. The place where traditionalists still shed a few tears. The pass ends down at Cockley Beck, where you can either continue up Hardknott or turn off for the Duddon Valley.

☆ Honister Pass 1,176 feet, 359m

From Seatoller, in Borrowdale, to Buttermere. There are 1-in-4 gradients in places and on the Buttermere side it can get narrow. Not a brilliant route for scenery. At the top is a green slate quarry. Not a difficult pass.

Newlands Pass 1,100 feet, 335m

The most direct route from Keswick over to Buttermere Village. Starts off yummy and easy looking, through Beatrix Potter type country, but gets steep and wild on the top.

Whinlatter Pass 1,043 feet, 318m

Goes from Braithwaite, near Keswick, to High Lorton. The easiest of all the passes, although there are occasional steep sections. Going up from the Keswick end, there are good views over Bassenthwaite, with parking places. A lot of the view is obscured, however, as you enter the Forestry Commission's Thornthwaite Forest.

A nice, easy route to Loweswater, Crummock and Buttermere.

Kirkstone Pass 1,489 feet, 454m

Connects Windermere and Ambleside with Ullswater. This is the pass all the TV crews rush to when snow begins and they want to show everyone that the Lake District is snowed in. From Windermere, the road is good, with a long, interesting descent to Patterdale. To get to the pass from Ambleside, you go up a very narrow, steep road, aptly called The Struggle (it is almost opposite the Bridge House). 19th century travellers used to have to leave their coaches and walk alongside the horses up this part. Not quite as bad as that today, but there are some sharp bends to trap the unwary.

Waterfalls

Most Lakeland becks or streams have a force or water-fall of some kind. Many of them are small, hidden and unsung. They do their own gentle singing. Tra la. Gurgle, gurgle. Here are some of the finest and most famous - but don't expect to see them at their best after a long, dry spell. Yes, that often does happen in a Lakeland summer. After a heavy rainfall, they're at their most spectacular . . .

☆☆☆ Taylor Gill Force

Above Borrowdale, at Stockley Bridge. This is what the experts generally consider to be Lakeland's finest water-fall. A spectacular setting with an ambling mountain stream transforming itself into a 140 foot cascade. Can be seen from below the bridge, but for the best views follow the path to the right of the falls.

☆☆ Scale Force

The Lake District's longest waterfall, at 172 feet. The path to the falls goes from Buttermere village and the falls are hidden in a narrow, tree-lined gorge. More for the real waterfall collector than the average visitor.

☆☆ Aira Force

Probably the most famous of the Lake District's falls. On the west side of Ullswater, near Dockray, the falls are a few minutes pleasant walk from the public car park. The main force falls 70 feet from below a stone footbridge. You also get a good viewpoint from the path which ends just below the falls. If the sun is shining, look out for the rainbow. Cafe beside the car park.

☆ Stock Ghyll Force

On the fellside behind Ambleside, this delightful little waterfall is easily reached by walking from the town centre up the road which runs behind the Salutation Hotel. A nice, wooded walk to a 90 foot cascade flowing under a stone footbridge. Not spectacular, but very pretty.

☆ Lodore Falls

At the southern end of Derwentwater, easily reached from the road but perhaps the nicest way to view it is by boat. This 40 foot cataract is in a chasm surrounded by woods and crags. You have to pay to see it and there is an honesty box, which must be unique for a natural feature of this kind. It is owned by the hotel, the Swiss Lodore.

Skelwith Force

Only a small waterfall, just a drop of 16 foot, but nicely situated on the River Brathay. Just above the Kirkstone Slate Galleries at Skelwith Bridge.

Best Views

Eight viewpoints, chosen because they're either good, brilliant or simply classics, in our own un-humble opinion.

☆☆ **Castle Crag, Borrowdale** One of the best viewpoints in the Borrowdale area. Marvellous views all round.

☆☆☆ **Border End** (At the top of Hardknott Pass.) A short walk up the fellside but providing spectacular views across to Scafell and Scafell Pike, over the River Esk.

☆☆☆ **Whinlatter Pass** From the brow of the hill, looking north across Bassenthwaite Lake.

☆☆ **Orrest Head, Windermere** Just above Windermere village. Brilliant views through all 360 degrees.

☆☆ **Corney Fell** From the summit, looking north west to the Isle of Man.

☆ **Loughrigg Terrace** Looking down into Grasmere Vale, with Helm Crag and Dunmail Raise in the background. A classic.

☆ **Ashness Bridge** Looking over Derwentwater. Another classic and in every postcard rack.

☆ **Gummer's How** At the south east end of Lake Windermere. Summit gives a view up Windermere and into the Lakeland fells.

Chapter Nine

WALKS

A LAKELAND SHEPHERD
(ABRAHAM'S SERIES)
445

Where to put those feet, especially family feet, with not too much danger. Also some Forests and other Natural Wonders.

I like a walk to be round. I don't like dragging straight up, that's for fell runners, only to come straight down again the same way. A sort of circle is best, slowly up a valley, through a gap, easily on to the top, then round the other side, preferably near a lake, back to base, without repeating one step. I don't like it too steep, especially coming down. Hurts the old knees. I like variety, smooth bits and rough bits. I don't want any roads, but I do like paths I can find easily, especially those grassy swards which look as if the Great Gardener in the sky had got out his celestial lawnmower to the side of the fell. I definitely want views, especially a lake, and I want to feel impressed by myself, look how far we've got, haven't we done well. I like a top that is a top, with a cairn we can crouch beside, scoffing the while. And back at the beginning, I like the thought of a pub or hotel nearby, for emergencies, such as more scoff.

My wife hates screes, so we are not allowed anywhere near them, certainly not. On family walks, the children have their own requirement - it must be a new walk, one we haven't done before. Oh the hours I have studied the OS and old Wainwright, getting further and further afield, trying to work out new routes which will keep us all happy. Many of those books of family walks you see are full of the obvious stuff, often lifted from each other, which any idiot can work out for themselves, such as round Grasmere, or Friar's Crag. I don't want them as easy as that, I like a walk which can spread itself across the day, with two hours up, a picnic and lots of rests, then two hours to stroll back. The joy when we find a new one, which we like to think we have created, carving it out of the contours, shaping it in our minds. And after all these years, we still manage to find them. So here's a dozen of them - all simple and fun. They make a pleasant change from the more arduous mountain and fell climbs of the previous chapter (and don't forget them, of course, when contemplating possible family outings). Right, best feet forwards.

Best Family Walks

Low-level walks, chosen for scenery and ease of walking, with a variety of pleasures and sensations, all possible with a relatively fit family party - and a good map.

☆☆☆ 1) Ullswater

Our all time favourite walking area is around the far shore of Ullswater, that section where there's no road. Everything is there, all the sights and sensations, and all in a fairly short space. There are two ways of doing it, either by driving round the lake to Howtown, then doing a round walk, ending back at your car; or by taking the steamer there and back across the lake. Either way, you are in for sheer pleasure.

(a) Park at the little church of Martindale, above Howtown, just on the top after the switch back road, then walk down the little twisting road and into Bore Dale. It starts off like easy Beatrix Potter country, all smooth and rounded, but as you proceed up the valley, the fields and farmhouses run out and it gets wilder and emptier. Climb up to the head of the valley, through the Hause or pass. The path is clear and the walking easy, though it gets a little steep towards the end. Once over the top, bear right, heading down towards Patterdale. Admire the views, then pick up the path which leads along the shore of Ullswater, underneath the flanks of Place Fell. The path twists and turns with the shape of the lake, giving a different but equally wonderful view at every angle. At Sandwick, you can carry on, if you're not tired, and take in the walk round Hallin Fell, or turn right up the little road, back up the hill to the car. About 10 miles in all. The perfect walk. Allow four hours.

(b) Leave the car at Glenridding and catch the steamer to Howtown. On leaving the pier, turn right through several gates and go onto the fellside track above Waternook. Continue along the footpath, descending to the water's edge before entering woodland below Hallin Fell. Cross the little road at Sandwick and walk up towards Townhead Cottage, where you should turn right and follow the wall before crossing Scalehow Beck. Descend to Long Crag and the lakeshore. The next mile is through attractive open and wooded slopes. Below Silver Crag, the bridleway divides. Keep to the path nearest the lake and follow it back to Patterdale, then follow the road to Glenridding.

A brilliant walk. Allow about four hours.

☆☆☆ 2) Buttermere

From Buttermere village car park, follow the path to the left of the Fish Hotel. Take the left-hand path through the kissing gate, cross the footbridge and follow the left-hand path around the lake's southern shore. At the head of the lake, go left across the fields and rejoin the road. As the road runs alongside the lake, watch out for a small car park on your left. Leave the road here and follow the shoreline once more, back towards the village.

A lovely, easy walk with good views. The walk takes about 2 1/2 hours.

☆☆ 3) Derwentwater

An easy, three mile walk along the west shore. Take the launch from Friar's Crag and get off at Hawse End. Follow the lakeshore footpath left (it goes through a field for a short while, leaving the shore). Keep to the path at the edge of the lake until it reaches the Brandlehow landing stage, then bear right until you reach a fork. Go left up some steps, through the kissing gate and then keep left between the cottage and boathouse. At the next fork in the path, go right across some rather boggy ground. Join another path going left to the shore. Follow the footpath until it joins the road, then go left to the Lodore landing stage, where you can catch a launch back to Friar's Crag.

Some good views on the walk, both of surrounding fells and of the islands, particularly St Herbert's. Watch out for the Floating Island at Lodore - you might be lucky.

☆☆ 4) Easedale

This one does go uphill a little bit, in fact it is quite steep in places, but it makes a good family walk if you take your time. Should require about 2 1/2 hours. From Grasmere village go along Easedale Road for half-a-mile until you come to a bend and a footbridge signposted 'Easedale Tarn'. Go through the woods along an obvious track and at the small, iron kissing gate take the path directly in front of you up the hill. This follows Sour Milk Ghyll (which has some nice little waterfalls and pools) up to the tarn. You can walk around the tarn, though it gets a bit boggy at the head.

Follow the beck back down the hill, this time on the opposite bank. Watch out for a footpath on your left waymarked with white dots and small cairns. This leads down to Far Easedale Gill. Cross by the footbridge, and follow the stream. Keep straight and ignore the farm on the right. Eventually you'll come to a gate and can follow the track as it becomes a road and takes you back into Grasmere.

☆☆ 5) Rydal Water

Park at White Moss car park, between Grasmere and Rydal on the A591. Cross over the Rothay via the footbridge and go south along the western shore of Rydal Water. Where the path splits, the lower path goes alongside the lake, the upper takes you a little way up the fellside and past Rydal caves (two disused mines, carved out of solid rock and perfectly safe - although you can only easily get into the larger of them). The path rejoins the A591 at Pelter Bridge. Cross up to Rydal Mount and, just beyond, turn left and follow the old packhorse route back to White Moss.

Good for Wordsworth buffs as you can take in Rydal Mount. Allow three hours. Can easily be extended into four to five hours by heading up to the top of Loughrigg Fell, rather than hugging Rydal lakeshore. But it is very popular walking country in the high season.

☆☆ 6) Mirehouse

Park at Dodd Wood car park and leave via the path which crosses the stream behind the Old Sawmill cafe. Join a tarmac forestry road and turn left for a few yards before turning right and walking uphill along a narrow track. This levels out and descends through the trees to bring you out on the A591 beside the Ravenstone Hotel. Turn right, in front of the hotel and cross the road just past the white bungalow on your left. Take the footpath beside the bungalow, down some steps and across a series of fields until you reach a minor road. Go straight across and follow the path through the fields to St Bega's Church. This may once have been a pagan site - notice the circular graveyard. It is certainly spectacular, set right on the shores of Bassenthwaite.

From the church, follow the stream towards Mirehouse, with Dodd rising impressively in the background. The right of way goes through Mirehouse's grounds, behind the house and back to the A591, near the car park.

A lovely, easy walk. Only three miles and easily done in a couple of hours. Go on Wednesday or Sunday during the season and visit the house.

☆ 7) Muncaster Castle

Park at Ravenglass railway station and leave via the footpath at the back, behind the Ratty terminus. This track takes you past Walls Castle, an amazing Roman ruin - once a bath house and now the tallest standing Roman building in the north of England. Continue along the track to Walls Mansion (not a Roman anything) and then turn left to Newtown House. Bear left again here and just past a small cottage look for a gate in the fence on your left. There is a permissive path across the conifer plantation which takes you up to a field. Cross the stile and once in the field, the path disappears. Use this as an excuse to run to the top of the hill in front of you for superb views across the valley to the fells of Lakeland. Look a little to your left and you'll see a wood at the far side of the field. Head towards it - but first turn round for the view out to sea where, if you're lucky and it's a clear day, you might see the Isle of Man.

As you approach the wood, you'll see a gate in the stone wall. Go through and into Muncaster Castle grounds (don't worry - it's a right of way). Go downhill through an amazing bamboo plantation until you arrive at the Castle. The right of way goes straight across and up the drive to the main road. You should stick to this if the grounds are closed, but if open detour right for more wonderful views (you may also spot a few wallabies - bet you haven't seen many of those elsewhere in the LD).

Go out to the main road and turn left for 3/4 mile until you reach Home Farm. Cross here and follow the footpath through the farmyard and across fields to bring you back to the track leading to Walls Castle. Retrace your steps to the station.

3 1/2 miles, allow two hours; a super walk well away from the crowds.

☆ 8) La'al Ratty

Opportunities to cheat on this walk and use the miniature railway to ride back.

Park at Dalegarth Station in Eskdale and walk back along the road towards Hardknott. Turn right at the crossroads, beside Brook House, and follow the lane to St Catherine's Church and the River Esk. Turn left along the riverbank and follow this very pretty route for about 3/4 mile you come to a hump-backed stone bridge. Cross over and head back towards Dalegarth. The track climbs away from the river, through a farm and then meanders across several fields. Ignore the path signed 'St Catherine's Church' (unless you want to cut the walk short) but continue through a wood and across a campsite, via a rather impressive footbridge across Stanley Gill. Cross the track and into the next field (signed 'Force Bridge') and through more woods until you enter an attractive park. Follow the tarmac track to the minor road at Forge Bridge. Cross the bridge and continue to the road junction (beside the George IV pub). Turn left and walk to the railway station at Eskdale Green and enjoy the train ride back to Dalegarth.

A beautiful riverside walk, covering about 3 1/2 miles in total. Good for children, who will love the train ride. Allow about two hours.

☆☆ 9) Loweswater

One of Lakeland's forgotten lakes - a good place to escape the mid-summer hordes.

Start at the Kirkstile Inn and follow the road past the church, towards Loweswater lake. Turn left at the road junction and then straight on, signposted Ennerdale and Mockerkin. Follow the narrow, twisting road (beware boy racers) until you reach the fell road. Turn right up here and follow this uphill, towards Mosser. Good views from the top. At a prominent footpath sign, turn left and go downhill to a farm gate. Follow the track to Grange Road. Turn right and then, just past the second entrance to the Grange Hotel, left and follow the bridleway to Hudson Farm.

Keep to the main track. By the farm, turn onto the gravel track and then through the left-hand of two gates. This track takes you down to the lake. A nice, grassy path follows the shore, through Holme Wood and brings you to Watergate Farm. Follow the track left, across several fields, and it brings you back to the road. Turn right and go back to the inn.

Four miles, 2 1/2 hours - dead easy. Good views of Mellbreak and - from the fell road - the Isle of Man.

☆☆ 10) Arthur's Pike, Ullswater

A quiet, unusual way of seeing a familiar view.

Park at Howtown, if you can, which means getting to the pier before the crowds or, if you're cheeky enough, park at the hotel, telling yourself you are going to be a guest, once you've done the walk. Go through the hotel grounds to Mellguards, then left through a gate and onto a long, very easy grassy path which hugs the side of the hill, almost parallel with the road to the left below. Just after the little reservoir thingy, cut up steeply through some ferns and climb up to White Knott, which is the first cairn. All very easy. It looked hard from below, but come on, you'll be on top in no time. Carry on to Arthur's Pike itself - then continue to Bonscale, a lovely ridge walk, but take care not to come down into Swarthbeck Gill. When you're above Fusedale, then cut right, zig zagging down the grassy slopes, heading back to Howtown Hotel. If the bar is closed, try their afternoon teas, especially the hot scones.

Perfect round walk, about three miles, takes 3 1/2 hours, with lots of stops on top to admire the brilliant views of Ullswater. Nice, easy beginning, just to warm yourself up, then the satisfaction of a brisk climb. Always uncrowded. Not many know this walk.

☆☆ 11) Barrow

No, not that beautiful town, but another relatively unknown fell, yet right within top tourist country. On a bank holiday, when the world and his wizened grandad is doing Cat Bells, try Barrow instead.

Park in Braithwaite village, then leave as if heading for Newlands, turning right off the road at Braithwaite Farm. It looks private, but head straight up to it and then on and upwards, trying to ignore the sound of the A66 below in the distance as it will soon disappear. Having reached the top of Barrow, where the views of Derwentwater are magnificent, you can either head back by going right, down on the path to High Coledale, that's if the weather is bad or the party is lazy (which would give a two hour round walk), or better still, carry on, veering to the left of Stile End, which there is no need to climb, round Outside (no need to climb that either) and you'll emerge above Coledale. Cut right down the grassy slopes to the valley bottom, heading for the old mines, then straight along the very good Coledale Beck track, back to Braithwaite. Time perhaps for tea in Book Cottage, or drive straight to Keswick and lash out at Maysons on something nourishing.

Very satisfying, really round walk, impressive views, no hard climbing. About four miles. Allow four hours.

☆☆ 12) Gowbarrow

Yes, another Ullswater stroll, but this time on the main road side, where it is very attractive, but hard to work out a decent family amble without hitting millions of other families, or the dreaded road. Park at the Aira Force car park, which has smart toilets and a cafe nearby, and usually hordes of coaches. Depending on the crowds, go up and explore the waterfall at once, or save it for later. The walk proper begins by heading right over a stile, aiming for the towers of a house called Lyulph Tower. As you climb the flank of Gowbarrow Fell, there are excellent views of Ullswater. Eventually start going up above a stream, following a wall, to the top of the fell. It's usually empty on top, as the softies have all stuck to Aira Force. Back along the top and then descend by a steep but easy grassy path, which children usually try to slide down, the fools, to Aira Force.

Easy, satisfying three hour family stroll, with great views, the famous waterfall to take in, Wordsworth's daffodils to look out for in season, and a caff at the end.

Forest Walks

Forests and woodland cover about 8.5% of the National Park, over half of them belonging to the Forestry Commission. These aren't, strictly speaking, natural features of the landscape and the Commission has earned itself some bitter enemies with its policy of covering the fells with dark, regimented conifers. To balance this, they have of late taken to opening up some of their plantations to the public, providing waymarked walks and setting up centres to explain what they are doing. The Forestry Commission has three main forests where this has taken place:

Forestry Commission Forests

1) Grizedale

The best known and one the Forestry Commission apparently feels terribly very proud of.

The forest lies between Esthwaite and Coniston. The main access points have car parks and toilets and there is a visitor centre just north of the village of Satterthwaite. This area was one of the first to be opened to the public. Perhaps for this reason it is not as good as its northern counterparts. The forest trails are often poorly marked and the paths can be confusing. The forest 'sculptures' are a brilliant diversion in the woods - often well camouflaged, so have to be sought out. The Visitor Centre does a good map of them, with details of the artists, some of whom have gone on to become very well known. Even the adventure playground at the Visitor Centre is sculpted. There are now mountain bike trails through the forest - a good way of keeping them off the fells.

☆☆ **Grizedale Visitor Centre** contains a forestry exhibition and displays relating to the industry and how it affects the area, with fascinating computer displays where you can try your hand at forest management. Shop with range of crafts; nice cafe.
Open (Visitor Centre only) April to October, daily 10.00-5.00. Nov.-March weekends. The forest itself is open at all times. Tel: 0229 860010.

2) Thornthwaite Forest and Dodd Wood

Two separate plantations, though usually publicised on the same leaflet, so we'll treat them as one.

☆☆ **Thornthwaite Forest** lies over to the west of Bassenthwaite Lake, and Whinlatter Pass goes through it. At the top of Whinlatter is a car park, the starting point for a number of good walks which give some great views over Derwentwater and Keswick. Also childen's trails, orienteering trails.

☆☆☆ **Whinlatter Visitor Centre** Right at the top of Whinlatter Pass, on the right, coming from Keswick. Used to be a bit stodgy and worthy but now, fresh from a most imaginative revamp, it's an excellent all round attraction. And free. (Though you now have to pay for parking). The new Exhibition is terribly hands-on, with loads of things to push and pull, watch and wonder at. You start with an audio visual presentation which is in Cumbrian dialect, very brave, with some brilliant visual devices. Outside, there's an amazing badger sett you can walk through, though I fear for vandals. Good book shop, mountain bikes for hire, loads of educational trails. Excellent caff, Hampers, for tea and light meals, all pine, with great views. Like sitting in the Alps. Tel: 07687 78469.

☆ **Dodd Wood** is leased from the Mirehouse estate and lies on the east shore of Bassenthwaite Lake. There is an excellent walk which leads you to the top of Dodd, giving a good view over Bassenthwaite and the fells. The car park down at the start of the walk also has the excellent Old Sawmill cafe.

☆☆ 3) Ennerdale

One of the most dramatic Lakeland forests. Cars must be left at Bowness Knott car park. The main forest trail - Smithy Beck - goes along the edge of Ennerdale Water and is clearly waymarked. Openings in the trees reveal fine views.

Thirlmere also has nature trails: Swirls Forest Trail - east shore; Launchy Gill - west shore.

Forestry information Walk sheets are available from most Tourist Information Centres, or direct from the Forestry Commission. For Grizedale, write to District Officer: South Lakes Forest District, Forestry Commission, Grizedale, Hawkshead. Tel: 0229 860373.

For Thornthwaite and Ennerdale: North Lakes Forest District, Forestry Commission, Peil Wyke, Bass Lake. Tel: 07687 76616.

National Trust Woodlands

The National Trust also owns some major woodlands. Good walks can be found at the following:

Windermere North west shore (Claife shore); a nature trail with an illustrated guide available (from National Trust information centres).

Coniston Park-a-Moor and Nibthwaite Woods on the east shore.

Derwentwater Great Wood (east shore), Manesty and Brandlehow (west shore) and Friar's Crag.

Specialist Walks

Nature Trails Many authorities in Lakeland have them these days, apart from the Forestry Commission. Enquire at local TICs for leaflets, but some of the best include: Ambleside (round Loughrigg and White Moss); Appleby (Castle Nature Trail); Barrow (South Walney Nature Trail); Carlisle (Kingmoor Nature Trail); Coniston (Brantwood Nature Trail); Dalton-in-Furness; Eskdale (Stanley Ghyll

Nature Trail); Glenridding (guided walk); Grasmere (guided walk); Hutton-in-the-Forest (Woodland Walk); Kendal (Serpentine Woods); Keswick (Friar's Crag); Ulverston (Hay Bridge Nature Reserve); Nether Wasdale. The National Park folk have an excellent range of "discovery" and guided walks on offer - mostly free, but some need booking in advance. Details fron TICs or Brockhole headquarters. 05394 46601.

Town Trails These are often marked or guided walks round towns and larger villages, or do-it-yourself trails with the appropriate leaflet. They include: Ambleside; Appleby; Furness Abbey; Carlisle; Cockermouth; Dalton-in-Furness; Grasmere; Hawkshead; Kendal; Keswick; Kirkby Lonsdale; Maryport; Pooley Bridge; Sedbergh; Whitehaven; Windermere/Bowness.

Industrial Trails Don't mock. Carlisle had its industrial revolution before Lancashire, and those West Coast towns led the nation at one time in coal and shipping and town planning. Lots of interesting Victorian industrial stuff to be seen, especially in Carlisle (Industrial Trail); Barrow (Vickerstown Town Trail); Whitehaven (Town Walkabout); Maryport (Harbour Walks).

Historical Trails It's becoming popular to link places with a historical theme into walks. They're often outside cental L.D., but that can sometimes add to their attractiveness, not to mention the peace and quiet. 'Cistercian Way' - 33 miles of walks from Grange to Piel Island - with lots of monks and monasteries en route. 'The Lady Anne Clifford Trail' - quite a walk, as this begins in Yorkshire and ends in Cumbria - but it successfully links properties involved in the life of that redoubtable 17th century lady. Leaflets from TICs.

Phallic symbolism? No, Giant's Grave, Penrith

Eden Valley Although we're mainly concerned with Lakeland proper, the good folks on the other side of the M6, still in Cumbria, have recently been setting out many fine walks in the Eden Valley and the Pennines. Leaflets available from Eden Tourism, Penrith. 0768 890256.

Farm Walks Another recent development. There are now regular Open Days on Lake District farms, mainly upland farms, on the hills, the sort peculiar to Cumbria. Most start around 2 o'clock, and the farmer usually does the guided walk. Get a leaflet from the National Park people, or a TIC. "Cumbria Farm Attractions Group" can give information on farm and nature walks. 05396 25331.

Wildlife The Cumbrian coast is especially rich in wildlife, thanks to the mudflats and saltmarshes. Large numbers of wintering waders and wildfowl can be seen, in some cases more than in any other spot in the world. You might also see rare animals, such as natterjack toads.

For information about Cumbria's trees, flowers, birds and mammals, and about the conservation work going on, contact - Cumbria Wildlife Trust, The Badger's Paw, Church Street, Ambleside. 05394 32476.

Geology After Cornwall, Cumbria is probably the most interesting county in England, geologically speaking. In fact, American geologists come all the way here for things they can't get at home, such as fluorites. Even an amateur, with no knowledge, soon can spot bits of the stuff, scattered over the fells. The two most popular Lakeland areas for finding specimens are:

Northern Fells, just south of Caldbeck, especially Roughton Gill, Carrock Fell and Driggeth. Beware the old mine workings. They can be dangerous. Very good for pyromorphites, malachite, pyrite. You might even find campylite, if you're lucky.

West Coast, round Beckermet and Frizington. Good for haematite, barytes. I met a man from Sussex who found a piece of Pallaflat Calcite at Egremont, which he sold for £450. Lucky. Britain's (some say Europe's) last working iron-ore mine is at Egremont. They have occasional guided tours. Contact West Cumbria Groundwork Trust. Tel: 0946 813677.

Walking Books and Leaflets

In addition to the general guide books listed already in Chapter 1, there are a number of others which give good low-level walks.

☆☆☆ **Walks in the Countryside** The National Park people publish an excellent series of walk sheets, 14 in all, each based in a particular area and offering two or three fairly easy walks, with a description and sketch map. They only cost 20p each, so are great value. Or you can buy the set in a special pack for £1.99. Highly recommended, because you don't have to take a whole book out with you. Cheap to replace if lost or damaged. The maps, I mean, not you. You are irreplaceable . . .

Enjoy the Fells in Safety - free. Leaflet published by the National Park Authority is worth a mention. Gives advice, safety hints, suggested equipment and - best of all - fell ascent times.

Nature Book Best book which covers Cumbria's mines, soils, animals, plants and such like is *A Field Guide to the Lake District*, by Jim Taylor Page, published by Dalesman, 1984. Rather school masterly, so it would be very useful if you are a teacher, or in charge of a group, but comprehensive and fairly easy to read.

Long Walk Book Just in case you've exhausted all those short family ones, or even those quick mountain climbs, why not try the Cumbria Way, a 70 mile walk from Ulverston, on the shores of Morecambe Bay, right through the heart of the Lake District, up to Carlisle in the north. You could do it in a week, taking in bed and breakfast places or youth hostels along the way. It's a Ramblers' Association enterprise and easily followed. Good booklet all about it called *The Cumbria Way* by John Trevelyan, published by Dalesman in 1987.

Guides

If you now feel you've got the hang of it, managing to place one foot in front of the other, or walking as we normally call it, you might want to venture up onto the hairy stuff. In that case, a proper mountain guide might be useful, one who knows the terrain and has reached the professional standards set down by the ABMG.

There are about 15 professional ABMG guides in Lakeland. Philip Poole of the Lakeland Guides Bureau acts as a clearing house for requests for guides 05394 44033. The British Mountaineering Council also have a list of qualified guides 061 273 5835.

Chapter Ten

Museums and Galleries

The Lake District has a large number of museums and galleries for such a small area. And not all of them are simply about Lakeland fells and sheep. I bet you didn't expect to find the largest collection of Laurel and Hardy possessions here, or a five hundred year old cat, or a seven foot pencil.

A lot of museums are now transforming themselves into highly imaginative interpretative centres, with up-to-date audio-visual displays and light, airy buildings. But in some ways the ones which are being left behind can be the nicest - old fashioned and badly displayed, but ideal for just pottering.

Admission charges
> **A** - under £2
> **B** - £2-£3
> **C** - over £3

Children are normally half price. Last admission time is often 1/2 hour to an hour before closing time. Opening months are inclusive - ie 'March-October' means 1st March to 31st October.

We have arranged them alphabetically, according to the nearest town or village. Note those which offer tea facilities - very few of them do.

Warning: Museums are obvious places to go in rainy weather, so if there's one you really want to see at its best, take a day off from the fells and go when it is sunny. Particular ones to avoid when wet are those in areas where there is little else to do when the weather is bad (e.g. Grasmere and Hawkshead).

We have tried our very best to give correct opening times, but they can change, so ring in advance if it's a vital visit.

Note: Literary Homes are in Chapter 11; Stately Homes in Chapter 12.

Ambleside
Armitt Collection

Public Library, Kelsick Road, Ambleside. Tel: 05394 33949.

It all began with three Bronte type sisters, Marie Louisa, Annie Maria and Sophia Armitt, who devoted themselves to writing and the arts. They founded a library in 1912, subsequently supported by the great and the good of the times, such as Canon Rawnsley, Beatrix Potter, Arthur Ransome, G. M. Trevelyan.

Best things: The Armitt Library now owns the largest collection of fungi water colours done by Beatrix Potter (that was an early passion, before she wrote Peter Rabbit); early Lakeland photographs; rare books of literary and Cumbria interest; archaeological relics; literary manuscripts.

At present, the collection is housed above Ambleside Public Library, but there are plans to house it in a new building beside Charlotte Mason College. We hope.

In the meantime, you can become a Friend of the Armitt Trust, just £5 a year. Write to Armitt Trust, Ambleside, Cumbria LA22 0BZ. Enquiries, telephone the Librarian, 05394 33949.

Open: Mon-Fri. 10-12.30, 1.30-4.00 (closed Thurs.).

Barrow
Furness Museum

Now here's a mystery. Where is it? Finding the Furness Museum these last two years has been harder than finding Nobby Ludd. Remember him? There are plans to re-house the social history stuff from the old Furness Museum, plus the new Maritime Museum (another mystery), into one new wonderful building. But where and when? It's promised for late 1993. They say. For details, or more mysteries, ring Barrow Town Hall 0229 825500. Or try the Curator direct on 0229 870871 who, as we write, is sitting there, all on his own, waiting for his new museum to open.

Caldbeck
☆ Caldbeck Mining Museum

Priests Mill, Caldbeck. Tel: 06974 78369.

Ian and Jean Tyler have been exploring Cumbrian mines for years, when they haven't been running their Carlisle sports shop. Now they've put their passion on show. Small but perfectly formed museum, ever so neatly done, in just three rooms, showing the history of mineral mining in Lake District, particularly the Northern fells. Photos, tools, lamps, specimens. The bigger objects can be picked up and handled. Good selection of mining books. Guided tours of local mines available.

Best things: Five Elizabethan mining tools, including chisels and hammer. They don't look much, but very rare.

Open: 11.00-5.00, March-Oct. Closed Mondays. Admission, A.

Carlisle
☆☆☆ Tullie House Museum and Art Gallery
Castle Street, Carlisle, Tel: 0228 34781.

Carlisle's award winning cultural wonderland - top UK national heritage Museum in 1991, thanks to its massive £5 million re-development. You can actually see where the money has gone, which is not always the case when they tart up something old, and sense the care and imagination lavished on all the exhibits, from the Romans to the railways. Manages to be fun, yet tasteful and informative, well laid out, for young and old, and worth two hours of anyone's time. Easy to find, as it's just past the Cathedral, before you get to the Castle, but hell for parking. Try over the road beside the Castle in Devonshire Walk. Restaurant, souvenir shop, always lots on - special exhibitions, lectures, films, concerts, so pick up leaflets.

Best things: In the Museum parts, Border Reivers and Roman Wall are very good, especially climbing up the Turf Wall. Great sound effects. Good on Lakeland wild life. Don't miss the battle arrows in the glass, looking over at the Castle. Sit in the old railway carriages. The Gallery shows change all the time, but the best is the pre-Raphaelite paintings. Carlisle has works by Burne-Jones, Millet, Pisarro, Whistler, Augustus John, Paul Nash, Stanley Spencer - amazing for a small provincial city. (They got them cheap in the 1930s when Sir Willam Rothenstein became their London art advisor.)

Before leaving, examine the original Tullie House, Carlisle's only remaining Jacobean building. The ornate lead drain pipes are works of art in themselves.

Open: All year round, 10.00-5.00, except Xmas Day. Admission - Museum B, Art Gallery and ground floor, free.

☆ Guildhall Museum beside Old Town Hall.
Tel: 0228 34781.

Built 1405, the last remaining medieval timber framed building in Carlisle, now beautifully restored. Eight rooms, displaying work of the various guilds who once use the building - shoemakers, tanners, butchers, weavers, merchants. All lovely, except for butchers room which has a horrible modern pine wood wall.

Best thing: the House itself. How did it survive.

Open: Same as Tullie House. Admission, dead cheap. (50p in 1993, including sound guide.).

☆ Cathedral Treasury

Carlisle Cathedral Tel: 0228 35169.

A new museum, in a superb underground gallery, housing all the Cathedral's treasures - ancient copes, historic plate, books, silver, plus displays which tell the story of Christian Cumbria. Open from 7.30 to 4.45. Free.

☆ Border Regiment Museum

Queen Mary Tower, Carlisle Castle. Tel: 0228 32774.

Part of the Castle, which is well worth a visit in itself. Free parking on the Castle's parade ground which is a great help.

Best things: The Border Regiment has served in battles all over the world for the last 300 years - from the Duke of Marlborough's days, the Napoleonic Wars to the last two World Wars. Of great fascination to all those with local connections, as the regiment's roots are well explained, but still of interest to all military fans. Good displays of regimental trophies and uniforms.

The full name, by the way, should be the Border Regiment and King's Own Royal Border Regiment Museum (making it the Longest Museum Title in Cumbria).

Open: April to Sept., daily 9.30-6.30; Winter, Mon-Sat, 9.30-4.00, Sunday, 2.00-4.00. Admission - A (entrance to the Castle also gets you into the Museum).

Solway Aviation Museum

Crosby on Eden, near Carlisle.

Open only on Sunday afternoons, but worth a mention as it's Cumbria's only plane museum. It's actually on Carlisle Airport, an amusement in itself. Local aviation memorabilia displayed in a little hut. Fascinating booklet on sale about the history of Carlisle Airport. Did you know it was used by Battle of Britain heroes and visited by De Gaulle?

Best things: Outside they have five real planes from the 1950s and '60s: Gloster Meteor, Canberra bomber, Vulcan bomber, Lightening, Vampire. The Vampire and Vulcan can be climed into and inspected. No phone.

Open: Sundays, 2.00-4.00 all year. Admission - A.

Carnforth
☆ Steamtown Railway Museum

Warton Road, Carnforth. Tel: 0524 732100.

Rather out of the way, though it tends to get advertised in the Lake District and they do promote Carnforth as

'The Gateway to the Lakes' (they'll be saying that about Manchester soon). Go down the A6 to Carnforth, then follow the signs to 'Railway Museum' - it's behind the British Rail depot (recognise it from 'Brief Encounter'?). Parking on site. Carnforth has few other attractions (apart from a superb secondhand book shop) so it is unlikely that you'll be walking from anywhere.

Best things: Thirty diesel and steam engines. It boasts that it's Britain's largest steam loco depot. (There are now so many exhibitions of old industries in Lakeland - what with bobbin mills, water-mills and steam engines - you sometimes get the feeling that if the rest of industrial civilisation collapsed, the Lake District could just turn the clock back 100 years and carry on as normal.)

Look out for a miniature railway (NB it doesn't run every day, so ring to check first), a Midland Railway signal box (how did that get there?); they used to have the Flying Scotsman, but it has now gone elsewhere (shame). Steamtown is often visited by mainline locomotives, so it could reappear. Full steam days are public holidays and Sundays in April, May and June. Wednesday, Saturday and Sundays in July and August. Also Sundays in September and October. Well worth a visit for railway buffs.

Open: Easter to September, daily 9.00-5.00; winter, 10.00-4.00. Closed Christmas Eve to Boxing Day. Admission - B/C - depending on whether it is a steam day or whether the miniature railway is running (why does anything to do with British Rail have to be complicated?). There's a small tea shop on site which is OK for snacks.

Cartmel

☆ Cartmel Priory Gatehouse

Cartmel, near Grange-over-Sands. 05395 36691.

Cartmel is a lovely little village, best reached from the north by coming down to Newby Bridge and turning left, then taking the turning for Cartmel about a mile further on. You can park in the village square, but if full (which it always is if the pubs are open), carry on through the square down the little road on the left of the post office and park by the racecourse. The Gatehouse is under the arch, just opposite the pump in the centre of the square.

Best things: The building itself dates from around 1330 and is owned by the National Trust. It is now let to a local artist, who has a display of work on show, often painting whilst visitors look around.

Open: April to October, daily 11.00-5.00 (closed Monday). Admission free.

Cockermouth

☆ Toy and Model Museum

Bank's Court, Market Place, Cockermouth.
Tel: 0900 827606.

Rod More, ex-electronics engineer, gets upset if you call him a 'collector' of toys. He accumulated them - either to play with, or make them work. On show he has British toys from 1900 onwards, including all the famous names you've ever played with - Hornby, Meccano, Triang; 60% of them to do with trains.

Best things: Hornby 0 gauge railway; Scalextric race track.

Open: Feb-Nov. 10.00-5.00 daily. Admission - A.

☆ Wm Creighton Mineral Museum

Crown Street, Cockermouth.
Tel: 0900 828301.

Just along from Wordsworth House. Part of a gift shop, so don't get confused. The museum is to the right as you go in, three little rooms, packed with over 200 minerals, all from the North of England, plus over 100 miner's lamps and tools.

Best thing: Wm Creighton, ex-stone carver, says his calcite lump from the Florence mine, 12 inches across, is world class. Best thing for amateurs, and all children, is to go into his flourescent room. All the rocks light up. Wondrous.

Open: 10.00-5.00 daily, except Sunday. Admission A (50p).

☆ Printing Museum

102 Main Street, Cockermouth.
Tel: 0900 824984.

David Winkworth has been collecting printing presses, machines, type faces for decades, and boasting about the museum he's going to open one day. Now he's done it, at the back of his antiquarian bookshop. You have to go through the shop to get to it, but it turns out to be surprisingly spacious. Shows the history of printing from 1800 onwards. Lots of good memorabilia.

Best thing: Imperial press, *c.* 1830. Columbian Eagle press, 1840.

Open: 10.00-4.00 daily. Closed Sundays. Admission - A.

☆ Castlegate House Gallery

Cockermouth, Castlegate. Tel: 0900 822149.

A recently opened commercial gallery, specialising in Cumbrian paintings by living, local artists. You don't have to buy of course, just admire the art, savour the ambience.

Best things: Depends on the current show, but the house itself is worth a peep, as it's one of Cockermouth's larger

Georgian gems, just opposite the Castle, with a surprising garden. (Ask to see it, and the inscription over the back door. It's private, but you could be lucky.)

Open: March to October, Monday-Saturday 10.30-4.30, except Wednesday, which is open 10.30-7.00. Closed Thursdays. Admission free.

Castle Brewery Cockermouth. Tel: 0900 823214.

Not a museum, but where else can we fit it in. This is the home of Jennings, Cumbria's leading traditional brewer, who now do guided tours of their old established site where you can see the beer in action. No children under 12 allowed, and I should hope not. Souvenir shop.

Open: Twice daily tours. Mon-Fri, at 10.30 and 2.00, plus summer Saturdays at 11.00. Advanced bookings advisable. Admission - B.

Coniston
☆ The Ruskin Museum
The Institute, Yewdale Road, Coniston. Tel: 05394 41541.

Right in the centre of the village, so parking is pretty hopeless. Use the main car park and walk back. You have to look carefully for the museum as it's only tiny.

Best things: Once inside there are some interesting displays relating to Ruskin and his circle. There are also some fine mineral specimens. A good example of a typical, old fashioned museum. The BBC film of the Donald Campbell record attempt on Coniston aroused a lot of interest, so the Museum is now trying to display more of its collection of photographs of Campbell and Bluebird.

Open: March to October, daily 11.00-1.00 and 2.00-5.00. Never terribly busy so no particularly good times to go - best to avoid it on wet days, though. Admission - A.

Finsthwaite
☆☆ Stott Park Bobbin Mill
Finsthwaite, near Newby Bridge. Tel: 05395 31087.

On the west side of Lake Windermere, just north of Lakeside on the Hawkshead Road (about a mile away), at the Finsthwaite road junction. Free car park on site.

Completely out of the way and set in wooded countryside. Can sound like any other little craft gallery, but is actually a major site of what used to be one of the Lake District's most important industries. Can be combined with a pleasant walk through the woods to Finsthwaite High Dam.

Best things: The place itself - this really *is* a bobbin mill, not a reconstruction. It was built in 1835 and was turning out bobbins right up until 1971. After it closed down, English Heritage bought the property and reopened it as a museum in 1983. It is now run by the Abbot Hall people. The massive mill building houses much of the original machinery, including the old water turbines and steam engines. The two resident curators, Mr Dixon and Mr Steeley, will give guided tours and demonstrations. They have both worked in the industry (though not at Stott Park) and are full of stories. There are also static displays and a small exhibition. A fantastic place, unique and well worth leaving the beaten tourist track to find.

Open: 1st April to October, daily 10.00-6.00. Admission - B.

Grasmere

☆☆☆ Grasmere & Wordsworth Museum

Town End, Grasmere. Tel: 05394 35544/35547.

Next to Dove Cottage, just off the A591, opposite the southern turning to Grasmere village. The museum is in a converted stable block which used to belong to The Prince of Wales Hotel. Limited parking if you're early, but impossible later in the day during the summer. Best to park in the village and walk up.

Best things: After Abbot Hall, this is probably the best and most 'professional' museum in the Lake District. They are very proud of the fact that it is the only 'Grade A' museum in the North-West, which means it has its own internal climate and air-conditioning. (Very refreshing on a sweltering summer day. You can wander about inside and get cool.)

The museum houses the best collection of original Wordsworth manuscripts in the entire known universe. Look out, too, for a copy of Dorothy's notebook, where she kept her famous journal. Not all the manuscripts are in William's own hand - he used to get his wife, Mary, or sister to write out his poems for him and would then go through and make corrections. It is fascinating to compare his handwriting later in life with a handwritten poem composed when he was at Hawkshead Grammar School - it got much worse. The display is brilliantly presented and it's all in chronological order, telling the poet's life story, so don't worry if your knowledge of Wordsworth is confined to a single poem about daffodils. There are many of Wordsworth's possessions on display, including a coat and waistcoat mounted on a dummy torso so that you can get an idea of his size. There are also paintings of many of his contemporaries. Each summer there is a special exhibition in the downstairs gallery.

It's not all Wordsworth and there are two rooms devoted to local history. Downstairs is a display showing the history of tourism in Grasmere, including some wonderful old optical instruments. Upstairs is a reconstruction of a farmhouse interior, as it might have been around 1800.

The Museum host three residential courses each year - a Winter School (Feb), Book Collectors Weekend (February or March) and the Wordsworth Summer Conference (August). More details in chapter 14.

There is a restaurant, just on the main road (well, there's always been one there but now the Dove Cottage lot actually own and run it). Open during the day and for evening dinner. Tel: 05394 35268.

There is quite a lot of reading to be done in this museum, so it is best to get there early in the day to avoid the crowds. It is often quiet around lunch time.

Final tip - do the museum before you do Dove Cottage. You'll appreciate it more.

Open: Now almost all year (they're closed Xmas Day and from mid-Jan to mid-Feb), daily 9.30-5.30. Last admission - 5.00. Admission - C (includes Dove Cottage and special exhibitions). Special rates for families and groups.
Warning: It can get very crowded during wet weather, especially during school holidays.

Hawkshead
☆☆ Hawkshead Grammar School
Hawkshead, near Ambleside. No telephone.

Dead easy to find - it's opposite the main car park. Leave the car in the car park, visit the grammar school, then walk into Hawkshead via the path round the back of the grammar school. This brings you into the centre of Hawkshead and avoids all the crowds panting to get into the sheepskin and gifte-shoppes.

Best things: The school is a lovely old building, though now painted up and looking somewhat different than in Wordsworth's day. It is famous, of course, because the young William Wordsworth went to school here. Inside you can see the desk where he carved his initials. (Or at least, that's what they tell you - very hard to find.) The main room is a school room set out as it was in the late 18th century. The curator is always on hand to answer questions about the school or Wordsworth. (Go early and catch him when few visitors are about and make the best of his local knowledge.) Upstairs there is a small library and a small exhibition on the history of the school. If you want to know how they made quill pens, there's a display which tells you. There is also a new room recently opened - the headmaster's study (potential for an exhibition of canes through the ages?). A nice, relaxing little museum, quiet even in summer. Opening times can be 'variable' according to moles.

Open: March to October, Monday -Sat. 10.00-5.00 (closed for lunch 1.00-1.30), Sunday 2.00-5.00. Admission - A.

☆☆ Beatrix Potter Gallery

Main Street, Hawkshead. Tel: 05394 35355.

For several years now, visitors to Hill Top have been disappointed to find that the original water colours from the Beatrix Potter books have not been on show. Taken, and hidden away, or so it seemed. Now they have reappeared, and in a marvellous setting. The National Trust have converted the original legal offices of William Heelis, BP's husband, and turned it into an excellent little gallery.

Best things: The Potter paintings of course. Don't miss them. Especially if you were amongst the thousands who couldn't see a thing for the crowds at the Tate show of Potter stuff. It is nice to be able to compare the printed illustrations with the early sketches and paintings. A shame the NT have concentrated on Peter Rabbit et al, to the exclusion of Beatrix Potter's other watercolours (such as her flower paintings which are exquisite). There's also a recreation of Mr Heelis's office, complete with his desk ledgers and period files.

Open: April-Oct. Mon-Fri 10.30-4.30 and Bank Holiday Sundays (last admission 4.00 pm). Admission - B.

Holker

☆☆ Lakeland Motor Museum

Holker Hall, Cark-in-Cartmel, Grange-over-Sands. Tel: 05395 58509.

Holker Hall is on the B5278 between Haverthwaite and Cark. The easiest way to get to it is turn right at Newby Bridge along the A590 and turn onto the B5278 at Haverthwaite. It's about 7 1/2 miles from Newby Bridge and the Museum is in the grounds of Holker Hall. Parking in the grounds. Can be visited as part of 'Lakeland Link' which includes steamer and rail travel. (See chapter 7 Lakes - Windermere for details.)

Best things: A northern Beaulieu in many ways - it even has Campbell's Bluebird, though this one is a replica, made for a BBC television play. There are over 80 historic vehicles - cars, motorbikes, cycles, engines, as well as various motoring bits and pieces (otherwise known as 'automobilia'), such as Princess Margaret's scooter, illuminated petrol pump signs, toy cars and a walk-round 1920's garage. Fascinating stuff. They now also have an East German Trabant, driven over when The Wall came down, and probably expired where it now resides. Favourite exhibit is likely to depend on your particular mechanical bent, but their prize exhibit is the 1922 Bentley. An excellent 'fun' museum, but it is expensive. Friendly manager though who will lift up the bonnet of their 1938 Lagonda, if you ask nicely.

Open: April to October, daily (closed Saturday) 10.30-5.30. Last admission 4.30. Life is too short to explain Holker's very complicated admission rules and charges - let's just say - B/C.

Kendal

☆☆☆ Abbot Hall Art Gallery

Abbot Hall, Kendal. Tel: 0539 722464.

Situated in Kirkland, at the southern end of Kendal. It's just behind the Parish Church and has one of the loveliest settings in town - right by the river and looking up towards Kendal Castle. Free car park - get to it by going through the Council car park.

The Gallery is in an immaculate Georgian building, set in a small park along with some of the oldest buildings in Kendal. Just because Kendal is not a major city, don't expect another small, provincial gallery. It is generally reckoned to be the finest art gallery in the North West and one of the top 20 in the whole country.

Best things: Abbot Hall itself, for a start. Built in 1759 for Lt Col George Wilson (at a cost of £8,000) it has been open as an art gallery since 1962, restored in 1992 to decorative splendour of 1760s. Downstairs houses a small but impressive collection of 18th and 19th century paintings, displayed along with period furniture, porcelain and glassware. It's set out in such a way that you feel as if you're wandering around someone's stately home - only without all those ropes. Upstairs the house becomes a more traditional art gallery setting to display the contemporary collection, works by Barbara Hepworth, John Piper, William Johnstone, Norman Adams, Elizabeth Frink. There are also changing exhibitions each year which are well worth looking out for.

Open: May to October, Monday-Saturday 10.30-5.00, Sunday 2.00-5.00; rest of year Monday-Friday 11.00-4.00, Saturday & Sunday 2.00-5.00. Admission - B, or you can save money by buying a combined ticket for the Art Gallery and the Museum of Lakeland Life and Industry.

Can also now purchase a Triple Ticket which includes Museum of Archaeology and Natural History as well as Art Gallery and Lakeland Life and Industry. Excellent value at £4. Use different bits at different times.

☆☆☆ Museum of Lakeland Life and Industry

Abbot Hall, Kendal. Tel: 0539 722464.

A separate establishment in its own right, housed in what used to be Abbot Hall's stable block. Part of the collection spills over into the adjacent 17th century grammar school, so watch out for the diversion sign as you go round the upstairs part of the museum. Small but prestigious, it won the first ever Museum of the Year Award in 1973.

Best things: Definitely the lack of glass cases. Most of the exhibits are on open display - you can touch them, walk round them, peer under them, even sniff them if you want to. Some of the drawers are worth opening, too. It's a fantastic little museum, full of reconstructed workshops with genuine, hand worn tools and instruments. There's a beautiful old 19th century printing press, made of cast iron and once used by the Westmorland Gazette; a hundred year-old weaving loom (sometimes used to give demonstrations by local experts); engineering and wheelwright's workshops; massive old clocks and signs; there's even a bedroom and living room, a delight to walk round, fully furnished as they might have been around 1900. This is definitely the best museum for anyone interested in Lakeland and its people. One of the nicest things about it is that many of the tools and exhibits came from local people. It is all so well done that it looks as though the people who used these tools have just knocked off for lunch and might be back at any minute to carry on working. Look out for the paint shop door upstairs, covered in 'stalactites' of paint where the brushes used to be worked out.

There is also a replica of Arthur Ransome's study, with many of his possessions, including his desk and chair.

Adjacent to the Ransome Room is the new John Cunliffe Room. Who 's he? Dum dum. He wrote Postman Pat, while teaching in Kendal, setting the stories in the Longsleddale Valley, with the addition of a lake, similar to Grasmere. The walls show murals from the stories, and some of the original drawings. Aimed at today's kiddies, but is he really in the Ransome league?.

Part of the success of the display relies on its minimal use of labels and text, but this has its drawbacks - quite often you find yourself wondering what on earth you're looking at. The only remedy is to arm yourself with the guide book before you go in and think of it as part of the admission fee.

Queens Gate is the new replica of a Kendal street scene, circa 1890, along the lines of the Castle Museum at York. Excellent chemist's shop and perfumery but were streets really this dark 100 years ago? Opened in 1985 by the Queen.

There is also a farming gallery which is easily missed as you have to go through the new Craft Shop to enter it. A nice, airy display of wonderful old farming implements, complemented by a refreshingly witty text (some of which is displayed actually inside the machines). A sign reads: "Cumbria contains two million sheep and half-a-million people". Some might say it doubles to four million on a Bank Holiday.

Open: May to October, Monday-Saturday 10.30-5.00, Sunday 2.00-5.00; rest of year Monday-Friday 11.00-4.00, Saturday & Sunday 2.00-5.00.

☆☆ Kendal Museum of Archaeology and Natural History

Station Road, Kendal. Tel: 0539 721374.

It's up by the railway station, about 10 minutes walk from the town centre. Limited parking at the museum.

Owned by the Town Council but administered by Abbot Hall, it is gradually changing from a typical municipal museum of the old school, into an imaginative 'interpretative' centre. Don't let that put you off though . . .

Best things: Kendal is full of surprises. Not only does it contain one of the best art galleries in the country, it also has one of England's oldest museums. Kendal Museum was first opened in 1796 when a gentleman by the name of William Todhunter staged an exhibition of 'curiosities'. Admission was 'one shilling per person; children, workmen and servants 6d each'. The museum has three main galleries, all designed to involve rather than simply explain. The dioramas are excellent; you can wander back and forth in time in the Westmorland Gallery, go on a nature trail around Morecambe Bay in the Natural History Gallery and wonder what on earth big-game were doing in the Lake District in the World Wildlife Gallery. This last gallery is fun, but doesn't have a lot to do with the area - the museum inherited a massive collection of stuffed animals and had to make a special gallery to display them in. Latest addition is a Wainwright display - telling the story of the local lad.

Open: Monday-Friday 10.30-5.00, Saturday and Sunday 2.00-5.00 (Saturdays, Spring Bank to Oct 10.30-5.00).

Keswick
☆☆ Keswick Museum and Art Gallery

Fitz Park, Keswick. Tel: 07687 73263.

Beside Fitz Park, on the left on Station Road, going up the hill towards Keswick Leisure Pool. Parking usually quite easy.

One of Cumbria's oddest museums, more an idiosyncratic collection of strange objects than a normal little municipal museum. Almost gets three stars, just for not trying, but that would be unfair on the really professional ones at Kendal and Grasmere. Often referred to as Fitz Park Museum.

Best things: Excellent collection of letters and documents to do with Wordsworth, Southey, Coleridge and Walpole.

Look out for an original copy of The Three Bears. Did you know that Southey wrote it? Bet you didn't. (In his original version it's an old woman who eats their porridge - Goldilocks is a later addition.) Of the dafter exhibits, there's a box marked '500 year-old cat - lift lid carefully'; and a set of 19th century musical stones, probably the best loved item in the museum, though the literary letters are much more valuable. Each stone gives out a different note when struck, so musical visitors can play tunes - and are allowed to, but using hands only. Can be very tiring. They were played before Queen Victoria in 1848. She was not amused.

There's a small art gallery, where exhibitions are changed each month. The Museum will also open in winter, but only for groups of ten or more.

Open: April to October, daily except Saturdays, 10.00-12.00 and 1.00-4.00. Admission - A.

☆☆ Cars of the Stars Museum
Standish Street, Keswick. Tel: 07687 73757.

Peter Nelson, Keswick dentist, has collected almost 30 vehicles which have appeared in TV and films, including Chitty Chitty Bang Bang, Lady Penelope's FAB 1 pink Rolls-Royce as used in Thunderbirds, Del Boy's Reliant, The Saint's Volvo and three James Bond cars. The 'Laurel and Hardy Model T Ford' is a genuine Ford, of the right period, and was owned by a film company, but there's little proof it was used by L. and H. But all the other cars are your actual ones. An amazing and unique collection, got together in only five years. Why did no one in America think of it. The setting is a bit barn like, in an old garage, but the tableaux and sound systems are improving all the time. Souvenir shop, little tea room.

Best thing: The whole notion is the best thing. Best single item - Chitty.

Open: Easter to New Year, daily, 10.00-5.00. Admission – B.

☆☆ Cumberland Pencil Museum
Southey Works, Keswick. Tel: 07687 73626.

In the north west part of Keswick. Follow the main road out of town and it's beside the river, just before the A66 turning to Cockermouth. Plenty of parking on site. It is about 10 minutes walk from the centre of Keswick.

The museum is part of the pencil factory, now owned by Rexel.

Best things: A good museum for children - and fantastic if you happen to be a pencil freak. It has been billed as 'the story of the pencil brought to life' and lately "home of the world's 1st pencils". (You could also call it a museum to industrial inertia, since the graphite for the pencil works now comes from abroad.) They have pencil making machines, a video display about pencils, a drawing competition, and a shop. (Where you can buy, wait for it . . . pencils.) There's even a replica of a graphite mine, so you can see where the stuff comes from. Don't miss the very clever Wartime Pencils - with a secret compartment, containing a compass and a map of Germany. The museum also boasts the World's Longest Pencil (it's in the Guinness Book of Records) - 7 feet long, over 15lbs in weight, with a 1-inch diameter lead core. It was made in 1978 to raise money for Keswick Mountain Rescue. Nowadays it's a celebrity and often out and about, raising money for charity. So if you particularly want to see it, ring in advance to make sure it's in residence.

Open: All year, seven days a week, 9.30 - Last admission 4.00. Admission - B.

Beatrix Potter's Lake District
Packhorse Court, Keswick.

Yet another twee BP experience for the trippers? Not quite. This is the National Trust, flying its own flag, letting us know about the wonderful work it has done on Lakeland since Beatrix Potter left it 4,000 acres. Today, it protects and conserves 140,000 acres, one quarter of Lakeland.

It opens April 1993, so we haven't seen it yet, but the NT promises 'a multi media show'. Don't they all.

Open: April-Oct, daily 10.00-5.00. Nov-March, weekends only, 10.00-5.00. Admission - B.
Ring NT HQ for further details - 05394 35599.

Maryport
☆☆ Senhouse Roman Museum
The Battery, Maryport. Tel: 0900 816168.

One of the country's oldest and most important private collections of Roman relics. It was begun in 1570 by John Senhouse, who collected bits from the old Roman Fort at Maryport, then kept through twelve generations of his family. Finally opened to the public in 1990 in a converted Victorian naval battery, overlooking the town. Only three rooms, but take them slowly, if you want to savour the sexual undertones, such as the Serpent Stone, probably Celtic, and what a big one, a phallus over 5 feet high, or the 'Pin Up Girl', a naked girl carved in stone to welcome soldiers going on leave. Naff modern paintings, showing Roman life, let you realise how artistic the Romans were. Don't miss the earthworks outside, where the old fort used to be. Or walk northwards and try to find the site of milefort 21. The whole of this coast has its own defence system, an extension of Hadrian's Wall, with Maryport as its HQ, hence the importance of this site.

Best things: the 24 altars, especially the lettering.

Open: July-Sept, every day, 10.00-5.00. April, May, June plus Oct, Nov. closed certain days - ring to check.

☆ Maryport Maritime Museum
1 Senhouse Street, Maryport. Tel: 0900 813738.
    Quite easy to find as it's right beside the quay.

Best things: Typical in many ways of Lakeland's small museums, but neat and attractive. It is devoted almost exclusively to the history of Maryport as a maritime centre. Very important at one time. It is small, but well run on a shoestring budget using enthusiasm and invention rather than the latest wonder display techniques. A nice change from the Heritage Interpretative Visitor Centres of this world. Houses collections of photographs of old Maryport and of general maritime interest. There are also items relating to Fletcher Christian (remember Mutiny on the Bounty?) and to Thomas Henry Ismay, the founder of the White Star Line. Both local lads. The museum houses a small tourist information centre and shop.

Open: Easter to October, Monday-Friday 10.00-5.00, Saturday 10.00-1.00, 2.00-5.00, Sunday 2.00-5.00. Rest of year Monday-Saturday 10.00-1.00 and 2.00-4.30. Free admission.

☆ Maryport Steamship Museum
Elizabeth Dock, Maryport Harbour. Tel: 0900 815954.
    New name for two old boats. (If you have one object, it's an exhibit - if you have two, you can call it a museum). Both worth seeing as they come as a pleasant surprise, hidden away in this rather sad corner of Maryport harbour.
    The Flying Buzzard is an old Clyde tug, built 1951, now fully restored and painted a foul orange to match Allerdale Council's corporate colour. Alongside it is *Vic 96*, a naval supply ship. Both ships can be toured - and most things touched..

Best Things: Engine room of the *Buzzard* is pretty neat - and *Vic 96* is fun when occasionally it lets off steam.

Open: Easter to October, 10.30-4.30, except Thursday.

Millom
☆ Millom Folk Museum
St George's Road, Millom. Tel: 0229 772555.

If you can find Millom, finding the museum should be easy, though it is very tiny. Park in the town.

Best things: Another small museum, 'intimate' is the best description. It's a bit overcrowded, but visitors are encouraged to handle the exhibits. Pride of place goes to a reconstruction of an authentic iron ore mine drift, with a real lift cage from one of the local mines, complete with a tape recording of the lift's last journey down the mine (I wonder if the miners came up again before they took the lift away?). You can crawl round the mine drift and get an idea of what working underground must have been like. There is also a reconstruction of a miner's cottage kitchen. It is one of those places where they try to get you interested, rather than just looking at objects. Puts the rise and fall of this coast's prosperity into perspective. Good fun. There is also an exhibition about the life and work of local poet, Norman Nicholson, known locally as "our most famous son". Curator who also runs small TIC at entrance, gives enthusiastic commentary if provoked. Shows N.Ns personal artefacts with loving involvement . . . .

Open: Easter week, May Day weekend and Whitsun to September, Monday-Saturday 10.00-5.00. Admission - A.

Penrith
☆☆ Penrith Steam Museum
Castlegate Foundry, Castlegate, Penrith. Tel: 0768 62154.

It is down Castlegate from the railway station. (Or up Castlegate towards the railway station, if you're coming from the centre of town). Can sometimes park outside the museum, but it is probably best to park at the station and walk back.

The outside of the museum is a bit unimpressive - it looks rather like a shop - but it conceals all manner of wonders inside.

Best things: This is one of the Lake District's best 'fun' museums - a good place to take the family. On display are several massive steam engines, plus various agricultural and engineering exhibits. The engines are all in working order and most days are in operation. (But ring in advance to make sure if you want to see them in steam.) It's a specialist museum but it doesn't take itself too seriously and there's enough going on to interest the casual visitor as well as the enthusiast. One of the best museums in Lakeland and highly recommended by all the experts. Look out for the period cottage and works office.

Open: Easter weekend and Spring Bank Holiday to

September, Monday-Friday 10.00-4.30. Open Saturday and Sunday at Bank Holidays only. Admission - B. Small tea shop on the premises, often closed, so try pub next door.

☆ Cumbria Police Museum

Carleton Hall, Penrith. Tel: 0768 64411.

Well, you never know, you might want to frighten the kids on a wet afternoon. Just a little museum, recently opened, in Cumbria police's handsome HQ, but full of fascinating stuff - handcuffs, ankle cuffs, truncheons, guns, early police radios, uniforms. What a toff a Chief Constable looked in the old days, dressed in his best. School and other parties encouraged. Worksheets available.

Best thing: The monocle of Percy Toplis, the Monocled Mutineer, yes, they really have it; the actual guns and break-in tools used by the murderers Rudge , Martin and Baker in 1885. Ugh.

Tours by appointment only. Ring and ask for Mr McKenzie.

Penrith Museum

Robinson's School, Middlegate. Tel: 0768 64671.

The building was a school at one time, a charitable foundation for poor girls, then became the Tourist Information Centre. Since 1990, it also houses the town's local history museum, a modest collection of photos, document, artefacts about Penrith's history, and assorted worthies. Of little interest to outsiders. Probably pretty boring for most Penrithians.

Best thing: the outside of the building.

Open: June-Sept, 10.00-7.00, daily, plus Sunday, 1.00-6.0. Oct-May, 10.00-5.00, closed Sundays. Admission - Free.

Ravenglass
☆ Ravenglass Railway Museum

Ravenglass. Tel: 0229 717171.

Not hard to find as it's at the Ravenglass end of the Ravenglass and Eskdale Railway. Parking easy.

Best things: The museum tells the story of the miniature railway and its place in the valley. There are relics, models and slides - all quite interesting. The best exhibit is the Synolda engine - a twin of the original Ravenglass railway engine which was built in 1915. It was rescued from Bellvue Zoo and is smaller than the current railway engine.

Open: April to October, daily, 10.00-5.00 + winter weekends (ex. Jan, early Feb.). Visits by appointment at any other time. Admission - A. Tea shop on site. Also has gift shop and TIC.

Seascale
☆☆ Sellafield Visitor Centre
Seascale. Tel: 09467 27027.

Yes, this is Windscale, the atomic place. Seascale used to be a little fishing village, right out on the west coast of Cumbria, miles from anywhere. Rail (either from Barrow or Carlisle) is probably the easiest way to get to it. There are also combined trips to get here, tying in with the Ravenglass and Eskdale Railway. Once you're within 10 miles, you can't miss it by road. (Local wits suggest you go by night and follow the glow.) Parking on site.

Best things: One of Lakeland's most biased exhibitions (probably rivalled only by the National Trust), this is basically a public relations job for British Nuclear Fuels. The present exhibition opened in June 1988 in a new, purpose-built building. The first thing which greets you as you drive in is a sign reading "Overspill Parking", which seems ominous until you realise what they're on about.

Once through the sliding doors and past the carpeted reception area, it is all very slick and impressive, with great use made of multi-slide and video presentations. Safety and the effects of radiation are dealt with straight away, though Chernobyl gets dismissed in a line (are people really soothed to learn that the average person received the same amount of radiation from Chernobyl as you'd receive from cosmic rays whilst on an airliner?). The simulated reactor interior is fairly stunning (the floor used to shake as part of the effect, but it had to be turned off because the first lot of visitors panicked). Plenty of interactive displays and buttons to press at the end of the exhibition. Ultimately, however, it is difficult not to get the impression of a controversial industry selling itself very professionally. You can easily spend a couple of hours on the exhibition itself, and there are regular bus tours of the site itself.

Hard not to recommend a visit, whatever your feelings about nuclear power. It is a great place to wander around if the weather is foul and if it encourages visitors out to the West Coast, so much the better. The easily impressed will be instantly converted by the exhibition's high tech displays, suave men in suits and the attractive ladies behind desks. Sceptics are liable to come out feeling vaguely unsatisfied.

Good cafe on site and there's a shop where you can buy rock with 'Sellafield' printed all the way through.

Open: April to October, daily 10.00-6.00; November-March 10.00-4.00. Closed Christmas Day. Free coach tours round the site available throughout the day. Day and half-day trips can be arranged by ringing 09467 27735 (note that there is a long waiting list for these). Free admission. Of course.

Threlkeld
Cumbrian Museum of Mining and Quarrying
Threlkeld. Tel: 07687 747.

"Definitely, I promise, something will be open by Whit. 1993", said Dr Chris Lane, one of the three enthusiasts who formed a charitable trust to create this long awaited new venture. "The only thing is, I'm not sure what . . . ".

So you have been warned. Not that this will stop the fans coming to look, if only at work in progress. They had 1000 visitors in 1992, just to gape. Hard to find, so study the map first. On no account follow any signs to Threlkeld village. It's on the other side of the A66. Head for Blencathra Business Centre. It's just behind, up the hillside. The site is enormous, in an old quarry, and the exhibits should be good, eventually - they've collected miles of narrow guage railway line and trucks, plus 4,000 other items.

Best things: who can tell?

Open: we hope so. Ring and find out.,

Ulverston
☆ Laurel and Hardy Museum
4c Upper Brook Street, Ulverston. Tel: 0229 552292.

Tucked in a little side street, between King Street and The Ghyll. Easy to miss, as it's in a private house. Park at the Ghyll and walk down.

Best things: Ulverston seems an unlikely place to have 'the world's largest collection of Laurel and Hardy memorabilia', but that's because you didn't know that Stan Laurel was born in Ulverston. This museum was set up by L & H fanatic (and one-time Mayor of Ulverston), Bill Cubin. There is tons of stuff; posters, letters, portraits, possessions. You can even see L & H films - the museum has virtually every one available and shows them continually.

A definite curiosity (and not a little bonkers) but worth seeing. If you're really keen, Stan's birthplace is on the other side of town - the curator or his wife can direct you there, but all there is to see is a plaque.

Open: All year, daily except Christmas Day, 10.00. (Genuine fanatics can get in almost any time by ringing Bill Cubin at home on 0229 586614.) Admission - A.

Whitehaven
☆ Whitehaven Museum
Civic Hall, Lowther Street, Whitehaven. Tel: 0946 67575.

Used to be an excellent little local museum when it resided in the Market Place. Unfortunately its new home is less sympathetic. It has the air of a temporary exhibition staged in a local library.

Best things: The displays are good with lots of information about the town and its industries - especially mining. There are some great model ships and a fascinating bird's eye view of the town painted by Matthias Read in 1736. Look out for the St. Bees Man, the story of a 600 year old local, unearthed in 1981.

A society called the Friends of Whitehaven Museum publishes an excellent series of leaflets about the area, which are available from the Museum. They also give lectures which anyone is welcome to attend.

Open: Throughout the year (except winter Wednesdays, Sundays and Bank Holidays), Monday-Friday 9.00-5.00, Saturday 9.00-4.00. Admission free.

☆ Michael Moon's Bookshop and Gallery

41-43 Roper Street, Whitehaven. Tel: 0946 62936.
Can be tricky to find, as the bookshop lurks in a side street, away from the shops and Whitehaven's endearing one-way system. No parking outside the shop.

Best Things: Once again, Michael Moon sails in where others fear to tread. Whilst Whitehaven Museum languishes in the anonymous surroundings of the Civic Hall, our intrepid bookseller has opened up a small, one room gallery at the back of his large, second-hand bookshop. It is liable to exhibit anything which takes his fancy, from bookmarks to paintings. The main problem is getting past all the books without spending all your time browsing.

Open: All year round, Mon-Sat 9.30 - 5.00 ex bank hols

Windermere
☆☆ Windermere Steamboat Museum

Rayrigg Road, Bowness. Tel: 05394 45565.
Just out of Bowness, on Rayrigg Road. In its own grounds by the lake and finding it is easy. Car park on site

Best things: Virtually anything set so close to a lake is bound to be nice. This is another fairly recent museum. There are 12 antique and vintage steamboats, well displayed but not always in steam. The best thing is undoubtedly the steam launch Osprey, which takes passengers out onto the lake. As anyone who has been on the Gondola will know, steamboat is the only way to travel. It is only operating on fine days, running six or seven trips a day, and it can only take 12 passengers. Ring in advance to check if it is running. The museum has one of the finest collections of steamboats in Europe. Still no proper tea shop. Passengers can book for an afternoon tea trip aboard Osprey - no prizes for guessing how they heat the water . . . Worth looking out for is the recently and beautifully restored SL Esperance - the model for Captain Flint's houseboat in Swallows and Amazons.

The Museum hosts a couple of model boat weekends, in May and August, plus a Steamboat Association Rally in August, and occasional art exhibitions.

Open: Easter to October, daily 10.00-5.00. Admission - B.

☆☆ The World of Beatrix Potter Exhibition,

The Old Laundry, Crag Brow, Bowness. Tel: 05394 48844.

Lakeland's most popular new exhibition, packing them in every day, all round the year. The pulling power is old - Beatrix Potter's lovely books - but the staging of the tableaux is new and the 9 screen video show very state of the art. See Peter Rabbit in his radish patch, Mrs Tiggy-Winkle in her cave, Jeremy Fisher in his pond. The video intro lasts five minutes, then you walk round the tableaux, finishing with a 16 minute film of her life. Highly organised, with groups of 25 led through at a time. Shell suits and Japanes love it. Superior Tate Gallery types prefer the original water colours at Hawkshead. Cafe and souvenir shop.

Best things: Bending down and spotting little windows and rooms you never noticed first time.

Open: all year, except Xmas Day. Summer 10.00-8.00, winter 10.00-4.00. Admission - B.

Workington
Helena Thompson Museum

Park End Road, Workington. Tel: 0900 62598.

Yes, even Workington has its own little museum, set in an eighteenth century house near Workington Hall. It has been here for a number of years, but only has a minuscule budget, so it doesn't go overboard on the advertising (unlike its neighbour, a few miles down the coast).

Best Things: Probably the house itself, plus the gardens. One or two nice costumes and some interesting examples of decorative art.

Open: April-October, Monday-Saturday, 10.30-4.00. November-March, Monday-Saturday, 11.00-3.00. Admission free.

Chapter Eleven

Literary Lakes

Wordsworth's House, Cockermouth

On the trail of Wordsworth and the Lake Poets, plus Miss Beatrix Potter, Mr John Ruskin and some other Literary Notables.

Admission Charges
A under £2; **B** £2-£3; **C** over £3.

Wordsworth

William Wordsworth gave us the Lakes and the Lakes gave us Wordsworth. No one should leave Lakeland without communing with Wordsworth, either by visiting one of his homes in person or remembering in spirit some of the things he wrote. As well as his poetry, he also wrote a Guide to the Lakes, a best seller in its time and still on sale today in a facsimile version. At the height of his literary fame, Poet Laureate and all that, a vicar is said to have asked him, "Excuse me, Mr Wordsworth, have you written anything else, apart from your Guide Book ? . ."

It is possible today to do a tour of the Lakes, following his life biographically. There are people, such as American and Japanese scholars, who come to the Lakes for this sole reason.

Cockermouth (born 1770)

☆☆ **Wordsworth House**

Main Street. Tel: 0900 824805. Owned by the National Trust.

Wordsworth was born here in 1770, the second of five children of a lawyer who was an agent for the Lowther family. The house, which went with the job, is still the handsomest in Cockermouth. He wrote about it in his long poem the Prelude, bathing naked in the local river, chasing

169

butterflies with his beloved sister Dorothy. The house and fine garden is structurally as it was, though the furniture is not Wordsworth's. Interesting china collection. A painting by Turner. Excellent coffee kitchen.

Open: April-Oct, daily 11.00-5.00 (closed Thursday), Sunday 2.00-5.00. Admission - B.

Penrith (1775-78)

Wordsworth's parents, on both sides, came from Penrith and he spent some time there as a young boy. His mother's parents had a draper's shop in the market square, though there is nothing of it now to be seen. His Penrith days were not happy. His mother died when he was eight and his father when he was 13. There was no money, as it turned out the Lowther family had not paid his father's wages. His guardians did not like him, considering him wild and unruly, and they separated him from his sister Dorothy. She was sent to live with relations, while William went to board at a little grammar school on the other side of the Lake District.

Nothing Wordsworthian can be seen in Penrith today, though you can climb the Beacon, a hill just outside the town, mentioned in the Prelude, which has good views of the Lake District. St Michael's Church, Barton, Pooley Bridge, has his grandfather's grave.

Hawkshead (1779-87)

✩✩ **Hawkshead Grammar School** No longer a school but open as a museum. The desks and books are laid out, just as they were in Wordsworth's time. (See Chapter 10.)

St Michael's Church Wordsworth described it as snow white, but it has now been un-whitewashed. Interesting church. Fine situation.

Anne Tyson's Cottage Wordsworth boarded with a 'dame', or landlady, who became a substitute mother. Now a private dwelling, called Wordsworth Lodge, but you can admire it from outside.

Old Windebrowe (1794),
Brundholme, Keswick.

William and Dorothy lived here for a short time in 1794, after he had been to Cambridge and returned from France. (He had an illegitimate daughter by a French girl, a fact which was kept a secret in his own life time.) This was William and Dorothy's first home in the Lakes since childhood. Here, William nursed his friend, Raisley Calvert, who subsequently died, leaving William enough money to be able to concentrate on a career as a poet. The Wordsworth room is not normally open to the public: the premises are used by the Calvert Trust for the disabled. Contact their main centre at Little Crosthwaite, Under Skiddaw for access. 07687 72254.

(There is a small plaque outside the Robin Hood Inn, in King Street, Penrith, where Raisley Calvert died.)

Dove Cottage, Grasmere, Wordsworth's Home   Abraham's Series No. 621   Keswick.

Grasmere (1799-1813)

☆☆☆ Dove Cottage

Town End, Grasmere. Tel: 05394 35544/35547.

This is the Wordsworth shrine and the main pilgrimage centre for tourists and scholars alike. It has come to symbolise Wordsworth's philosophy of 'plain living and high thinking'. He lived longer at Rydal Mount, but by that time he was past his best as a poet. It was at Dove Cottage that his greatest works were written.

He moved in at Christmas time, 1799, with his sister Dorothy. Later he married Mary Hutchinson and three of their children were born here. He was also joined by Sarah Hutchinson, his wife's sister. Add to that a frequent flow of friends staying at this tiny, seven-roomed house and things became pretty crowded. They moved out in 1808 to a much-larger house, across the valley, but still in Grasmere.

Dove Cottage is much as it was in Wordsworth's day and is very lovingly cared for. The garden has been restored and even the old summer house rebuilt. Except during the height of summer, log fires are usually kept burning in the grates and visitors are offered a chatty and well-informed guided tour. Inside, most of the furniture is Wordsworth's and the general aim is to keep it the way it was when he lived there; the only jarring note are a few items which belonged to Wordsworth later in life, but Dove Cottage got them first and rivalry between the Wordsworth places can be fierce.

Next to the Cottage is the excellent Wordsworth Museum. Go there first, if you can. During the summer, you have to visit the Cottage early in the day as it can get very, very crowded (though even then you might run into the early morning coach parties, fresh from their hotels and wanting to blast round the cottage before heading off to Gretna Green). Wander around on your own and it's easy to imagine what it must have been like to have lived there.

Open: Now almost all year (they're closed from mid-Jan to mid-Feb), daily 9.30-5.30. Last admission - 5.00.

Admission - C (this includes Dove Cottage and special exhibitions). Special rates for families and groups.

Warning: It can get very crowded during wet weather, especially during school holidays.

Wordsworth had two other homes in Grasmere, neither of them open to the public. **Allan Bank**, where he moved in 1808, is a large house, easily seen from down by the lake as it is above the village, directly under Helm Crag. Quite a nice old house, with magnificent views over Grasmere. It is owned by the National Trust, but rented privately. Used to be white, but was repainted buff for Ken Russell's Coleridge film.

The second house is the **Old Parsonage**, opposite St Oswald's Church. Wordsworth moved there in 1811, because the chimneys at Allan Bank smoked too much and he fell out with the landlord. By 1813, two of William's children had died at the Parsonage, so he and Mary decided to quit Grasmere Vale altogether and move to Rydal.

Grasmere valley seethes with Wordsworth associations. William, Mary and Dorothy are buried in the churchyard, and they also left some of their 'pet' names on the surrounding landscape. On the road above Town End, walking towards White Moss, there is a field gate which Wordsworth used to call the 'wishing gate'. Now it is somewhat unromantically covered in barbed wire. Behind the Swan Inn, at the foot of Dunmail, is Greenhead Ghyll - the setting for Wordsworth's poem, *Michael*. Down in the village, there are no Wordsworth cafes, though it is probably only a matter of time. There is the Wordsworth Hotel, emblazoned with a facsimile of his signature, and featuring various horrors such as 'The Dove and Olive Branch Bar' (Dove Cottage was originally an inn, called the Dove and Olive Branch), the Prelude suite, etc. The hotel has no connection of any sort with Wordsworth. The same might be said of the portrait - supposedly of the poet - which hangs in the entrance hall. The whirring noise you can sometimes hear in Grasmere churchyard is Wordsworth spinning.

Rydal (1813-1850)

☆☆☆ **Rydal Mount**
Rydal, Ambleside. Tel: 05394 33002.

Rydal Mount was William's final home, until his death in 1850. In his own lifetime, it became a poetical shrine to his fans - he would sometimes receive as many as a hundred visitors a day, flocking to the gate just in the hope of a glimpse of the great man. He became Poet Laureate and would issue great pronouncements on the purpose and structure of poetry. (He has the distinction of having been a Poet Laureate who never wrote a line of official verse.) It is a somewhat grander house than their previous homes and William and Dorothy both thought they had gone up in the world. Once something of a rebel, by now William was a staunch supporter of the old order. The cuckoo clock that now hangs in Dove Cottage was once at Rydal Mount and its ticking used to soothe him to sleep. One night in 1850 it struck midnight and on the twelfth stroke, William died.

Originally a 16th century farmhouse, the house is still owned by a descendant of William's. Rather unimpressive from the outside, it is set in beautiful grounds - originally landscaped by William - and contains a lot of his furniture, manuscripts and possessions. When William died, most of his effects were sold off and bought by local people. Over the years, they have gradually been returned to their former homes.

On a fine day, Rydal Mount can be lovely and the magnificent view from the garden has hardly altered since William last saw it.

Open: March to October, daily 9.30-5.00. November to February, 10.00-4.00 (closed Tuesdays during winter and late Jan). Admission - B. (Groups can book evenings, complete with wine and poetry.)

At the bottom of the lane to Rydal Mount, just behind the church, is an area of land now owned by the National Trust and called Dora's Field. This has nothing to do with the daffodils of William's poem, as some visitors assume, but was a field given to his daughter by the poet. The real site for those notorious daffodils is on the west shore of Ullswater, in Gowbarrow Park (also owned by the National Trust and accessible). William and Dorothy passed through the park in 1802, when on their way to visit their friends, the Clarksons, at Eusemere, near Pooley Bridge.

The Lake Poets

Wordsworth gathered about himself quite a circle of other literary notables of the period. They became known as the Lake Poets, though in style there was little connection between them.

Samuel Taylor Coleridge was the first. As soon as the Wordsworths were installed in Dove Cottage, he moved up to Greta Hall, in Keswick, just to be near them. He would often walk over to Dove Cottage for the evening, often coming via Helvellyn. Coleridge was a notable walker and toured the Lakes extensively. In 1802, he made the first recorded ascent of Broad Stand on Scafell - a walk which has since become too dangerous to follow without ropes.

Greta Hall is now part of Keswick School and is not open to the public. Details of Coleridge's life and work can be found in the nearby Fitz Park Museum. He eventually left his family, took to drugs, lived abroad then moved to London where he died in 1834.

Robert Southey

Robert Southey joined Coleridge at Greta Hall in 1803. They were brothers-in-law and Southey eventually ended up supporting Mrs Coleridge when her husband was pursuing Sarah Hutchinson (Wordsworth's sister-in-law) - which perhaps explains his frequent visits to Dove Cottage. Southey wrote hardly any verse directly connected with the area, but he wrote the original version of the Three Bears, a good piece of children's verse about the Lodore Falls and a fine biography of Nelson. He also wrote the first official history of Brazil and the government of that country paid for the memorial to him which is now in Crosthwaite Church, Keswick. He never went to Brazil.

Southey spent almost all his adult life in the Lakes. He became Poet Laureate in 1813 and between them, Southey and Wordsworth made the Lakes the centre of English poetry for several decades. Southey died at home in Keswick in 1843 - and Wordsworth took over as Laureate.

Thomas De Quincey

Thomas De Quincey is now most famous for writing a book called *Confessions of an English Opium-Eater*, but he also wrote a wonderful book of gossip and memories of the Lake Poets, called simply, *Recollections of the Lakes and Lake Poets*. He was an early fan of Wordsworth - although the great man treated him rather badly later in life - and made three separate attempts to visit his hero at Dove Cottage, coming up all the way from Oxford. Each time his nerve failed him and he retreated. He finally got there in 1807 and eventually took over the lease when Wordsworth and family moved out. Dorothy made him some curtains and was amazed at the huge quantities of books he installed in the house. He upset the family almost at once by knocking down their summer house and cutting down the orchard to let more light into the Cottage. Dorothy refused to speak to him after that. The Wordsworths further snubbed him when he began an affair with a local farmer's daughter, whom he eventually married. She came from Nab Cottage. It is beside the A591, looking over Rydal Water. it is not strictly open to the public, but they still have De Quincey's desk there. He moved into The Nab in 1829, though he still kept on Dove Cottage to house all the books. In 1835, he tried to buy it for £130.

De Quincey became the second editor of *The Westmorland Gazette* but got the sack for not going to the office. He was a tenant of Dove Cottage for 27 years, though only lived there for 15 years. He died in Edinburgh in 1859.

Dove Cottage still houses several items of interest to De Quincey enthusiasts, including his opium balance (he wrote *Confessions* whilst he was there) and some fascinating portraits. The house is described very well in *Recollections*.

Sir Walter Scott, the novelist, was a frequent visitor to the Lakes and a friend of the Lake Poets. He first came as a guest of Wordsworth and stayed with him at Dove Cottage. He was so put off by the meals (too much 'plain living' for his tastes) that he used to climb out of his bedroom window every morning and go to the Swan Inn in the village for a proper breakfast, before returning and getting back into bed as if nothing had happened.

He used Castle Rock in St John's-in-the-Vale as the setting for 'The Bridal of Triermain'.

William Hazlitt, the writer, visited Southey at Greta Hall, but left in a rush, pursued by villagers, having got himself rather too involved with one of the local girls.

Keats came to the area in 1818, visited Rydal Mount to see Wordsworth and climbed up to the waterfalls at Stock Ghyll in Ambleside. He also climbed Skiddaw and described Castlerigg Stone Circle as:

> like a dismal cirque
> 'Of Druid stones, upon a forlorn moor'.
> *(Hyperion II, 34-5)*

John Ruskin

☆☆☆ **Brantwood**

East of Lake, 2 miles from Coniston Village. Tel: 05394 41396.

John Ruskin, art-critic, writer, philosopher and champion of many social causes, first came to the Lakes as a young boy in 1824. In 1871, at the age of 52, he decided to settle here and bought Brantwood on Coniston for £1,500, without even first seeing the place. "Any place opposite Coniston Old Man *must* be beautiful", he said. In the event, he got "a mere shed of rotten timbers and loose stone", but he transformed it into a beautiful home, stocked it with art treasures (particularly the paintings of Turner, of whom he was an early champion) and lived there for the last 30 years of his life. Today, Brantwood is open to the public (which was Ruskin's original wish) and its enthusiastic curator, Bruce Hanson, has transformed it into an excellent museum and country house. It now rivals the other Lake District big guns (Dove Cottage, Hill Top and Rydal Mount).

The house contains many of Ruskin's paintings and possessions. Look out for the Ruskin designed wallpaper in the downstairs rooms. Nice to see the political message of his writings coming across in a video of his life and work, on constant show in one of the downstairs rooms. Ruskin fought hard against the worst aspects of Victorian society and values. Sobering to realise how much of his message is relevant today.

Landscape gardener, Sally Beamish, is developing the 15 acre garden in the spirit of Ruskin (he abhorred 'fashionable' gardens). Brantwood stands in 250 acres of grounds and there's a good nature trail. There is now a new jetty to bring people across to Brantwood by the Gondola service, plus a privately-run launch open to the public operating from the Coniston Boating Centre, and the head of the lake, and linking up with Coniston Rambler bus service.

Excellent tearooms, now called The Jumping Jenny (named after Ruskin's boat) and open to non-visitors to the house (the wood stove is very welcoming in winter). Upstairs is the Coach House Gallery. Also a good book shop, in the house. Thursday evenings in summer - Dinner & Theatre. Dine in JJ's restaurant and retire to R's dining room to watch professional actors recreate spirit of R's time and thoughts.

Open: Mid-March to mid-November, daily 11.00-5.30. November to March, Wednesday-Sunday 11.00-4.00. Admission - C.

There is a **Ruskin Museum** down in Coniston village, which is of interest, and a monument to him at Friar's Crag on Derwentwater, which bears the following quote from him: "the first thing I remember as an event in life was being taken by my nurse to the brow at Friar's Crag on Derwentwater".

Beatrix Potter

Beatrix Potter was a Londoner, born there in 1866, but her family had connections with Lancashire cotton and she spent her holidays from the age of 16 in the Lake District, in rented, but rather grand houses, round Windermere and Derwentwater. Her parents were genteel, upper middle class Edwardians and she was educated at home and expected to devote her life to her parents, or get married. She found an outlet for artistic talents in drawing and painting "little books for children" and encouraged by the family's Lakeland friend, Canon Rawnsley, her first book, Peter Rabbit, was published in 1901.

The money she made with her books she used to buy Hill Top Farm at Near Sawrey in 1905. Over the next eight years, she wrote another 13 children's books, mostly while she was in the Lake District. In 1913, she married William Heelis, a local solicitor, and after that devoted her life to her farms and to the preservation of the countryside, doing a great deal to help the work of the National Trust, thanks again to the friendship and encouragement of Canon Rawnsley.

Beatrix Potter died in 1943. All her property, 15 farms with their Herdwick flocks, many cottages and 4,000 acres of land, came to the National Trust. She asked that the Herdwicks, her favourite sheep, should continue to be bred, and that both farms and cottages should have local, reliable, tenants. Most of her original paintings eventually came to the Trust and can now be seen in the new Hawkshead Gallery -

☆☆ Beatrix Potter Gallery
Hawkshead. Tel: 05394 35355. For details see Chapter 10.

☆☆ Hill Top
Near Sawrey. Tel: 05394 36269.

Beatrix Potter built an extension on the house for her tenant farmer, but kept the original 17th century building for her own use. She wrote many of her books there and sometimes was able to stay for a few nights but at no time did she actually live there. Nearby Castle Cottage became her home after she married William Heelis.

Hill Top, which contains Beatrix Potter's furniture, is small and very popular, with 90,000 visitors going through it in the peak year of 1979. It is the duty of the National Trust to protect its properties, in this case against the fabric of the building being eroded by the sheer number of visitors, so restrictions have been introduced by limiting numbers allowed into the house at any one time, making no reductions for parties, not permitting coaches and shutting the house on Thursdays and Fridays. It must be one of the very few houses open to the public where they go to such lengths to restrict the public. Best to go mornings.

Open: Easter to October, 11.00-5.00, daily except Thursday and Friday. Admission - C.

☆☆ Mirehouse

Bassenthwaite Lake, Keswick. Tel: 07687 72287.

The final major literary home in the Lakes which is open to the public is Mirehouse on the eastern shore of Bassenthwaite, four miles north of Keswick on the A591. It was once the home of James Spedding, a noted literary figure of the 19th century, the author of a 14-volume biography of Francis Bacon. One of his more notable visitors at Mirehouse was Tennyson, who stayed there whilst working on his version of the Arthur Legend. He used Bassenthwaite in his description of Arthur's death - it was on this lake that the black barge bore away King Arthur's body in *Idylls of the King*.

Thomas Carlyle was a frequent visitor to Mirehouse. He said that it was "beautiful and so were the ways of it . . . not to speak of Skiddaw and the finest mountains on earth". Not only was James Spedding the host for some of the literary notables of his day, his family also had literary connections. His father, John, spent six years in the same class as Wordsworth at Hawkshead Grammar School. Some of Wordsworth's letters - along with those of Southey and Hartley Coleridge - can be seen at Mirehouse.

Still in the Spedding family, Mirehouse today is the epitome of the English country manor house. Very often a pianist is playing. The rooms are delightful, the house historic and the setting majestic. It has a nature trail in the grounds and Bassenthwaite Lake's only east-shore walk.

Mirehouse has only been recently opened to the general public and is still relatively unknown and uncrowded. The Speddings are likely to be on hand - if so, ask them to let you hear their Tennyson recording, reciting the Charge of the Light Brigade. Altogether a house not to miss.

Open: Easter to October, on Wednesdays, Sundays and Bank Holiday Mondays, 2.00-5.00. Admission - B. Grounds and tearoom daily 10.30-5.30.

There is an excellent coffee shop nearby in the Old Sawmill, Dodd Wood, to which there is no admission charge.

Other Literary Connections in Lakeland

Most of the writers of the 19th century seem to have visited the Lake District and many took on holiday homes or even settled there.

Harriet Martineau, built the Knoll, at Ambleside, and lived there for 30 years. She wrote *The Complete Guide to the English Lakes* (but didn't give star ratings to anything). She was a friend of Wordsworth and her visitors included at various times Charlotte Bronte, George Elliot and Matthew Arnold.

Felicia Hemens also became a resident of Ambleside and lived at Doves Nest. Not very famous today, but she wrote *The Boy Stood on the Burning Deck* and spawned a host of parodies.

Charles Dickens and **Wilkie Collins** toured the area in 1857, describing their travels in *The Lazy Tour of Two Idle Apprentices*. They stayed at the Queen's Head Inn at Hesket Newmarket (now a private house) and went on an ill-advised expedition to climb Carrock Fell, getting caught in rain and mist.

Sir Hugh Walpole moved to Brackenburn in 1923, a house on the south-west shore of Derwentwater. His four famous *Herries* novels were set in Borrowdale. The home of Judith Paris can be seen at Watendlath, beside the tarn.

Arthur Ransome lived near Coniston and used settings from Windermere and Coniston for his *Swallows and Amazons*.

Literary Events

Winter Wonderland A winter service on Windermere, pointing out all the literary associations. Followed by coach to Grasmere and a visit to Dove Cottage, tea at the restaurant, and finally, a nice highlight to the trip, a candlelit wine reception and poetry reading at Rydal Mount. Runs Saturdays, November to March. Details from Bowness Bay Boating Company on 05394 43360.

Wordsworth Winter School, and also Summer Conference and Book Collectors Weekend. Details from Dove Cottage.

Literary Lunch. An annual lunch, open to the public, in which prizes for the Lakeland Book of the Year are awarded. Details from Cumbria Tourist Board.

Chapter Twelve

Homes and Gardens

No, this is not a chapter about glossy magazines but a look at some of the more stately and historic delights of Cumbria. As elsewhere in Britain, many owners of grand homes have had to open up in recent years and let the rest of us come in and gape, or have handed them over to public or other bodies who now care for them. We also consider the Best Gardens, Open Farms, Castles, Old Mills, Churches, Ancient Monuments.

Admission Charges

A under £2
B £2-£3
C over £3.

Note well: Several of the big Stately Homes now close on Fridays and Saturdays, so check in advance.

Castle Dairy

Wildman Street, Kendal. Tel: 0539 721170

Originally the dairy which served Kendal Castle and was in use when Katherine Parr lived there. It is now the oldest habitable stone-built house in the area. Of Tudor design, it was restored in 1564.

Open: Easter to September, Wednesdays only, 2.00-4.00. Admission - A (It is STILL only 5p).

☆☆☆ Dalemain

Penrith. Tel: 07684 86450

A large, Georgian-fronted house visible from the A592, with extensive grounds. The house itself is medieval, Elizabethan and early Georgian. Fascinating architecturally and contains family portraits of the Hasells, who have lived there since 1665. A magnificent garden and a fantastic tea shop in a baronial hall. Probably *the* best house to see in the northern lakes, if you've only time for one.

The garden is famous for its rare trees and shrubs. Small museum of agricultural bits and pieces in the 16th century barn.

Open: Easter to mid-October, Sunday-Thursday 11.15-5.00. Admission - C.

☆☆ Holker Hall

Cark-in-Cartmel, Grange-over-Sands. Tel: 05395 58328

An outstanding country house, dating back to the 17th century. Owned by the Cavendish family. The site itself used to belong to Cartmel Priory. Contains some beautiful examples of panelling and wood carving and some rare paintings. Including works by Van Dyck and Joshua Reynolds. It is a magnificent 'stately home' but without ropes and restrictions. The gardens are wonderful and contain what is said to be the oldest monkey puzzle tree in the country. Garden Festival in June which they hope will be annual.

There's a lot going on at Holker, which can sometimes put you off as it sounds more like a country fair than a stately home. There are often model aircraft rallies, hot-air ballooning, vintage car rallies. All very professionally done, but if you want to see the house and grounds at their best, go when none of these wonders are on. The gardens are best in early summer. Cafeteria, playground, twee gift shop.

Open: Easter Sunday to October, daily (except Saturdays) 10.30-6.00. Last admission 4.30. Admission - B/C (very complicated). Also the site of the Lakeland Motor Museum (see Chapter 10) for which there is yet an additional fee.

☆☆ Hutton-in-the-Forest

Penrith. Tel: 07684 84449

Situated just off the B5305 between Penrith and Wigton, this was originally a 14th century pele tower with 17th, 18th and 19th century additions. It is the home of Lord and Lady Inglewood. It has a nice, amateur feel to it and you sense that the running of it isn't too severely professional. You get the distinct feeling that the occupants are around. Which they usually are. Very satisfying, architecturally, it is like visiting three stately homes in one.

Good gardens with some excellent tree specimens. Tea shop very good. The Gardens are open daily except Saturday, but the House has some peculiar opening days. You have to be smart to catch it open.

Open: Easter Bank Holiday, then May to September, Thursday, Friday, Sunday and Bank Holidays; 1.00-4.00. Parties by arrangement at any time. Admission - C (children free).

☆☆☆ Levens Hall

Nr. Kendal. Tel: 05395 60321.

Five miles south of Kendal, situated by Levens Bridge. Magnificent Elizabethan mansion, although it originally began as a Norman Pele Tower. Some fine paintings, furniture and plaster-work to be seen. Fascinating fire-place in the south drawing room with carvings depicting the four seasons, the four elements and the five senses. Very good topiary garden laid out in 1692.

Levens Hall is trying very hard to be a stately home on the southern model, providing lots of fun for kiddies, of all ages, such as their Steam Collection (in steam on Sunday afternoons and Bank Holidays). The House is run, owned and lived in by the Bagot family. It can be a bit too commercial for some tastes, but they are trying. Look out for their special exhibition on Admiral Percy who started as a midshipman with Nelson on HMS Victory.

There are occasional guided tours of the garden, con-ducted by Chris Crowder (the ex-Blue Peter gardener). These are very good - informative and relaxed, and the gardens are improving all the time. Telephone for times and details. (Incidentally the gardens are now exporting yew clippings to Europe to further research into anti-cancer drug.)

Gift shop, of course, and licensed tearooms which do light lunches and ices. Plants for sale

Open: Easter Sunday to September; daily, except Friday and Saturday, 11.00-5.00. Admission - C (gardens only - B).

☆ Lowther Leisure Park

Hackthorpe, Penrith. Tel: 0931 712523.

Not exactly a stately home but in the tradition of some of the more modern commercial ones. Lowther Castle is now a facade, most of the interior having been pulled down. It was, in any case, an early 19th century Gothic mansion, rather than a true castle. Lowther Park now boats 40 different activities - adventure playgrounds, assault course, mini race track and a resident circus, which is included in the admission price. A fun day out for all the family, so they say. Lowther connection apart, however, it's not unique and there are similar attractions farther south. Surely you aren't already bored with mountains and lakes?

Open: Easter to mid September. Some closures during these dates. Check before liberating kids here. Daily 10.00-6.00, last admission 4.00 pm. Admission - C(+). Children under three years old, free (wow).

☆☆ Muncaster Castle

Ravenglass. Tel: 0229 717203/717614.

The Scots are indirectly responsible for the architecture

of many of Cumbria's historic homes. Like many others, Muncaster Castle is based on a defensive pele tower, built in 1325, to keep them at bay. In the 1860s, the fourth Lord Muncaster had it rebuilt to make a tasteful mansion, still lived in by the Pennington family as their ancestral home since the 13th century. Contains furniture, tapestries and paintings, including some by Reynolds and Gainsborough.

The gardens are magnificent in early summer, when the rhododendrons and azaleas are at their best. Viewed against the background of the Lakeland fells, they are spectacular. One of the finest displays in Europe.

The bird garden also contains wallabies, the only chance to see wallabies in Lakeland. (Not wallies - they can be seen any time in Bowness during the summer.) Muncaster Castle is now the headquarters of the British Owl Breeding and Release Scheme, run by well-known local ornithologist Tony Warburton.

Tearooms, but rather poor. Plus a shop and small garden centre.

Open: Castle - Easter to October, 1.00-.4.00 Tuesday-Sunday (but open Bank Hol Mondays). Grounds and owl centre daily 11.00-5.00. Admission - C (castle and grounds - half price for grounds only).

☆ Naworth Castle

Near Brampton, Carlisle. Tel: 06977 41156.

A relative newcomer to the stately home stakes, Naworth has been the home of the Earls of Carlisle for the last 700 years. Present castle dates back to 1335. Rather dour, sandstone building, but fine courtyard and inside the Great Hall has some magnificent French tapestries and there's interesting alabaster by Burne-Jones in the Library. The Hall also houses the heraldic crests and family tree of the Howard family. Not as yet a great deal to do or see, though the family is trying hard. Lady Carlisle took the tickets the day I arrived while the Hon Philip Howard was the guide. (He was wearing a rather worn 'Lonsdale' sweatshirt, tut tut. The Howards, you see, have traditionally been the rival top Cumbrian family to the Lonsdales of Lowther Castle.)

Open: Easter Sunday and Monday; then May to September, Wednesday and Sunday only - plus Saturdays in July and August - 12.00-5.00. Admission - B.

☆☆ Sizergh Castle

Kendal. Tel: 05395 60285

The home of the Strickland family for 700 years. There was an original house there, but this was replaced in 1340 with a pele tower. Those Scots again. Largest tower in

Cumbria still standing. The great hall was added in 1450 and some very fine panelling and carving added in Elizabethan times - some of the finest in the country. A lovely house, the gardens date from the 18th century. Great on a warm, sunny day. Now owned and run by the National Trust. And there are teas available, at long last.

Open: Easter to October, Sunday, Monday, Wednesday and Thursday 2.00-6.00. Last admission 4.00. Closed Good Friday. Admission - C (castle and grounds; grounds only are half-price).

☆☆ Townend

Troutbeck, Windermere. Tel: 05394 32628

This is a 1626 statesman farmer's home - rather more prosperous than your average farmhouse - in an interesting, unspoilt hamlet.

Original and surprisingly elaborate furniture and panelling. A dark little place, it contrasts with all the stately homes, but it is very typical of its period. Run by the National Trust, who have recently opened three new rooms, once used by servants. The small garden is laid out to resemble a photograph of Townend from the late 19th century.

Open: Easter to October, Tuesday-Friday and Sunday (but open Bank Holiday Monday) 1.00-5.00. Last admission 4.30. Admission - B.

Note: No electric light, so it may close at dusk if this is earlier.

Gardens

Many of the above mentioned homes have fine gardens which are open to the public - notably Dalemain and Sizergh. If it is only the garden you wish to see, here are the ones already listed which let you in at a reduced rate:

> Holker Hall
> Hutton in the Forest
> Levens Hall
> Muncaster Castle
> Mirehouse, Keswick (see 'Literary Lakes')
> Sizergh Castle.

There are also a few more worth seeing in their own right which are not part of a stately home or park -

☆☆ Acorn Bank

Temple Sowerby, near Penrith. Tel: 07683 61893
(Six miles east of Penrith)

An outstanding collection of over 140 types of herbs in this small, walled garden belonging to the manor-house of

Acorn Bank. Now owned by the National Trust. Excellent spring display.

Open: Easter to end of Autumn Half-Term, daily 10.00-6.00. Admission - A.

☆☆ Graythwaite Hall
Newby Bridge. Tel: 05395 31248
(4 1/2 miles south of Hawkshead.)
    Seven acres of garden, landscaped by Thomas Mawson. Marvellous for rhododendrons and azaleas.

Open: April to June, daily 10.00-6.00. Admission - B.

☆☆☆ Lakeland Horticultural Society Garden
Holehird, Troutbeck, near Windermere. Tel: 05394 46008
(On A592, 3/4 mile north of mini-roundabout with A591.)
    Extensive grounds with vast range of plants, alpines in glass houses, hundreds of heathers. A gardener's garden.

Open: 11.00-5.00. Free admission (but there is a donation box).

☆☆☆ Lingholm Gardens
Keswick. Tel: 07687 72003.
(shore of Derwentwater, near Portinscale).
    Formal and natural gardens, with extensive rhododendrons and magnificent woodlands. A wonderful view over the lake to Borrowdale. Garden tour. (Just a short walk from the boat landing at Low Brandlehow.)
    They now have a tearoom (excellent apple pie) and small garden centre - good fuchsias.

Open: April to October, daily 10.00-5.00. Admission - B.

☆☆☆ Nunnery Walks
Nunnery House, Staffield, Penrith. Tel: 0768 898537.
(About nine miles north of Penrith, just off the Kirkoswald Road, in the Eden Valley)
    Two miles of paths through wild woodlands on the banks of the River Eden, to one of the best waterfall displays in Cumbria. Go on a nice day after heavy rainfall and it's terrific.

Open: All year, daily 9.00-6.00. Admission - A. Tearooms.

☆☆ Rydal Hall
Rydal, Ambleside. Tel: 05394 32050.
(Between Ambleside and Grasmere, turn off the A591 at the sign for Rydal Mount)
    The Hall itself is mainly Georgian, though parts go back to before 1600, and is owned by the Diocese of Carlisle. Used for conferences, holidays and retreats, the Hall

itself is not open to the public, but it stands in 30 acres of grounds and the formal gardens have recently been opened up. The gardens were originally laid out by Thomas Mawson.

It means the public can once again visit the famous Lower Falls, much painted by the Early Tourists. Nearby is the Grotto, a summer house once regularly visited by Wordsworth. The gardens also have a nice fountain and splendid views over Rydal to Lake Windermere.

Open: Daily, all year. Admission - free, but donations welcome. Self-guiding leaflet available at the gate.

Halecat

Witherslack, nr. Grange-over-Sands. Tel: 05395 52229.

This was opened in 1988 and features a small garden, nicely laid out with shrubs and trees. Good views across Morecambe Bay. Nursery gardens with home grown plants for sale.

Open: All year, Monday-Friday, 9.00-4.30; Sunday, 2.00-4.00. Admission free.

☆ Stagshaw Gardens

Ambleside. Tel: 05394 35599
(3/4 mile south of Ambleside on the A591)

Rhododendrons, azaleas, magnolias, all in eight acres of woodlands. Constantly developing as a memorial to the founder, Cuthbert Acland.

Open: April to June, July-October by appointment with National Trust, daily 10.00-6.30. Admission - A.

Note: No tearooms and only a very small car park. Park at Waterhead and walk.

Other Gardens

Another method of seeing well laid-out formal gardens - which used to belong to the people that used to *live* in the Lakes - is to visit some of the larger ex-country houses, eg, Brockhole, which has 30 acres of grounds. Just up the road towards Ambleside is the Langdale Chase Hotel - go in for a bar lunch and then walk around the grounds. Great display and one of the best views over Windermere to the mountains from the hotel's terrace. The Storrs Hall Hotel, about three miles south of Bowness, has another good garden (and good bar lunches).

Each year the *National Gardens Scheme* publishes a list called **Gardens Open in Cumbria and the Lake District.** - this lists a number of interesting gardens which are not normally open to the public on a regular basis, but open on selected dates during the year. Gives opening times, admission charge (if any) and who does teas. It is a free sheet, available from information centres, or send SAE to:

> The National Gardens Scheme
> Hatchlands Park
> East Clandon
> Guilford GU4 7RT.

Open Farms and Farm Parks

Working farms which open up to the public. Increasingly popular, judging by the number of little home-made leaflets now littering every TIC. Having chased us away for centuries, more and more farmers are now urging us, nay imploring us into their fields and farmyards. Diversification, it's called. Here's five which sound interesting:

Low Plain Farm Park

Brigsteer, Kendal. Tel: 05395 68323.

Easter-mid October. 10.30-5.00. Variety of animals, all readily accessible. Old farm equipment, tearoom, shop.

Holme Farm   Sedbergh. Tel: 05396 20654

March-September. 11-.00 on. Winter by arrangement. Nature trail, conducted tours, seasonal demonstrations.

Ponsonby Farm Park

Cumrey Kitchen, Ponsonby, Seascale. Tel: 0946 841426.

Easter-September 10.30-5.00 daily except Mondays. Old Home Farm of 17th century Ponsonby Hall. Mixed farm with pets corner, farm walks, seasonal activities, tearoom, shop. Also 3 llamas.

Waterside House

Howtown, Pooley Bridge, Penrith. Tel: 0768 86332.

Feb-Oct daily. Working farm with seasonal activities plus space to camp, picnic, launch boats and to fish.

Craigburn Animal Farm

Catlowdy, Penton, Carlisle. Tel: 0228 577214.

May-mid September, 11.00-6.00. Working farm, demonstrations, unusual breeds (no, not the Sellafield sheep again), farmhouse restaurant.

Castles

There are quite a few castles dotted about the fringes of the Lake District, a lot of them designed to repel the onslaughts of the marauding Scots. Some are little more than pele towers, others Neo-Gothic mansions, some simply follies, others romantic ruins.

☆☆☆ Carlisle Castle

Tel: 0228 31777.

Carlisle is the best by far and houses the Border Regiment Museum. Stirring history with Mary Queen of Scots and Bonny Prince Charlie connections. *Looks* like a real castle, dark and grim, not like your soft and fancy turreted Southern castles. Visit the prison rooms and find the graffiti.

Open: All year. Summer, 9.30-6.00; winter 9.30-4.00. Admission - B.

☆ Appleby Castle

Tel: 07683 51402.

At the top of the main street (opposite end to the church). Good car parking on site.

The castle dates from the 11th century though was largely restored by Lady Anne Clifford in 1653. The Norman keep and earthwork defences remain. Now listed as a Rare Breeds Survival Trust Centre with a wide range of unusual breeds on display - goats, cattle, sheep, ponies, chipmunks and wildfowl; plus bantams, heron, flamingos and ibis.

The Norman keep is open to the public with displays of medieval and 17th century furniture. There is also a collection of 19th century bicycles (not for breeding purposes) and you are allowed out onto the roof for wonderful views over the town. The great hall now houses a collection of Nanking porcelain salvaged from S. China Seas in 1986. Also Lady Anne Clifford's "Great Picture" - huge 3 sectioned affair of Clifford family. Cafe on site.

Open: Easter to October. Sunday-Thursday, 1.00-5.00. Admission - C.

Wray Castle

Low Wray, Ambleside. Tel: 05394 32320.

Two miles south of Ambleside, turn off the B5286 for Hawkshead at the sign for High Wray.

Not a real castle but a Victorian folly now owned by the National Trust and leased by the Wray Castle College of Marine Electronics (the only private college in the world training people for the merchant navy). Grounds have been open to the public for a number of years, but 1986 was the first year the public were allowed inside. Not a lot to see - just the hall and music room. They've really only opened it to satisfy everyone's curiosity. Beatrix Potter stayed here on her first visit to the LD at the age of 16 (her father rented it as a holiday home). Later she bought most of the land surrounding the building, though she never owned the castle itself. The grounds are very pleasant; look out for the mulberry tree planted by Wordsworth.

Open: In July and August, by arrangement only. Contact Ian Gordon at the above address.

Note: Muncaster Castle, Sizergh and Naworth Castles are covered in the Stately Homes section.

Ruined Castles

The following are ruins, open to the public or visible from the roadside:

☆☆ Brougham, Nr. Penrith. Tel: 0768 62488.

Well preserved ruin of an important castle built within the ramparts of a Roman fort. One of the castles restored by Lady Anne Clifford, and the place where she died. Best of the ruins. Run by English Heritage, with a shop on site.

Open: April to 30 September, 10.00-6.00 daily. 1 October to March, Wednesday to Sunday, 10.00-4.00. Admission - A.

Cockermouth

Part ruined, part lived in and very rarely open to the public, except occasionally during Cockermouth Festival. Good view of the walls from beside the river.

Egremont, Nr. Whitehaven

In a public park at the south end of the town. It stands on a mound in a loop of the River Ehen. Some stylish herringbone masonry.

Open: When park open. Free admission.

Kendal

An impressive stone-built affair which stands in a public park to the east of the town centre.

Open: all time. Free.

Kirkoswald, Nr. Penrith

A ruined tower in a farm field to the south east of the village. One of a group of castles built to deter the Scots from penetrating south and east through Millerstang and Stainmore.

Free admission, but check with farmer.

Penrith

In the public park, opposite the railway station. A favourite dwelling of Richard, Duke of Gloucester (later Richard III) when he was Warden of the West Marches.

Open: 9.00-dusk. Free.

Piel (on Piel Island, off the coast by Barrow-in-Furness)

Built by the monks of Furness Abbey to protect their harbour from the Scots. Boats go out to it from Roa Island in summer. Details of access Barrow TIC.

Still in Cumbria, are **Brough**, also built within a Roman fort, and **Pendragon**, with its suggestion of Arthurian connections (they turn up all over Cumbria). Pendragon once guarded Mallerstang and Brough Stainmore. In the far north, uncomfortably exposed, is **Bewcastle** - you can see it when you go to see the stone cross.

Mills

There seems to be a little growth industry in Cumbrian Mills in the last few years with several being renovated and reopened, either as museums or as working mills, following centuries-old systems. Great to look at and listen to and, best of all for families, many of them do first class teas and cakes, often using their own products, made on the premises.

Here are a few of the best mills currently open to the public:

☆ Gleaston Watermill

Ulverston. Tel: 0229 869244.
(Off A5087 south of Ulverston).

Present building dates from 1774. One of three mills which served the now ruined Gleaston Castle. Lovingly restored by enthusiasts. Also Dusty Miller cafe, shop and evening activities.

Open: April-Sept. 11.00-5.00 (not Mondays), winter 11.00-dusk.

☆ Eskdale Corn Mill

Boot, Holmrook, Eskdale Tel: 09467 23335.

Again being restored by enthusiasts. Water powered mill in fantastic setting, near one of L'al Ratty's stations.

Open: Sunday-Friday and Bank Holiday Saturdays, 11.00-5.00.

☆ Heron Corn Mill

Waterhouse Mills, Beetham, Nr Milnthorpe. Tel: 05395 63363.

Hard to find, as you have to go through an untidy paper factory, but worth it. This was a working mill in a thriving farming community right up until 1955. There was a mill on this site as far back as 1220. Today, the mill is restored as a working museum, run as a charity, with fine displays and some old machinery grinding away. Newly opened from 1989, there is now a museum telling the history of paper making. Buy some stoneground flour before you leave.

Open: April to September, Tuesday-Sunday 11.00-5.00. Also open Bank Holidays. Admission - B. No teas - try the Wheatsheaf Hotel, just down the road.

Little Salkeld Mill

Penrith. Tel: 0768 881523

Another water-powered corn mill, fully working and producing quite a famous range of stoneground flour.

Only the shop is now open - mornings only. It's a family business - two of their children are called Snowdrop and Harvest. Ahh.

☆☆ Muncaster Mill

Ravenglass. Tel: 0229 717232

Yet another corn mill, this time at the *other* end of the Ravenglass railway. The mill and machinery dates back to the late 1700s, although there was probably a mill here before the 1400s. The watermill uses a millrace 3/4 mile long. It is in use as a working exhibition and flour is available for sale. It has a very homely, friendly atmosphere - especially when Ratty goes chugging past the door. Looks quite idyllic until you consider the amount of work which has gone into making it look that way.

Open: April, May and September, daily (except Saturdays) 11.00-5.00. June to August, 10.00-6.00.
Admission - A.

☆☆ Wythop Mill

Embleton. Tel: 07687 76394.
(1/2 mile off the A66, 4 miles from Cockermouth)

An old woodworking mill which uses a working overshot waterwheel. Originally a corn mill, it later became a sawmill around the mid-1800s. It has been fully restored and now contains a small exhibition of old woodworking machinery. Excellent restaurant, serving light lunches and week-end dinners. There is a small car park.

Open: Easter to October, 10.30-5.30, closed Mondays.

Churches

Cumbria has one Cathedral, several abbeys in various states of repair and a host of interesting churches. They tend not to be as ornate or rich, either outside or inside, as some southern churches. Many of them, especially near the Borders, were semi-fortified to repel raiders, but they are all rich in history and archaeological interest.

Impossible to list them all - it would take up most of the rest of the book. Here are seven of the most famous and interesting.

☆☆☆ Carlisle Cathedral

Began as an Augustinian church in early 12th century, promoted to cathedral in 1133 - the only Augustinian house in England to achieve this. Rather small, as cathedrals go, but has a magnificent east window, one of the best in England. The west end and transepts are the earliest parts. Most of the decorated features rebuilt following a great fire in 1292.

The Civil War took some toll on the structure and it had to wait for Victorian times for a decent restoration.

Don't miss the 15th century paintings behind the choir stalls. A tour is available of the Prior's Tower. Next door is the very good Undercroft Buttery and a bookshop.

☆☆ Cartmel Priory

Cartmel, Nr Grange-over-Sands.

Founded by William Marshall, the Baron of Cartmel, in the late 12th century. Now nothing remaining of the original priory except the gatehouse (National Trust) and church. The gatehouse is open to the public, just off Cartmel Square (see 'museums'). The church has been restored several times and is now a collection of styles; the east window is 15th century. The best feature is the carved oak misericords, with some delightful mermaids, apes, elephants and unicorns. A very quiet, impressive church.

☆☆ Furness Abbey

Barrow-in-Furness. Tel: 0229 823420.

Mentioned by Wordsworth, now a ruin in the care of English Heritage (the two facts are not connected). The remains are very impressive, some parts almost at their original height. It dates from around 1127 and the layout can be clearly seen - in sections, the walls rear overhead and you get the powerful feeling of the monastery's size and influence. Located in a small valley, midway between Barrow-in-Furness and Dalton, east of the A590.

☆ Holm Cultram Abbey

Abbey Town.

On the west coast, just east of Silloth, the little hamlet gets its name from the abbey, founded in 1150 (in fact, the houses get their stone from the remains). Largely destroyed by the dreaded Scots, the remains now serve as the parish church. The west doorway is Norman and there are some good carvings.

☆☆ Lanercost Priory Tel: 06977 3030

Sandwiched between Brampton and Hadrian's Wall, this was an easy target for the Scots (more so than for the tourist). The nave is used as the parish church and the ruins are surprisingly intact, almost as impressive as Furness, and now cared for by English Heritage.

☆ Shap Abbey

Set in a valley one mile west of Shap, it was founded in 1180. One of the few Premonstratensian abbeys standing. In a nice setting, you come upon in unexpectedly. The tower is the only part relatively intact, though you can still see the layout. If you want to see some of the stones that were once part of the Abbey, look closely at Lowther Castle.

☆ Quaker Meeting House

Mosedale

The Quakers have strong roots in Cumbria, dating back to George Fox's early years. (He married Margaret Fell of Swarthmoor Hall, Ulverston.) In 1653 he came to preach at Mosedale, a tiny hamlet south of Caldbeck, and later a Meeting House was built there which still stands today. It's been exquisitely restored and although small and humble, just one room, it's well worth stopping for, especially as in the summer, Tuesday to Saturday, they serve rather nice teas.

Other Churches

Almost every town or village in the Lakes has a church of some interest, although some are little more than a stone cabin (look at Wythburn). Some very remote, such as the ones in St John's-in-the-Vale and Wasdale.

In the towns, especially on busy days, they make a perfect escape from the noise and bustle and, apart from Grasmere Churchyard, where everyone is searching for the Wordsworth graves, their churchyards are usually completely ignored. Our favourite parish churches and churchyards are as follows:

St Martin's, Bowness. Excellent stained glass window.
St Michael's, Hawkshead. Brilliant views.
St John's, Keswick. More brilliant views.
St Kentigern's, Crosthwaite, Keswick. Southey grave.
St Anthony's, Cartmel Fell. Marvellous isolation.
All Saints, Cockermouth. Large, Victorian sandstone.
St Michael's, Isel. Perfect little Norman church.
St James's, Whitehaven. Spectacular Georgian interior.
St Andrew's, Dacre. Don't miss the four amazing bears, at each corner of the churchyard, but if the vicar sees you photographing them, there could be a fee . . .
St Mary's, Ambleside. Interesting memorabilia on Wordsworth, Mathew Arnold, W. Forstep.
St Oswald's, Grasmere. Follow the crowds to THE grave.

Ancient Monuments

Loads of good archaeological sites, but for many of them you'd need a magnifying glass and a portable archaeologist. Here are the ones where you can actually see something.

☆☆☆ Bewcastle Stone Cross

One of the oldest and most magnificent crosses in Europe. In the churchyard of the village (north of Hadrian's Wall and only just in Cumbria), it is a beautifully carved sandstone cross, over 1,300 years old and over 13 foot high. Covered with incredible carvings. Amazing that it is still left outside, exposed to all weathers, and not indoors at the British Museum. (Let's hope the sneaks don't steal it, hoping for a swap . . .). Both church and cross stand within the ramparts of a Roman fort.

☆☆ Gosforth Cross

Another sandstone cross, this one Viking and over 12 foot high. Tall and slender it looks frighteningly fragile and is covered with mythological heroes and Viking legends. Situated in the churchyard at Gosforth, on the west coast by Wasdale.

☆ Irton Cross

In Irton churchyard, just north of Ravenglass, near Santon Bridge a near perfect Anglian cross over 1000 years old. Intricately decorated with Runic inscriptions and patterns.

☆ Galava Roman Fort

The remains of a Roman fort at Waterhead, just south of Ambleside. Old local name is Borrans Fort. The foundations remain and the original fort probably dates from around AD79. The field in which it stands is owned by the National Trust. To get a really good view of the layout, climb Todd's Crag on Loughrigg and look down on it.

☆☆ Hardknott Roman Fort

Near the top of the pass, on the left as you go up from Eskdale. You can easily miss it from the road. One of the best Roman forts in Britain, set on a dramatic site guarding the road from Galava to Glannaventa (Ravenglass). The parade ground is fascinating and the views fantastic. The Roman name was Mediobogdum and the walls still stand, though not very high. Worth investigating.

Stone Circles

☆☆ Castlerigg

Just off the A66, before you get into Keswick from the south. It has a fantastic setting, surrounded by high fells, though the stones themselves are not very impressive; 38 of them in a circle, roughly 90 feet across. About 3 to 4,000 years old. Like the economy, no one can explain it.

☆☆ Long Meg and her Daughters

Near Little Salkeld, just north of Penrith, the circle is huge, nearly 300 feet wide. Long Meg is the tallest of 68 or so stones, about 9 foot high and covered with mysterious symbols. The 'daughters' are the other stones and the circle probably dates from around 1,500 BC. Off the beaten track, but an incredible place.

Now for an oddity -

☆☆☆ The Bowder Stone

One of Lakeland's most famous features, this is a large, isolated rock, apparently in a state of delicate balance (30 feet high, 60 long and about 1,900 tons of it). Stands away from the rock face, overlooking the valley. How it got there, no one knows. A ladder allows you to climb to the top. It is perfectly safe, but just try walking under the overhanging sides of it - quite unnerving. Located in Borrowdale valley, with a nearby car park and well-marked footpath to it.

Chapter Thirteen

People, customs, phrases

Apart from all those Big Literary Names, from W. Wordsworth to B. Potter, who will for ever be associated with the Lake District, there are quite a few other more local people, from different walks of life, whose names you might come across when exploring Cumbria. Here's a brief selection, plus some handy customs and curiosities, phrases and words which might be useful when talking to the locals.

People

Joe Bowman Huntsman of the Ullswater hounds from 1879 to 1924. Died in 1940, aged 90. Smart hunting folks maintain he was a better breeder than John Peel, though he is remembered only in local Cumbrian hunting circles.

Mary of Buttermere, or Maid of Buttermere. Mary Robinson, a innkeeper's beautiful daughter, was wronged by a blackguard who bigamously married her in 1802. Her case became the talk of the nation, was turned into a West End melodrama and mentioned by Wordsworth in the Prelude. She is buried in Caldbeck Church. Now recreated in a successful novel by Melvyn Bragg.

Lady Anne Clifford, 1590-1676, High sheriffess of the County of Westmorland. Owned vast estates, including the castles of Appleby, Brougham, and Pendragon, which she restored. Founded hospitals and charities. Now seen as an early feminist heroine. Leaflet available from CTB: *The Lady Anne Clifford Trail.*

The Lowthers Cumbria's ruling family. For 400 years they have been the most dominant, wealthiest and most innovative family in the whole region. The present head of the family is the Seventh Earl of Lonsdale, James Lowther, who lives at Hackthorpe, near Penrith. A recent survey named him as the 19th richest man in the UK, worth £100 million. Their ancestral home, Lowther Castle, which is nearby, is now empty, a romantic ruin. At one time, they were like feudal kings in Cumbria, lords of all they surveyed. Wordsworth's father worked for them and Wordsworth himself, having started off hating them, became very keen to have their patronage and friendship. They were behind the industrial mining and shipping development of West Cumbria from the 18th century. Throughout Cumbria today, you will still see references to the Lowther family, in street names, shops, cinemas, and now in horse trials and a country park. It was the fifth Earl, an eccentric spendthrift who was passionate about sport, and gave his name to the famous Lonsdale Belt for boxing. He was also passionate about the colour yellow, and made all his servants wear yellow livery. The Automobile Association, for whom he was first President, took their colour from him . . . To this day, Cumbrian Tories at election time always sport yellow, not blue as elsewhere in the land. All because of the Yellow Earl.

John Peel (1777-1854). Huntsman, born and lived in the Caldbeck area, a legend in his lifetime, if only a local one, for his passion for the hounds. He devoted all his energies to them, often at the expense of his own family. A much more selfish, unattractive figure than his legend might suggest. The famous song which commemorates him, now the Cumbrian national anthem and known throughout the English speaking world, was never heard by Peel himself. The words were put to the present tune fifteen years *after* his death. He died in 1854 and is buried in Caldbeck churchyard. His grave is well worth a visit, unless the anti-bloodsports supporters have vandalised it again.

Canon Rawnsley (1851-1920) of Crosthwaite Church, Keswick. A founder of the National Trust and one of Lakeland's great activists and preservationists. Friend of Beatrix Potter, loved bonfires, hated rude postcards.

197

Will Ritson (1808-1890). An innkeeper at Wasdale Head. He claimed to be a personal friend of Wordsworth and De Quincey. He also claimed that he was the biggest liar in England. An annual competition is still held in West Cumbria to find the biggest liar of the year. No politicians need apply.

Wonderful Walker Rev Robert Walker (1709-1802). Curate of Seathwaite in the Duddon Valley, known throughout Lakeland for his care and kindness. Despite living on a pittance all his life, gave endlessly to the poor. Written about by Wordsworth in his Duddon sonnets.

Famous Residents

People who were born, died or lived for some time in the Lake District.

Katherine Parr (wife of Henry VIII), lived Kendal 1512.

George Fox, founder of the Quakers, lived in Ulverston, 1670-75.

George Romney, artist, born Dalton-in-Furness 1734, died Kendal 1802. Buried Dalton.

Sir John Barrow, explorer and founder Royal Geographical Society, born Ulverston 1764.

Fletcher Christian, *Bounty* mutineer, born Cockermouth 1764.

John Dalton, atom theorist, born Eaglesfield, Cockermouth 1766.

James Boswell (biographer of Dr Johnson) Recorder of Carlisle, 1788-1790.

William Wordsworth, poet, born Cockermouth 1770, died Rydal, 1850.

Samuel Taylor Coleridge, poet, lived Keswick, 1800-1810.

Robert Southey, poet, lived Keswick, 1803-1843.

Thomas De Quincey, writer, lived Grasmere, 1803-30.

William Wilberforce, lived Windermere, 1780-88.

John Peel, huntsman, born and died Caldbeck, 1776-1854.

John Wilson (alias Christopher North), writer, lived Windermere, 1807-15.

Percy Bysshe Shelley, lived Keswick 1811-12.

Dr Thomas Arnold, headmaster, retired to Ambleside 1834-42.

Matthew Arnold, poet, son of Thomas, lived Ambleside 1834-42.

Harriet Martineau, writer, lived Ambleside 1844-76.

W E Forster, educational reformer, lived Ambleside, 1850.

John Ruskin, writer, artist, lived Coniston 1871-1900, died Coniston, buried Coniston.

Stan Laurel (of Laurel and Hardy), born Ulverston 1890.

Canon Rawnsley, writer, preservationist, lived Keswick 1901-20.

Beatrix Potter, children's writer, lived Sawrey 1906-43.

Ben and Winifred Nicholson (artists) lived Bankshead, Brampton 1920s.

Arthur Ransome, children's writer, lived Coniston 1930-1967.

Sir Hugh Walpole, writer, lived Derwentwater 1932-41, died Derwentwater, buried Keswick.

Lord (Norman) Birkett, judge, born Ulverston, 1883, died 1962.

Kurt Schwitters, German artist, died Kendal 1948.

Kathleen Ferrier, singer, 1912-1953, lived Silloth and Carlisle.

Norman Nicholson, poet, born Millom 1914, died 1987.

George MacDonald Fraser, writer, born Carlisle 1925.

Lord (Willie) Whitelaw, lives near Penrith.

A Wainwright, the one and only, lived Kendal 1941-91.

Lord Hoyle, scientist, lived Ullswater since 1970s.

Margaret Forster, writer, born Carlisle 1938.

Melvyn Bragg, author, broadcaster, born Wigton 1939.

Chris Bonington, mountaineer, lived Caldbeck since 1974.

Doug Scott, mountaineer, lived Hesket Newmarket since 1982.

Anna Ford, broadcaster, brought up in Wigton and Brampton.

Ken Russell, film director, has a home in Borrowdale.

Famous Visitors

Agricola, Roman governor, campaign in Cumbria AD79.

St Cuthbert, visited Carlisle and district 685.

David I, King of Scotland, died Carlisle 1153.

Edward I, Hammer of the Scots, died Burgh-by-Sands 1307.

Robert the Bruce, plundered Cumbria 1314.

Mary, Queen of Scots, imprisoned Carlisle Castle 1568.

Celia Fiennes, traveller, visited Lakes, 1698.

Bonnie Prince Charlie, captured Carlisle, 1745, marched through Cumbria.

John Wesley, evangelist, toured Lakes area, 1759.

Thomas Gray, poet, travel writer, toured Lakes 1767, 1769.

Benjamin Franklin, US statesman, stayed Derwentwater 1772.

J. M. W. Turner (painter) toured S. Lakes Summer 1797, 1816.

Charles Lamb, writer, stayed Keswick 1802.
John Paul Jones, US sailor, raided Whitehaven, 1778.
William Hazlitt, writer, stayed Keswick 1803.
Sir Walter Scott, writer, regular visitor to Lakes 1805-25.
Sir Humphrey Davy, scientist, stayed Grasmere 1805.
John Constable, painter, two months in Lakes 1806.
George Canning, statesman, visited Lakes 1814, 1825.
Robert Owen, reformer, visited Lakes 1817.
William Wilberforce, philanthropist, stayed Rydal and Keswick 1818.
John Keats, poet, visited Lakes, climbed Skiddaw 1818.
Ralph Waldo Emerson, American essayist, visited Lakes 1833.
John Stuart Mill, philosopher, stayed Keswick 1833.
Lord Tennyson, poet, stayed Bassenthwaite 1835, honeymoon Coniston 1850.
Branwell Bronte, worked as tutor, Broughton-in-Furness 1840.
Thomas Carlyle, visited Bassenthwaite, 1840s-70s.
Charlotte Bronte, writer, stayed Ambleside 1849, 1850.
Mrs Gaskell, writer, stayed Ambleside 1850.
Charles Dickens, writer, toured Lakes, climbed Carrock Fell 1857.
Wilkie Collins, writer, toured with Dickens 1857.
Donald Campbell, racing driver, killed Coniston 1967.

Customs and Curiosities

Buttermere Round A coach trip in the olden days from Keswick down Borrowdale and over Honister to Buttermere then over Newlands back to Keswick. Passengers had to get off and walk up all the steep hills. References still seen in old Lakeland engravings and writings.

Char Windermere contains a unique species of fish called Char. It's a form of trout, a very ancient fish, thought to have been left behind after the Ice Age and got stuck, unable to migrate. Potted char and char pies were considered a great delicacy in the last century and were exported to London. Now only a few amateur char fishermen survive on Windermere.

Dry Stone Walls Walls without mortar or cement, put together by hand, from natural stones and slates. A much harder art than it appears. Between 1750-1850, most of the open fells were enclosed, or divided by these walls, even up to the mountain tops, an enormous undertaking, yet many of them still stand intact to this day.

You can have a go at doing it yourself at Brockhole or join a properly organised Dry Stone Walling Meet which the National Park people run. You spend a day with a Ranger, learning how to construct a dry stone wall. Most people turn up just to watch, then find themselves joining in. In 1985, an elderly American lady joined in, wearing a white suit.

Fell Ponies A distinctive feature of the Northern and Eastern Fells. Mostly black, brown or bay, they roam wild in groups round the open fellside and commons. In bad weather, they gather near villages or on minor roads. They appear to be *completely* wild, and are allowed to breed and wander freely, but they do have owners, so don't try to steal any. Formerly they pulled small farm carts or worked down the mines. Now very popular as children's ponies.

Gurning A traditional event, going back 700 years, which is held annually at the Egremont Crab Fair. Much loved by the British Tourist Authority and Americans. Competitors have to put on a horse collar and make the most ridiculous or ugly face.

Hodden grey A type of undyed, grey cloth, very hard wearing, mentioned in the John Peel song, 'coat so grey'. On no account make the mistake of singing in 'coat so gay'. Tut, tut.

Merry Neet A merry night, Cumbrian style, with singing and entertainment, traditionally after fox hunting.

Ratty Or La'al Ratty, meaning Little Ratty. Nickname for the preserved railway line at Ravenglass.

Rushbearing Annual ceremony at Grasmere Church, and elsewhere, to commemorate the renewal of rushes which were laid on the bare church floor every August, then taken up in the Spring.

Spinning galleries Wooden balconies on farm buildings where the wool was spun. Best known example, see all those post cards, is Yew Tree Farm near Coniston.

Statesman Ancient name for yeoman farmer, independent small farmers, with perhaps no more than 50-100 acres. They still make up most of the central farming community.

Words and Phrases

They all speak English, so in theory you should not have too many problems . . .

Norse Origins Their accents and place names often betray the influence of earlier settlers, especially Norse, and it is as well when map reading to know the meaning of the more common words which are peculiar to Cumbria.

Beck = stream
Blea = blue
Fell = mountain, open hill slopes
Force = waterfall
Garth = enclosure, field
Ghyll/gill = narrow ravine, usually with a stream
Grange = outlying farm belonging to a monastery
Hause = narrow pass
Holm = island
How = small hill, mound
Intake = land enclosed from waste
Kirk = church

Mere = lake, pool
Nab = projecting spur
Nes = headland, promontory
Pike = sharp summit, peak
Scree = loose stones, debris
Skarth = gap in a ridge
Tarn = small mountain lake
Thwaite = clearing in a forest

Pronunciations

Rothay = Row-thee
Loughrigg = Loff-rigg
Langdale = Langdul
Aspatria = 'Spaytree
Holker = Hooker
Greysouthen = Grey Soon

Thornbarrow = Thornburuh
Bowness = Bo-nuss
Ravenstonedale = Ra'sundul
Brougham = Broom
Lamplugh = Lampluh

Sheep Names

The local names for ages and sex of sheep also betray their Norse origins and are still in common use. Yow means ewe, gimmer means a yearling, tup means a male, hogg is a last year's lamb, twinter is a two year-old, trinter a three year-old.

However, when Cumbrian farmers count their sheep they use an ancient Celtic form of counting. Even non farming Cumbrians, in the big smoke like Carlisle say yan for one and yance for once. Counting up to twenty sheep goes something like this:

Yan, tan, tether, mether, pimp, teezar, leezar, catterah, horna, dick, yan-dick, tan-dick, tether-dick, mether-dick, bumpit, yan-a-bumpit, tan-a-bumpit, tedera-bumpit, medera-bumpit, giggot . . .

Now you can go anywhere.

Chapter Fourteen

Sports and Entertainments

The native sports are what make Cumbrian gatherings so unusual. You will see sports which exist nowhere else in the world. They are fascinating to watch, even if you have no idea what is going on . . .

After the spectator events come the do-it-yourself activities, from fishing and riding to climbing and sailing.

Then finally entertainments for a more cultural type which are on offer in Cumbria, notably theatre, music and cinema. Yes, the National Park does boast cinemas. All two and a half of them . . .

Cumbrian Sports

Cumberland and Westmorland Wrestling

The most famous of the Lake District's native sports and you can see it practised at all the main sporting events. It began with Norsemen and at one time was widespread across the country. Today it is almost exclusively Cumbrian and a feature of many of the sports and agricultural shows. It looks like a trial of strength but is actually quite technical. The best wrestlers usually follow in family tradition and seem to be practically bred for it. Just like the best animals.

Two men face each other in a small arena, watched by two judges and a referee. The wrestlers are usually dressed in costumes which resemble combinations and embroidered bathing trunks. After shaking hands, the two men 'tak hod', that is, lock arms behind each other's back. The aim is to try to topple the other fellow to the ground and break his hold. If both fall, the one on top is the winner. The secret lies in tempting your opponent into a position of apparent security and then quickly over-balancing him. To the casual spectator, the technical subtleties are often not very obvious, but the events usually have a sense of atmosphere and tradition which make them well worth attending.

Fell racing

One of the principal attractions of a Lake District sports day. It consists of a race to the top of the nearest fell, often a gruelling 1,500 foot struggle, round a flag at the summit, then a breakneck dash back down into the arena. A straightforward, though torturous race. The best of all is the Grasmere guides' race (nothing to do with boy scouts and brownies) which can be quite spectacular and very exciting to watch.

Sheep dog trials

Nowadays, these take place all over the country and are well known to everyone through television, but they began in the north of England. The first took place in Northumberland in 1876 and the following year sheep dog trials were being held on Belle Isle, Windermere. In 1891, the 'Lake District Sheep Dog Trials Association' was formed.

Five sheep are released at one end of the arena - up to a quarter of a mile away - and the shepherd has to remain at his post whilst his dog - usually a Border Collie - gathers the sheep and brings them towards the shepherd through a series of obstacles. The final and most difficult part is to coax the sheep into a pen and it is only at this stage that the shepherd is able to assist, other than by whistling and calling.

Towards the end, the tension can build up quite rapidly and there is often a sense of magic about the way the shepherds can control their dogs. These events are very popular and set against the Lakeland fells on a fine, summer day, you are seeing them at their best. They often form a part of an agricultural or sports show but it is best to see them at the Rydal or Patterdale Sheep Dog Trials for the greatest sense of atmosphere.

Fox hunting

Not unique to Lakeland, though the sport's most famous exponent - John Peel - is buried in Caldbeck churchyard. Cumbrian fox hunting on the fells is radically different from the 'polite' social occasions of the south. The Lakeland farmer hunts primarily to kill foxes and keep down their numbers - and does it on foot. The hunt followers no doubt have reasons of their own. There are no horses and red coats - all the members hunt on foot and only one, the huntsman, wears the red coat. Hunt followers can be seen parked beside the road at the foot of the fells, from whence comes the disembodied baying of the hounds. There are six main packs in Cumbria:

Blencathra - reckoned to be the premier pack. Established in 1840. Its territory includes the countryside around Thirlmere, Derwentwater, Skiddaw and Caldbeck.

Melbreak - concentrates on the north west fells and out to the coast.

Ullswater - including territory around Kentmere, Fairfield and out towards Penrith.

Eskdale and Ennerdale - south west Lakeland, Scafell and into Langdale and out to the coast.

Coniston - concentrates on the central Lakes and east of Windermere.

Lunesdale - operates out over the Pennines.

The fox hunting season extends from the beginning of October through until the end of April. Neither the time nor the sport is particularly convenient for the holiday maker to the Lakes. But should you winter in Lakeland, look out for it. Full details of all the fixtures for the fell packs are published in the October issue of *Lakescene* each year. Or watch the local newspapers.

Hound trailing

A favourite sport in Cumbria for more than a hundred years and probably originally derived from the method used by huntsmen to train fox-hounds. It is really fox hunting without the fox. It's done in the summer off-season, so it's perfect for visitors to watch. From a starting point, a trail is set down by dragging an aniseed-soaked cloth over the fellside, making the course as difficult as possible by including fences, hedges, walls and a variety of terrain. For a fully-grown dog, the trail can be up to 10 miles long and can take 25 to 45 minutes to complete.

After the scent has been laid, the hounds are released; they pick up the scent from the 'trailer', then the whole pack rushes off into the hills. They might be out of sight until the finish, when they follow the trail back and the owners shout, whistle and wave to coax their animals over the line. The end can be quite exciting, but for most 'serious' spectators the attraction lies in betting which hound will win. The local Cumbrian bookies, who appear at most big sports, are a feature in themselves.

Trailing is held throughout Cumbria from April to October and the *Whitehaven News* (published Fridays) carries details of venues and times for the area (though tracking down the locations can be a problem - ask your friendly TIC). Hound trailing is also an important part of many of the shows and sports days.

Sporting Shows

There are several dozen sporting and farming shows held every year in the various Cumbrian towns and villages, all worth going to, and most of them include native

Cumbrian sports. Keep an eye out for the local papers or notice boards for the smaller village shows for they have a flavour of their own, but the two Big Sports Days are held at Grasmere and Ambleside. All visitors should try if possible to fit in one of them.

For more details and times nearer the day, contact the TIC nearest the show.

☆☆☆ Grasmere Sports

Third Thursday after the first Monday in August.

The major Lakeland sporting event and by far the most popular in the area with often up to 20,000 spectators. Held in the 'ring' - the field just outside Grasmere, across the A591 from Town End and Dove Cottage. A brilliant location with all the usual running, throwing and cycling events, attracting professionals from all over the country, along with the best of the traditional, local events, such as Cumberland and Westmorland wrestling (in addition, there is a contest for the best costume worn by the wrestlers). Also the famous guides' fell race and hound trailing. Gets very crowded, so go early, otherwise about the only place to park is Keswick. Full of atmosphere and excitement, despite its size and fame, this remains a local show, unique to the area and still administered mainly by Grasmere people.

☆☆☆ Ambleside Sports

Thursday before first Monday in August.

Held in Rydal Park, just north of Ambleside. Began before the first world war and was revived again about 30 years ago. Now one of the biggest events of its kind in the Lake District, with track events, fell races, Cumberland and Westmorland wrestling. An exciting event to go to in a lovely, fellside setting.

☆☆ Cartmel Races

Spring and late Summer Bank Holiday, Saturday and Monday.

Probably the smallest of the National Hunt courses, set at the opposite end of the village to the Priory. Apart from horse racing there is usually a small fairground, along with stalls and refreshment tents. Not worth families spending the whole day there as it can get very crowded, but perhaps worth using as a base for a day out exploring Cartmel itself and the surrounding area.

☆ Keswick Sports

Revived in 1992. Let's hope they keep going. August Bank Holiday.

☆☆ Lowther Horse Driving Trials and Country Fair

Weekend in early August.

Held on the Lowther Estate, near Penrith, this is the

largest established occasion of its kind and one of the country's leading sporting events. As well as the horse driving trials (in which Prince Philip has been known to take part) there are also supporting attractions and the country fair itself with a wide range of stalls and events.

Agricultural Shows

The distinction between an agricultural show and a sporting or field event tends to get a bit blurred in the Lake District, with many of the farming and country shows attracting people who have come to watch the sheep dog trails, hound trails or Cumberland and Westmorland wrestling. Nearly all the shows are intended for the general visitor, not just the farming community, so are worth seeking out if they coincide with your holiday. Here are some of the best:

☆☆ Cumberland Show
Next to last Saturday in July.

Held in Rickerby Park, Carlisle, and for many years has been the largest of the agricultural shows in Cumbria. Lots of traditional and modern events staged to make it a whole day's entertainment.

☆☆ Skelton Show
Third Saturday in August.

Formerly a little local show, centred on a village north of Penrith, which in recent years has exploded in size and content and enterprise. They now claim to have more animals on show than their rivals.

☆☆ Ennerdale Show
Last Wednesday in August.

Held at Bowness Knott, Ennerdale. What began as a small flower show has evolved into a delightful little agricultural and horticultural show, with hound trails, fell racing , sheep dog trials and gymkhana. It all ends with a dance in the evening.

☆ Eskdale Show
Last Saturday in September.

Primarily a sheep show, but including fell races, children's sports and singing and horn-blowing competitions. The mountains providing a superb setting.

☆ Gosforth Show
Third Wednesday in August.

Another traditional Cumbrian agricultural show, with additional entertainments in the form of terrier racing and a gymkhana. Along with the Eskdale and Hawkshead shows, this tends to be a mainly agricultural affair which is probably more fun for the local than the visitor. Worth taking in, but only if you happen to be in the area at the time. Or you could plan a day's outing around it and explore the area.

☆ Hawkshead Show
Changeable.
   On the lines of Gosforth, but this time with added hound trailing and horse jumping.

☆☆ Keswick Show
Late Summer Bank Holiday Monday.
   An important agricultural show with a bit more of a general appeal in the form of hound trails and Cumberland and Westmorland wrestling.

☆☆ Loweswater Show
Third Thursday in September.
   Thought by many to be the nicest small show of them all.

☆☆☆ Wasdale Show
Second Saturday in October.
   Now this one is worth going out of your way for. A superb setting at Wasdale Head, this is one of the best sheep shows in Cumbria, with lots of judging of sheep, sheep dogs, shepherds' crooks and even their boots. There are also tug-of-war competitions, pillow fights, fell races, hound trails and the notorious Cumberland and Westmorland wrestling. Very good.

☆☆☆ Westmorland County Show
Second Thursday in September.
   Held at Lane Farm, Crooklands and one of the best one-day shows in Cumbria. Better than the Cumberland Show, so Westmerians like to believe. All kinds of agricultural competitions and displays, dog shows, Cumberland and Westmorland wrestling, show jumping, horse drawn carriage driving and a 'welly' race. There is also usually a dance in the evening (you can always tell the best shows by this).

☆☆☆ Appleby Horse Fair
Second Wednesday in June.
   Not really an agricultural show, but set up by a charter of 1685 as a fair for horse trading. Today it is world-famous, the largest of its kind in the world, and attracts a huge gypsy gathering. Well-worth going to if it coincides with your visit for the sheer spectacle and bustle. Great if the weather is good. People arrive and camp out in the area up to a week before the day of the sales.

Sheep Dog Trials

In addition to trials found at some of the agricultural shows, there are five main events held in the Lakes:

☆☆ Rydal

Second Thursday after first Monday in August. Held in Rydal Hall grounds, just outside Ambleside on the A591.

Lake District

First Thursday after the first Monday in August. Held at Ings, near Staveley.

Threlkeld

Third Wednesday after first Monday in August. In Burns Field, Threlkeld, near Keswick.

☆ Patterdale Dog Day

Late Summer Bank Holiday Saturday. Held in the King George V playing fields, Patterdale.

Kentmere

Last Thursday in September. Held at Millrigg, near Staveley (about three miles up the Kentmere valley).

The best of the sheep dog trials is definitely Rydal. An excellent show which is fun and doesn't take itself too seriously. (Even the announcements over the PA system are entertaining.)

Rushbearing Ceremonies

Rushbearing is the survival of the old custom of strewing the old, earth floors of churches with rushes. Today the 'rushbearing' is a cross made of rushes and flowers and carried by the children of the parish. A procession is led by a band, followed by the clergy and then the children of the village, carrying the bearings. The procession usually goes round the town or village and ends at the church with hymns and prayers. There are five rushbearing ceremonies remaining in the Lake District - any one of which is worth going along to watch. The children of Ambleside and Grasmere are traditionally given a piece of Grasmere gingerbread if they have carried one of the rushes.

Ambleside Rushbearing

First Saturday in July.

Grasmere

Saturday nearest St Oswald's Day (August 5).

Musgrave Rushbearing

First Saturday in July.

Urswick Rushbearing

Sunday nearest St Michael's Day (September 29).

☆☆ Warcop Rushbearing

St Peter's Day (June 29), unless it falls on a Sunday, in which case the previous Saturday (28th).

Warcop is the most interesting spectacle of the five and is accompanied by children's sports and a military band.

Miscellaneous Events

Things which aren't quite sports and aren't quite agricultural or traditional, but which are becoming a fixed part of the Lakeland calendar. Check in TICs or local newspapers for exact dates.

☆ Carlisle Great Fair

Third Saturday in August for about ten days.

A revived fair which was once old-established. The focal point is the open air market in the city centre and the fair begins with a charger, read out at 8.00am on the first day. Daily events are posted at the Tourist Information Centre. A sort of mini-Edinburgh Festival. In this case, very mini, but they are trying.

World Gurning Champion, with runner-up.

☆☆ Egremont Crab Fair

Third Saturday in September.

One of Cumbria's oldest and oddest annual events. Dating back to 1267, the fair begins when, at 12.30pm, about £40 worth of apples are thrown to the public. A greasy pole is erected at dawn in the main street and a five pound note placed on top. Anyone who can climb the pole can have the money. (It used to be a half-sheep, but presumably that got too expensive.) There are track and field events and hound trails during the day. In the evening there is a pipe-smoking contest and an event for which the fair is famous; the World Gurning Championships. The entrants to this revered competition put their heads through a horse collar and grin or 'gurn' - the object being to pull the most revolting expression; the most grotesque wins. Entrants with dentures tend to have an advantage here, though it is said that one year the contest was won by a sympathetic onlooker who was just watching.

☆ Cumbria Steam Gathering

Last weekend in July.

An impressive gathering of old steam cars, traction engines and commercial vehicles. There is also a fairground and market. Held in Flookburgh.

☆☆ Lake Windermere Festival

Traditional Lakeland event, revived in 1982, which takes over Bowness and Waterhead for a week in early July. Events include helicopter rides, brass bands, water-ski displays, 'Mr Lakeland' beauty competition, triathlons, power boat racing and, of course, Cumberland and Westmorland wrestling. Most of the action takes place on or around the lake. Lots going on, aimed at visitors and locals alike. Good fun but can make accommodation a bit scarce - be warned.

☆ Lakeland Rose Show

Second weekend in July.

Taking place in Grange-over-Sands (but no longer at Holker Hall - contact Grange TIC for location), this two-day event is one of Cumbria's most trumpeted summer attractions. Opened by royalty, at the very least, it has become something of a showcase for horticulturists all over the country. Not only flowers, but also car shows, massed bands, parachute displays, the Red Arrows. (Sponsored by North West Water Authority in 1989 - ironic seeing that rain caused massive problems for the show in the past two years.) *The* flower show to go to in the north of England. Costs a bomb to get in.

☆☆ Kendal Gathering

Late August/beginning September.

This two-and-a-half week event occurs in and around Kendal. Not a show as such but a sort of mini-festival with a number of contrasting attractions, including show-biz personalities, shows, exhibitions, band contests, dances, ceilidhs. It usually incorporates the Westmorland County Fair (turning a traditional attraction into another tourist honey-pot). But undoubtedly the star of the Gathering is its culmination in the Torchlight Procession, when hundreds of people join in a procession route, lit by torches and candles, which winds throughout the town on the final evening of the Gathering. If going to the Procession, get there early as the police close the town to traffic early in the evening. Best times are given in the *Westmorland Gazette*. (People seem to come from all over for the Procession - two years running UFOs were spotted overhead, according to the local papers.)

The Biggest Liar in the World Competition

Third Thursday in November.

This eccentric little competition, administered by

Copeland Borough Council, takes place every year at the Santon Bridge Inn. It dates back to Will Ritson, a 19th century publican who lived at the head of the Wasdale valley. 'Auld Will' was a genuine and sincere man who lied constantly; one tale was that turnips in Wasdale grew so big that the dalesfolk quarried into them for their Sunday lunch and then used them as sheds for the Herd-wick sheep. (Nowadays, according to the contest-runners, people live in turnips because they are natural features of the landscape and they do not need planning permission from the LDSPB.) In 1974, Tom Purdham won the contest by telling a visiting BBC tv team - who had turned up to film the winner - that he wasn't taking part in the contest. The BBC were convinced and went home without filming him. A recent winner was Jos Naylor, the fell runner. The 1985 winner was John Reeves who works for British Nuclear Fuels at Sellafield. (Jolly useful chap, I'd have thought.) His Big Lie was some nonsense about Halley's Comet really being an everlasting carpet woven from Herdwick sheep wool. The contest is held strictly for amateurs - politicians, journalists and lawyers are barred from entry. Price of admission includes an excellent tatie pot supper. Contact Copeland Council (see chapter 1 for address) and they will happily send you lots of lies about the contest.

Recreations

Having listed and described the spectator sports, and where you can go and see them happening, we now come to the do-it-yourself sports and activities; fishing, golf, riding, swimming, climbing, dry slope skiing, sailing and even parachuting.

Ballooning

It's now possible to take a trip over the LD in a hot air balloon, a real one, not one of those tethered things that you queue for hours to get in to at local shows. Both the following companies have air operators' certificates:

High Adventure, who have an outlet in Windermere 05394 46588 (They are a subsidiary of Gone With the Wind Ltd., of Bristol.)

The Windermere Balloon Company. Tel: 05394 47206 are a local lot and operate all year round.

Canoeing

Lots of lakes and rivers to paddle on, but check access first. The major lakes should provide no problem. The British Canoe Union has regional and local access officers who update and co-ordinate the latest info. on smaller lakes and on the rivers. Their updated info. is available from TICs. If planning in advance, you could contact BCU directly 0602 821100.

Climbing

Rock climbing was virtually invented in the Lake District by a group of climbers basing themselves at Wasdale Head. Nowadays if you're out on any of the fells which has a suitable rock face nearby you'll probably see little figures moving slowly across it, strung together with their gaily coloured ropes. Not something for the novice to try without proper instruction or equipment (see *Instructors*). A number of guide books to the crags are available, but if you're coming to the area and want to get in touch with any of the climbing clubs or with climbing individuals, often the best approach is to contact the two main climbing shops:

George Fisher
2 Borrowdale Road, Keswick. Tel: 07687 72178.

Frank Davies (The Climber's Shop)
Compston Road, Ambleside. Tel: 05394 32297.

Climbing Clubs

Barrow Mountaineering and Ski Club
D. R. Stanford, 56 West Shore Park, Walney Island, Barrow.

Carlisle Mountaineering Club
Roz Winter, 9 Tindale Terrace, Tindale Fell, Brampton.

Eden Valley Mountaineering Club
G. Baum, Barn Cottage, The Lea, Laithes, Penrith.

K Fell Farers
A. Bryan, K Shoes Ltd., Netherfield, Kendal.

Kendal Mountaineering Club
A. Bently, 4 Chelsea Court, Milnthorpe.

Over the Hill Club
B. Dawes, 5 Headlands, Glenridding, Penrith.

West Cumbria Mountaineering Club
D. J. Livesey, 62 Meadowfield, Gosforth.

All the above clubs are members of the British Mountaineering Council and should be happy to accept enquiries from interested people.

Falconry

Lakeland Bird of Prey Centre, Lowther Park.
Tel: 0931 712746.

The only place in Lakeland where you can learn falconry. Day courses available, or you can just watch their 70 birds of prey go through their paces. Flying displays 12.30, 2.00 and 4.00 daily, depending on weather. The Centre used to be at Appleby but moved to Lowther in the summer in 1992 and has proved very popular. They are in the grounds of the original walled garden of Lowther Castle - and have no connection with the nearby Lowther Leisure Park. Open all year from 10.30. Cream teas available. Admission, 1993, £2.75.

Fishing

Every angler must hold a National Fishing Licence and will probably also need a permit, since most water seems to be either owned or let to clubs, associations or some other body. A complete list of licence and permit distributors is available from any of the tourist information centres.

A couple of good Lakeland fishing books are available: *Angler's Guide to the Lake District* by James Holgate and Geoff Parkinson, 1987, £2.50, Westmorland Gazette (part of their *Castabout* series) and the cleverly titled *The Lure of the Lakes* by Angus Berry, 1986.

Fishing licences are administered by:

The National Rivers Authority
N.W. Region,
PO Box 12,
Warrington, Cheshire WA4 1HG
Tel: 0925 53999.

They can supply a licence if you write to them in advance, and permits can be obtained locally from fishing tackle shops, TICs and on-site distributors.

Fishing Tackle Shops

Ambleside Angling, The Old Post House, Millans Park, Ambleside. Tel: 05394 31242.

Eddie's Fishing Tackle, 70 Shaddongate, Carlisle. Tel: 0228 810744.

Field and Stream, 79 Main Street, Keswick. Tel: 07687 74396.

Lakes Tackle Shop, 3 Belsfield Terrace, Kendal Road, Windermere. Tel: 05394 45978.

J. Norris, 21 Victoria Road, Penrith. Tel: 0768 64211.

They will all supply fishing licences and permits for particular waters.

Fish Farms

There are a number of these where it's possible to fish, and in some cases receive tuition. A selection:

Crossfield Sport Fishery, Staffield, nr. Kirkoswald. Tel: 0768 898711. Private lessons in Eden Valley.

Hawkshead Trout Farm, Hawkshead. Tel: 05394 36541. Fishing on Esthwaite Water. Boat hire, fish for sale, and Feed the Fish for children - pay to feed 'em, pay to catch 'em, pay to eat 'em . . . No, that's unfair, they are trying to provide a day out for all the family.

New Mills Trout Farm, Brampton,. Tel: 06977 2384. Lake stocked with trout. Also have restaurant and tearoom - wonder what's on the menu?

Whins Pond, Ewan Way, Edenhall, Penrith. Tel: 0768 62671. 20 acre stocked lake.

Flying

Cumbrian Aero Club, Carlisle Airport.
Crosby-on-Eden, Carlisle. Tel: 0228 73333.
    They undertake aircraft leasing, hire, sales, charter work and train people for private pilot's licence.
    Also a much smaller organisation called *Furness Aviation*, based at Walney Island Aerodrome, Barrow-in-Furness do flying lessons, but on more of a part-time basis at present. Tel: Club House on 0229 472404.

Gliding

Lakes Gliding Club, Walney Island, Barrow.
Tel: 0229 41458.
They have a clubhouse and run weekly courses as well as day flights and lessons.

Golf

    Golfing in the Lake District has its special attractions due to the scenery. The following five are amongst the best situated:

Kendal Golf Club, The Heights, Kendal. Tel: 0539 724079.

Keswick Golf Club, Threlkeld Hall, Threlkeld. Tel: 07687 79324.

Cockermouth Golf Club, Embleton. Tel: 07687 76223.

Grange Fell Golf Club, Grange Fell Road. Tel: 05395 32536.

Windermere Golf Club, Cleabarrow, Windermere. Tel: 05394 43123.

Parachuting

    For the really adventurous:

North West Parachute Centre
Cark Airfield, Flookburgh,
Grange-over-Sands. Tel: 05395 672.

    If you only want to spectate, Humphrey Head - the headland near Grange-over-Sands - has a grandstand view, also Carlisle Parachute Centre, Carlisle Airport. Tel: 0228 573365.

Paragliding

    The sort where you struggle to a high lump of land and hurl yourself off then float gracefully down, courtesy of a mini parachute. A well-established local school is:

Eagle Quest School of Mountaineering and Paragliding. Rookin House Farm, Troutbeck. Tel: 07684 83888.

Riding and Pony Trekking

Anyone contemplating trekking and making extensive use of the various bridleways throughout Cumbria can contact the Cumbria Bridleways Society, who will help with route-planning and local knowledge.

Cumbria Bridleways Society Secretary, 2 Compston Villas, Ambleside. Tel: 05394 33188.

Riding Schools

Seven recommended by our horse riding moles:
Armathwaite Hall, Coalbeck farm, Bassenthwaite. Tel: 07687 76239.
Bigland Hall, Backbarrow, Nr. Ulverston. Tel: 05395 31728.

Holmscales Farm, Old Hutton. Tel: 0539 729388.

Trekkers, The Stables, Hall More Farm, Hale. Tel: 05395 63265. Who do early morning rides (breakfast included) and also pub rides. Very civilised.

Yew Tree Trekking, Yew Tree Farm, Wilton, Egremont. Tel: 0946 820105.

Western Trail Riding Centre, Tindale Fell. Tel: 06977 46671.

The Calvert Trust for the Disabled, Old Windebrowe, Brundholme Road, Keswick. Tel: 07687 74395.

Sailing and Windsurfing

Plenty of opportunity for weekly courses and holidays - more so then ever since several Educational Outdoor Centres are opening up their courses to the public. The standard of tuition and equipment is usually excellent and prices competitive.

For Arthur Ransome fans, there's "Swallows and Amazons" week at the YMCA's national centre at Lakeside on Windermere. You can go chasing AR's elusive locations. A certain island on the lake is becoming so unelusive that it's going to have to be relocated. Tel: 05395 31758 for details.

Hiring boats and equipment on the larger lakes isn't difficult - see Ch. 7 for details. It's rather more difficult to find tuition by the day or by the hour. However we recommend trying:

Windermere
Windermere Sailing Centre, Millerground. Tel: 05394 88107.

The only one of its kind financed by a District Council - good for them. Very reasonably priced.

Low Wood Watersports Centre. Low Wood Hotel, Ambleside. Tel: 05394 34004.

Formerly announced itself as a water ski centre, now diversifying (in anticipation of 10 mph speed limit I wonder?).

Derwentwater
Nichol End Marine, Portinscale, Keswick. Tel: 07687 73082.

Ullswater
Glenridding Sailing School, The Spit. Tel: 07684 82541.

A well-established school with Royal Yachting Association recognition (which means good standards).

An alternative is to contact a local instructor - there are a number of these who offer a variety of activities tailored to personal needs including watersports. (see Instructors below).

Or try 'Wind and Water Activities Centre' based at 23 Church Street, Windermere. Tel: 05394 44020. They act as a 'clearing agency' for enquiries about a wide range of activities - and will put you in touch with relevant instructors. They also sell windsurfers, canoes etc. from their premises.

Ski-ing

Several ski clubs exist in the LD. If you're interested in cross country stuff, contact Christine Woods, tel: 0539 733112 of the LD Cross Country Ski Club. Those who prefer downhill ski-ing will need the Lake District Ski Club. They ski on the back of Helvellyn, at Raise, complete with proper tows. An elusive bunch to get hold of, they will nevertheless welcome you if you choose to walk up to their club. They certainly should. It'll take you about 1 1/2 hours, carrying all your gear.

If you want to go dry ski-slope ski-ing, there's an excellent little slope in Kendal. Run entirely by volunteers, it nevertheless has very good instructors. Also provides daytime tuition - phone John Lowther 0539 821636 or Judy Raynor 0539 724247 for details.

Swimming

Until August and September, the lakes can be very cold, but if you are feeling cowardly there are number of indoor and outdoor pools around. (See Chapter Four for hotels with pools.)

Outdoor
Appleby
Chapel Street. Tel: 07683 51212.

Askham (near Penrith)
Behind the Queen's Head Inn. Tel: 09312 570.

Grange-over-Sands
The Esplanade. Tel: 05395 33053.

The first two are heated. The Grange pool is an open-air, salt water pool with a splendid situation along the sea promenade, overlooking Morecambe Bay.

Indoor
Schools all over Cumbria are opening up their pools to visitors during the summer holidays, evenings and week-ends. The following are purpose-built swimming pools - some public, some school. All are indoor and all offer more than just a pool (usually training pools, saunas):

Barrow-in-Furness
The Park Leisure Centre, Greengate Street.
Tel: 0229 871146.
Carlisle
City Baths, James Street. Tel: 0228 22105.

Cockermouth
Sports Centre, Castlegate Drive. Tel: 0900 823596.

Egremont
Wyndham Baths. Tel: 0946 820465.

Kendal
South Lakeland Leisure Centre, Burton Road.
Tel: 0539 729511.

Keswick
Keswick Spa Leisure Pool, Station Road. Tel: 07687 72760. Lacks depth, but scenic to float around in. Not really for swimmers, this is really a souped-up kiddies' paddling pool, with waterchute, sloping 'beach' and a rather unpredictable wave machine. Great for kids, not so hot for adults (which seems a missed opportunity).

Maryport
Netherhall Swimming Pool. Tel: 0900 812161.

Penrith
Eden Swimming Baths, Southend Road. Tel: 0768 63450.

Ulverston
Priory Road. Tel: 0229 554110.

Whitehaven
Copeland Swimming Pool, Cleator Moor Road.
Tel: 0946 695021.

Wigton
Swimming Baths. Tel: 06973 42412.

Windermere
Troutbeck Bridge Swimming Pool, Troutbeck Bridge.
Tel: 05394 43243.

Workington
Moorclose Swimming Pool, Newlands Lane.
Tel: 0900 61771.

Waterskiing

Low Wood Watersports Centre
Low Wood Hotel, Ambleside. Tel: 05394 34004.

Leisure Centres

Two big ones worth mentioning:

South Lakeland Leisure Centre
Burton Road, Kendal. Tel: 0539 729511.
For concert bookings, telephone 0539 729702.

Has a range of facilities: squash, badminton, weight training, swimming. The centre houses the *Westmorland Hall*, where concerts, plays and performances are held. Also has a bar and cafe.

The Sands Centre
Carlisle. Tel: 0228 25222.
All the usual sports facilities, plus concerts and entertainments - especially during July and August.

Instructors

In addition to the specialist schools and centres, for those interested in climbing, canoeing, caving, orienteering or windsurfing, there are a number of individual instructors operating in the Lake District. Some of the ones who have been reliably around the longest:

R & L Adventures
Knotts Farm, Patterdale Road, Windermere.
Tel: 05394 45104.
(Abseiling, canoeing, fell walking, map reading, orienteering, rock climbing and general mountaineering catered for.)

Lakeland Experience
Green Lodge, Eskdale Green.
Tel: 09467 23228.
(Abseiling, canoeing, caving, fell walking, map reading, orienteering, rock climbing and mountaineering.)

Summitreks
14 Yewdale Road, Coniston.
Tel: 05394 41212.
(Abseiling, caving, fell walking, mountaineering, map reading, orienteering, mountain biking, canoeing, rock climbing and windsurfing.)

White Mountain
Lake Road, Ambleside. Tel: 05394 32752.
(They have a 'guides desk' information bureau which will put you in touch with relevant instructors for walking and climbing activities.)

Theatre and Music

There are five main venues in or close to the Lake District (if we ignore Carlisle) which cater for music and drama. With the exception of the Blue Box Theatre, they all host a variety of events - concerts, plays, lectures, recitals - and most tend to be one or two night occasions; the advantage is that these centres can sometimes attract some of the best touring companies in the country.

☆☆ **Blue Box Theatre**, Lakeside Car Park, Keswick. Tel: 07687 72282.

It's that rather unsafe-looking collection of jacked-up portacabins that greets you as you walk to the lake shore from Keswick town centre. It used to be the Century touring theatre but has now put down roots and the new resident company are raising funds for a proper building. It's a lot nicer inside than the outside would have you believe.

The resident company operates during the summer months and put on three plays, running them in rotation so that you don't get the same play for more than three consecutive days. The plays are usually 'standards' and are well-performed. Well worth a visit. The Moot Hall Information Centre usually has leaflets telling you what they are putting on.

☆☆ **Old Laundry,** Bowness-on-Windermere. Tel: 05394 88444.

A new theatre in the round, holding up to 300 people, built as part of the World of Beatrix Potter complex. It started off in the summer of 1992 with an Ayckbourn, then who doesn't, but this was a new one, direct from Scarborough. Promises to have touring companies and local shows in future.

☆☆ **Theatre-in-the-Forest**, Grizedale Forest. Tel: 0229 860291.

A nice little theatre in a unique position, tucked away miles from anywhere in the Grizedale Forest. (It is easy to find - just north of Satterthwaite on the Hawkshead road.) Provides a range of entertainment throughout the year, mainly concerts, talks and the odd theatrical production. BBC North tend to make a lot of use of it for folk concerts and the like. Programmes appear each week in the *Westmorland Gazette* - otherwise you often have a job finding out what is going on there without a visit. Hawkshead Tourist Information can usually help, though. A nice drive on a summer evening, but don't underestimate how long it takes to get there. It is easiest to find from the Hawkshead direction.

☆ **Rosehill Theatre**, Moresby, near Whitehaven. Tel: 0946 692422.

Rather a trek from the central Lakes, but another very

good arts centre which puts on a range of concerts, films and productions throughout the year. They also have workshops regularly and there is an adjoining bistro. Events listed in the *Whitehaven News* and sometimes at Whitehaven, Keswick and other Tourist Information Centres.

☆☆ Brewery Arts Centre, 122a Highgate, Kendal. Tel: 0539 725133.

An active arts centre in a restored Brewery building. It has become the cultural heart of Kendal and puts on a very good range of plays, concerts, films and special events throughout the year. There is a good bar and it has a photographic gallery and a number of workshops. Very good on mime and folk. This is really a community arts centre run on very professional lines. The Centre sponsors two very good music festivals each year:

Kendal Jazz Festival - around the end of summer, with some big names often appearing.

Kendal Folk Festival - in late August, featuring a wide range of events over a week or more, from concerts and ceilidhs to workshops, displays and competitions.

The Centre itself always has a wide range of information on display about arts activities generally in and around the Lakes. Also houses Kendal's only cinema.

Renaissance Theatre Trust, 17 Fountain Street, Ulverston. Tel: 0229 552299.

Not a theatre as such, but a small coffee shop and arts centre which houses the Trust itself. They are responsible for promoting and organising concerts and shows throughout South Cumbria and the Furness area. They book other venues (such as Civic Halls) and bring in outside artists. The Centre has rooms for a small-scale concert or lecture and a very good cafe. It also operates at the Ulverston Tourist Information Centre.

West Walls Theatre, West Walls, Carlisle. Tel: 0228 33233.

☆☆ Lake District Summer Musical Festival

Held in early August for two weeks. Becoming increasingly well known and attracts excellent musicians and orchestras to the area. Concerts are held in Ambleside, Grizedale, Troutbeck Bridge (the Lakes School with their impressive grand piano), Kendal and other local venues. There are also daytime activities, based at Charlotte Mason College, including masterclasses. Details from Heather McBain. Tel: 0629 823733, or TICs nearer the time.

Grizedale Piano Festival

Held every year in early summer. Contact Theatre in the Forest.

Cinemas

The National Park contains only three public cinemas.

Bowness

☆☆ **Royalty Cinema**, Lake Road. Tel: 05394 43364.

A small, but quite good cinema which can sometimes get big feature releases surprisingly quickly, especially during the summer. It tends to spoil this by repeating blockbusters throughout the height of the season. Okay for visitors, but a bit boring for the locals. **Warning:** they have a vile habit of breaking films halfway through so they can flog ice creams; if this is liable to cause apoplexy, wait and see it at Zeffirelli's.

Ambleside

☆☆ **Zeffirelli's Cinema**, Compston Road. Tel: 05394 33845.

Very good, with some nice decorative touches, such as fan lighting and old projectors as ornaments in the foyer. Doesn't get the blockbusters as quickly as Bowness, but amply compensates for this by putting on interesting films slightly out of the crowd-pulling mainstream. This is definitely a cinema run by an enthusiast and a rather classier affair than the Royalty. To get a balcony seat you need to book in for their meal in Pizzeria and cinema ticket afterwards.

Programmes for these two usually change Friday and details appear in *The Westmorland Gazette*.

Keswick

Alhambra Cinema. Tel: 07687 72195.

A small cinema tucked away in St. John's Street. Now rather bijou, since refurbishment.

Other Cinemas

There are of course a lot more cinemas around the outskirts of the Lakes, especially in the larger Cumbrian towns. They include:

Barrow: Astra 1, 2 and 3, Abbey Road. Tel: 0229 825354.

Carlisle: Lonsdale Cinema, Warwick Road. Tel: 0228 514654/ 25586.

Kendal: Brewery Arts Centre, Highgate. Tel: 0539 725133.

Millom : Palladium Cinema, St George's Road. Tel: 0229 772441.

Penrith: Alhambra Cinema, Middlegate. Tel: 0768 62400.

Ulverston: Roxy Cinema, Brogden Street. Tel: 0229 552340. Trying very hard with enthusiastic film club.

Whitehaven: Gaiety Cinema. Tel: 0946 693012.
Rosehill Theatre - for upmarket films you'd never otherwise see in Cumbria.

Workington: Rendezvous Twin Cinemas, Oxford Street. Tel: 0900 602505 . (wonder if one needs binoculars for this?).

Chapter Fifteen

Shopping

Yes, we know you haven't come to the Lakes to shop, or so you think. But just look at all those crowds on the pavements of Bowness and Keswick. Where do they all come from. So we have surveyed five types of shops which visitors, and residents, might well want to use at some time.

Antique Shops

Cockermouth

☆☆ Antique Market
Old Courthouse, Cocker Bridge, Main Street.
Tel: 0900 824346.

☆☆ Cockermouth Antiques
Station Street. Tel: 0900 826746.

High Newton

Shire Antiques
High Newton in Cartmel.
Tel: 05395 31431.

Kendal

Cottage Antiques
151 Highgate. Tel: 0539 722683.

☆ Highgate Antiques
Georgian House, Highgate. Tel: 0539 724527.

Keswick

John Young & Son
12 Main Street. Tel: 07687 73434.

Kirkby Stephen

Haughey Antiques
30 Market Street.Tel: 07683 71302.

Newby Bridge
☆☆ Townhead Antiques
Townhead, Newby Bridge Road. Tel: 05395 31321.

Windermere
Joseph Thornton Antiques
4 Victoria Street. Tel: 05394 42930.

Bird Cage Antiques
College Road. Tel: 05394 45063.

Book Shops
Well, you might want to buy more copies of *The Good Guide to the Lakes* - go on, spoil the friends back home.

Lakeland book shops are terribly good on Lakeland books and maps - not so hot on the latest sensitive novel from London. All Lakeland book shops which stock this book are of course excellent, but here's a small selection:

Ambleside
Fred Holdsworth
Central Buildings. Tel: 05394 33388.

Wearing's Bookshop
Lake Road. Tel: 05394 32312.

Bowness
Cumbria Books
Crag Brow, Bowness. Tel: 05394 47200.

Lakes Bookshop
Quarry Rigg, Lake Road. Tel: 05394 45780.

Cockermouth
The New Bookshop
42/44 Main Street. Tel: 0900 822062.

Grasmere
Sam Read
Broadgate House. Tel: 05394 35374.

Hawkshead
Seddon's Bookshop
The Square. Tel: 05394 36650.

Kendal
Bookworm
93 Highgate. Tel: 0539 724419.

Henry Roberts
7 Stramongate. Tel: 0539 720425.

Keswick

Lake Road Bookshop
Lake Road. Tel: 07687 72910.

Chaplin's
19 Station Road. Tel: 07687 72440.

Millom

Duddon Books
2 St George's Road. Tel: 0229 774307.

Penrith

Bluebell Bookshop
Angel Square. Tel: 0768 66660.

Ulverston

James Atkinson
6 King Street. Tel: 0229 553097.

Whitehaven

Cribbs Bookshop
Church Street. Tel: 0946 695111.

No ratings this time for bookshops - they get terribly jealous of each other. However, in our personal opinion, the two most interesting are probably Fred Holdsworth's, in Ambleside, and The Bluebell, in Penrith. Fred Holdsworth's stocks more of the out-of-the-way books and it is amazing what he has got hidden in the crowded shelves of his little shop. The Bluebell, by contrast, now in new posh premises, boasts that it is the biggest bookshop in all Cumbria, with 3,500 square feet.

For anything on Wordsworth or the Lake Poets, try:

The Wordsworth Bookshop
Town End, Grasmere.
Tel: 05394 35544.

This is next to - and run by - Dove Cottage.

Even better, because they carry less of the souvenir stuff, is the bookshop at Brantwood, Ruskin's house in Coniston. The National Park Visitor Centre, Brockhole, also has a good selection of books on the area. The larger tourist information centres (especially the National Park TICs) also have books on the area.

Secondhand Book Shops
Ambleside

The Little Bookshop
1 Cheapside. Tel: 05394 32094.

Barrow

Mostly Books
247 Rawlinson Street. Tel: 0229 36808.

Carlisle

☆☆ Bookcase
17 Castle Street. Tel: 0228 44560.

Cartmel

Peter Bain Smith
Bank Court, Market Square. Tel: 05395 36369.

Cockermouth

☆ Winkworth Antiquarian Books
102 Main Street. Tel: 0900 824984.

Kendal

Ewan Kerr
No 1, Yard 51, Stramongate. Tel: 0539 720659.

Keswick

Appleby's Books
5 St John's Street.

Ravenstondale

The Book House
Grey Garth. Tel: 05396 23634.
    Actually a family home, but stuffed with books to browse through. Also do B & B (For a bit of bedtime reading?)

Sedbergh

☆☆ F R & G Hollett
6 Finkle Street Tel: 05396 20298.

Whitehaven
☆☆☆ Michael Moon
41-42 Roper Street. Tel: 0946 62936.
    A huge place, great for browsing. As a rule, he knows what he has got in stock, but he's not sure exactly where to find it. However, he'll tend to keep you amused whilst you're both looking for it. One mile of shelves. Boasts he can accommodate two full coach loads on a wet day, especially now he has opened up his new Art Gallery.

Craft Shops and Galleries

    Still seems to be a growth area, despite Economic Crises. Some give a good focus to a trip out - e.g. Wetheriggs Pottery is very near, and a blessed relief from Lowther Park. Some are small, one person operations, often the results of someone's desire to escape the rat race of a Big City (for the rat race of a small village). Others have been going for centuries and continue to use traditional working methods.
    The best present is something unique to the area so, if you've already stocked up with Kendal Mint Cake and want to find something smarter, you might try these:

Alston

Gossipgate Gallery
The Butts. Tel: 0434 381806.
Converted congregational church with arts and craft from
N. England. Interesting Pennine slant to things. Exhibitions, teas. Combines excellently with trip on S. Tynedale
railway, stopping off at Village Bakery, Melmerby en-
route. Fabulous views, deserted roads, bliss.

Ambleside

☆ Kirkstone Slate Gallery
Skelwith Bridge, Ambleside. Tel: 05394 33296.
A wide range of green slate ornaments and objects, produced on site and ranging from slate ashtrays to table
lamps. Range of quality craft objects - tries to avoid the
predictable.

☆☆ Adrian Sankey Glass
Rydal Road. Tel: 05394 33039.
Glass sculptures and glass ware. You can visit the new and
beautiful workshop and see the finished products being
made.

Appleby

Courtyard Gallery
32 Boroughgate. Tel: 07683 51638.
Attractive setting with original works of art and exhibitions. Cafe which extends into said courtyard.

Brougham

Brougham Hall Craft Centre
Nr Penrith. Tel: 0768 68184.
Developed by charitable trust to rescue 19th century Hall
from dereliction. Variety of crafts in workshops on site and
cafe.

Brough

Clifford House Craft Workshops
Main Street. Tel: 07683 41296.
Designs and makes jewellery on-site. Also sells other crafts.
Nice little coffee shop.

Cartmel

Cartmel; Craft Centre
Broughton Lodge Farm, Field Broughton. Tel: 05395 36009.
Housed in old home farm. Variety of craftspeople who also
give demonstrations and tuition. Goods for sale. Also Egg-
Pudding Stone Restaurant.

Coniston

The Coach House Gallery
Brantwood. Tel: 05394 41426.
Ruskin's outbuildings - interesting displays and sale of
paintings and crafts. Look out for tubular windchimes -
very haunting, hanging in the stable window with that
backdrop of fells.

Egremont

Lowes Court Gallery
12 Main Street. Tel: 0946 820693.
Provides display centre for West Cumbrian artists and craftspeople - not a commercial organisation, so particularly worth visiting. Has monthly exhibitions too. Nice selection of hematite jewellery, made locally. (Egremont has last working mine for this - see Chapter 9). Also home to small TIC.

Gosforth

Gosforth Pottery
Gosforth, Nr. Seascale. Tel: 09467 25296.
Ground floor workshop, upstairs gallery and shop. Can see work in progress.

Grasmere

The Heaton Cooper Studio
Tel: 05394 35280.
(Also at Quarry Rigg, Bowness. Tel: 05394 44766.)
The paintings of W. Heaton Cooper have become a major industry in the Lake District, on postcards and greetings cards everywhere. These two studios specialise in prints and reproductions but also have one or two originals on display. To some people, Heaton Cooper's paintings *are* the Lake District.

Kendal

Kendal Glass Engravers
177 Highgate. Tel: 0539 733800.
Hand-produced glass engravings, displayed in the adjacent gallery, all individually signed and dated.

Keswick

☆ Thornthwaite Galleries
Thornthwaite. Tel: 07687 78248.
(Off the A66, between Keswick and Cockermouth.)
Fascinating - if rather up market - art gallery with a range of work for sale by local artists.

☆☆ Lakeland Guild Craft Gallery (above sheepskin shop)
Lake Road. Tel: 07687 74636.
Run by Lakeland Guild of Craftsmen. Very wide range.

Kirkby Stephen

Langrigg Pottery
Winton. Tel: 07683 71542.
Interesting, reasonably priced pottery made on premises. Lovely old building.

Penrith

☆ Wetheriggs Country Pottery
Clifton Dykes.
Tel: 0768 62946.
Gallery, showroom and exhibition offering a range of pottery made on site. They use traditional techniques and

you can visit the workshop and see the work taking place. Also a very good cafe and they claim there has been a pottery on this site for nearly a thousand years. Have a try in your own throwing area.

Eden Craft Gallery
St Andrew's Churchyard. Tel: 0768 67955.
Good range of Cumbrian crafts. Coffee shop.

Rusland
Forest Spinners
Rusland. Tel: 0229 860255.
Spinning workshop near Grizedale Forest, using fleeces from their own sheep, so there. Demonstrations and articles for sale.

Sedbergh
Dent Crafts Centre
Helmside, Dent. Tel: 05396 25400.
Spinning, pottery, printing and hand-frame knitting.

Staveley
Wedge Hall Gallery
Windermere Road. Tel: 0539 821130.
Supports a range of small, local crafts producers. Also a nice tea room.

Ulverston
☆ Cumbria Crystal
The Auction Mart, Lightburn Road. Tel: 0229 554400.
Factory in which you can watch glass blowing and see all the stages of production of crystal glass, with a showroom selling seconds too. Small admission charge.

Underbarrow
Lyth Gallery
Town Yeat, Nr Kendal. Tel: 05395 68383.
A new venture in a converted barn - getting away from crafts and teas with everything type of gallery. Small but very out of ordinary displays of personally selected paintings and drawings. Deserves to succeed.

Windermere
Made in Cumbria
Tourist Information Centre, Victoria Street.
Tel: 05394 46499.
An enterprising new venture by the tourist folk. They've opened up the basement room and stocked it with high quality goods, all Cumbrian. A very welcome departure from the tea-towel and keyring image.

John Kershaw Pottery
40a Main Road. Tel: 05394 44844.
Stoneware pottery, made on the premises.

The NP people have Craft Days at Seatoller Barn in Borrowdale. Can be quite jolly as craftspersons come from all over to sell or demonstrate.

Factory Shops
Cumbrian industries that have been around for ages now realise that people will pay to see goods made before buying them.

Carlisle:
Eden Valley Woollen Mill, Armathwaite. Tel: 06974 72457.

Kendal:
Goodacre Carpets. Tel; 0539 723601.
K Shoes. Tel: 0539 724343.

Sedbergh:
Pennine Tweeds. Tel: 05396 20558.

Food Shops
If you're self-catering, or just feeling peckish, you will need to stock up. Beware. There are some places in the Lake District where you might starve to death, unless you can live off Kendal mint cake and leather Lakeland key fobs. Hawkshead, Coniston, Grasmere and even Bowness are rather like that - great for gifts and souvenirs, not so hot for food (though Open All Hours, Lake Road, Bowness can be a life saver if self-catering as it stays open late). Windermere is better for food shopping. Very few of the smaller Lake District villages have shops, you have to trek to the larger towns. In general, if you're in the northern Lakes, head for Cockermouth or Penrith, if you're in the south, go to Ambleside, Windermere, Kendal or Ulverston to stock up. The following is a summary:

Good for Food
Ambleside - good grocers, butchers and greengrocers. Especially good on market day (Wednesday). Try Lucy's Specialist Grocers, Church Street - brilliant Aladdin's cave of goodies
Kendal - lots of supermarkets and smaller food shops. Late opening in most of them on Friday nights. Also a good food market on Saturday.
Penrith - lots of food shops and one or two good supermarkets.
Cockermouth - also good for food shops, with a nice little market on Monday plus the new Walter Willson supermarket.
Windermere - needs to be mentioned for its Booths supermarket.

Towns round the fringes of the Lakes, where tourism is less important, are also quite good if you're stocking up for a holiday. These include Whitehaven, Workington, Ulverston and Grange-over-Sands. Carlisle, of course, being the largest town, has the biggest shops and supermarkets. They have an excellent Marks and Spencer Foodstore and the Lanes Shopping Complex.

Walkers' Shops

Shops which specialise in the great outdoors, supplying gear for walkers and climbers, are a feature of the landscape in the Lake District. Invaluable for guide books, maps, wet-weather and walking clothes as well as general advice. The two biggest - Fisher's and Frank Davies - are good sources of information on walking and climbing activities generally and frequently have notices displayed in the windows giving details of talks, lectures and local instructors. Some will also hire out specialised equipment. Keswick Mountain Sports, Fisher's and Frank Davies all hire boots, Frank Davies hires waterproofs too. Stewart Cunningham hires tents, bikes and baby packs.

Ambleside is becoming *the* centre for walking and outdoor shops; there were six and a half at the last count. Keswick isn't far behind, though.

For this type of shopping, it is best to stick to the specialist shops (such as those listed here) and ignore the ordinary sports shops and gift shops selling cheap rucksacks.

Ambleside
☆☆ Frank Davies
(The Climber's Shop), Compston Road. Tel: 05394 32297.

Stewart Cunningham
Outdoor Centre, 12 Rydal Road. Tel: 05394 32636.

Miniwalkers
Rydal Road.
Not really an outdoor shop, more a window display opposite Cunningham's. It features waterproofs and walking gear for children. Call if half a shop.

Rock and Run
4 Cheapside. Tel: 05394 33660.

John Gaynor's
Market Cross. Tel: Ambleside 33305.
Not really a specialist, but a good range of outdoor clothing and tents.

White Mountain
Lake Road. Tel: 05394 32752.
Gear shop with some out-of-the ordinary makes. Booking for climbing and paragliding. Satellite weather and weather charts.

Wilf. Nicholson
Central Buildings. Tel: 05394 32235.

Bowness
☆ Stuart's Sports
Lake Road. Tel: 05394 43001.

Broughton-in-Furness
Mountain Centre Sports
Brade Street. Tel: 0229 716461.

Kendal
Lakeland Mountain Centre
3 Kirkland. Tel: 0539 728356.

Peter Bland Sports
34a Kirkland. Tel: 0539 731012.
Good on footwear for the fells, but only if you plan to run
up them.

Kendal Sports
30 Stramongate.
Tel: 0539 721554.

The Survival Shop
Waterside. Tel: 0539 729699.
(A good shop for those achieving the feat of parking in
Kendal.)

Keswick
☆ George Fisher
2 Borrowdale Road. Tel: 07687 72178.

Mountain World
28 Lake Road. Tel: 07687 73524.

Rathbone's Outdoor Sports
26 Main Street. Tel: 07687 72700.

Keswick Mountain Sports
73 Main Street. Tel: 07687 73843.

Needle Sports
56 Main Street. Tel: 07687 72227.

Penrith
Survival Aids
Morland, Nr. Penrith. Tel: 0931 714444.
    The most specialised of the lot, perhaps. A wide range
of outdoor and travelling gear, some of it rather militaris-
tic. And yes, this is the same firm that sits rather strangely
in London, among the shops beside Euston Station .

Wasdale
A neat little climbing shop, right beside the Inn:
Barn Door Shop
Wasdale Head. Tel: 09467 26384.

Windermere

☆ The Fellsman
2 Victoria Street. Tel: 05394 44876.
Especially good for skiing equipment.

Buying a House in the Lake District

For the last 200 years, millions of people who have visited the Lakes have come away with the same fantasy - why can't we find a nice little cottage and settle down here for good. Today, such things are harder to achieve than they have ever been, either finding a cottage or getting a local job. Wordsworth himself had a hell of a problem. He never ended up in his own house, as both Dove Cottage and Rydal Mount were rented, and it took him years of begging letters to influential friends to get himself a nice local job, Distributor of Stamps for Westmorland. But it can be done, even for complete outsiders.

It is possible, if you look hard and stick to the West Cumbrian fringes, to find a small terrace house around the £30,000 mark. It won't be all that desirable and will need work, but they do exist. And if you have a good idea, plus a bit of talent and energy, you could even start your own business in Lakeland. Those two at Sharrow Bay, who now run England's nicest hotel, started from scratch. The Mountain Goat Bus Company was begun by an offcomer. It is very often the outsiders who do bring new life and new vitality, but there are problems peculiar to the Lake District, due to the fact that it's a National Park. Your chances of opening a hamburger haven on the top of Skiddaw are a bit slim. The National Park people are not frightfully keen on that sort of thing. But, you never know. Your particular dream might be the one to succeed.

First of all, there are a few basic guidelines . . .

Which area?

It is vital to decide as quickly as possible on the particular area you want to look at, choosing a lake, a town or valley you like the best. On the map, the National Park looks pretty small, but you just can't look through all of it. There's the travelling around for one thing and secondly, the local newspapers and estate agents strictly divide up Lakeland along that north-south divide.

National Park As a general rule, the south is more expensive than the north, thanks to the better road and rail communications. Folks from Liverpool and Manchester tend to settle round the southern Lakes. People from Newcastle aim for the northern bits.

Grasmere, despite the crowds, is still considered a very desirable place to live, especially near the lake. Ambleside and Coniston are also expensive. Windermere and Bowness are equally expensive, but thought a bit flash. Borrowdale is smart but Keswick is bourgeois. Furness has some discriminating fans while the Caldbeck fells are an acquired taste.

Cumbria Just outside the NP boundaries, there are some smart fringes and not so smart fringes.

No one wants to live amidst the industrial deadliness of West Cumbria, unless they have no alternative, so avoid Workington, Cleator Moor, Frizington, Distington. Barrow has few fans, outside Barrow. Whitehaven is coming up. Nicest of all, along that western fringe, is to look for something near Cockermouth.

Incidentally, the *real* landed-gentry of Cumbria neither live in central Lakeland nor on those western fringes - they tend to live just to the east, well away from either industry or the holiday hordes. The Lowthers are near Penrith and so are several other of Cumbria's landed nobs. Some of the biggest and nicest houses of all are in the Eden Valley.

Newspapers

Always buy all the local papers when house hunting. Though few people in Cumbria sell their properties privately, you will see all the agents' adverts.

For the south and central Lakes - the best is *The Westmorland Gazette*.

For northern Lakes - *Cumberland News* or *Keswick Reminder*.

The West Coast papers (see Chapter One for addresses) can also be useful. You can get a local newspaper by post, if you get on their circulation list, as this is the best way of keeping in touch with the market from outside.

House Prices

Now we come to the tough bit - tough to generalise about and tough when you realise just how much you will have to spend to get that really desirable cottage, the one everyone wants, with the cosy porch and the nice view of the lake and the pretty fell behind. Starting from the fringes and the most cheapest, this is what you might expect to pay.

Cumbria

For an undesirable terrace house, in a place like Workington or the slummer parts of Carlisle . . . £30,000.

For a remote cottage, in rotten condition, miles away near the Scottish Borders or on the Pennines . . . £40,000.

For a better situated though unconverted cottage, on the pleasant fringes of the National Park, such as near Cockermouth or Penrith, Kendal or Furness . . . £60,000.

National Park

Small terraced house in one of the Lakeland towns, such as Windermere . . . from £80,000.

Unconverted cottage on the fringes, such as Caldbeck . . . £80,000.

Village house without views . . . £100,000 plus.

Dream cottage, in a desirable situation and fully modernised . . . from £200,000.

Detached house, with lake frontage . . . from £500,000.

Flats

These are well-worth considering for holiday homes and have a number of advantages. For a start, they aren't isolated, so security is far better. They have no garden to look after, are cheaper to maintain and there's often a management company which will look after the property in your absence.

There are some splendid flats available; manor houses were built in the last century specifically to take advantage of position and views. Many have now been converted into flats. Expect to pay about £100,000 for a two-bedroom flat with good lake views in one of these houses.

Building a House

So what about building a new house? Well, for a start you are likely to be restricted to existing settlements. Nobody wants the fells cluttered up with expensive condominiums. One of the functions of the Lake District Special Planning Board is to try to control the amount and type of new building that goes on within the National Park. If you build a house in the NP, for example, it must have a local slate roof - both to blend in with existing buildings and to maintain local industry. The LDSPB is a Good Thing, though the amount of control it exercises has been undermined in recent years by successive Secretaries of State. However, political gripes aside, being in a NP does mean that building plots are comparatively rare and expensive - a small plot in or near Windermere, for example, would fetch in excess of £50,000.

For a while the Board had a Section 52 agreement, whereby it tried to impose occupancy agreements on new housing in favour of local people (who are gradually being forced out of the market by the increasing number of holiday homes). That was overruled and the current position is that there will be no occupancy restrictions on *new* dwellings erected within a settlement. Outside settlements, strict planning control is exercised so that it is unlikely that anyone without an essential need (eg, a farm or forestry worker) will get consent.

Barn conversions are a separate area altogether and the Board provides a free leaflet as a useful starting point.

One final point - if you are buying a house, particularly in a rural area, get your solicitor to check carefully that there is not an existing occupancy restriction in force (eg for agricultural workers). The Board *is* able to enforce these and is keen to do so.

Time Sharing

Basically, you are buying a share in a property for up to 80 years ahead, buying only the week or weeks of the year in which you take your holiday. For those weeks, the place is yours to do with as you like - you can rent it, lend it to friends, holiday in it yourself or even swap it with timeshare places elsewhere in the world. The advantage is that for the rest of the year, you have no worries about the property or its maintenance - and the standard of these places can be very high indeed, with plenty of facilities on site (swimming pools, bars, saunas, etc). The disadvantage is that you can only use the place for the week or weeks you have bought (unless you do a swap). There is never the feeling of it being 'your' holiday home. There can also be hefty maintenance expenses which can go up all the time.

Prices vary according to which part of the year you prefer, higher in the summer and Christmas period, lower in January and the tail end of the year. School holidays are always expensive, so October is best value.

The Lake District has around a dozen time share developments, ranging from large purpose built estates offering a high standard of accommodation and service to simpler conversions. On the whole, they have been well received, with none of the bad publicity or dodgy selling methods of the Mediterranean. The leading ones have proved popular with customers and proved good investments, even in hard times. These are the ones we think the best, with some 1993 prices.

☆☆☆ The Langdale Partnership, Great Langdale, Ambleside. Tel: 05394 37391.

This was the first of the Lake District's timeshare establishments, opened in 1982, and remains the most successful. Built at the old Langdale gunpowder works, they now offer a range of accommodation based around a large, landscaped estate near Elterwater. The original Swiss-style chalets are still there, but now there are also apartments in Chapel Stile and very plush (some might say flash) apartments in Elterwater Hall. All very up-market and a little cut off from the locals, though the Partnership is responsible for sponsoring several arts events locally. Facilities include a hotel, an excellent leisure centre, with swimming pool, sauna, squash court, solarium and gymnasium. There are also bars and a restaurant on site, some of which are also open to the general public (the leisure centre is restricted to timeshare or hotel residents, or to locals buying a yearly club membership, but offers membership on daily basis).

You can buy from one to ten weeks; a two-bedroom lodge will cost from £4,588 to £15,093 per week, depending on time of year. This price is for an 80 year ownership. On top, there is a management charge (which can go up each year), covering rates, maintenance, insurance of the house and contents and domestic services (cleaning, provision of towels, etc - they boast that you don't have to lift a finger to see that your property is well looked after). Each lodge has central heating, is furnished to a high standard and telephones are available. A Chapel Stile apartment costs between £3,622 to £12,075 and an apartment in Elterwater Hall is between £4,497 to £12,966. No price increase here because of state of market.

☆☆☆ **The Lakeland Village**, Newby Bridge, near Ulverston. Tel: 05395 31144.

This is a prestigious development built jointly by Douglas and Kenning on the banks of the River Leven. Centrepiece is the Whitewater Hotel which provides luxury hotel accommodation, plus restaurant, bar and conference facilities, in what was originally an old textile mill. Timeshare accommodation consists of traditionally-built Lakeland stone cottages, all finished to a very high standard and rather more homely than Swiss chalets. Pride and joy of the development is the leisure centre (called Cascades - they all have to have their twee names); it provides swimming pool, jacuzzi, squash court, gym and dance studio, and on the top floor they provide specialised health and beauty treatment on an appointment basis, available to timeshare owners and members of the outside world alike (for a fee). Used to be run by Champneys, the health farm people, but now run by the Lakeland Village themselves. Use of the leisure centre comes with timeshare ownership or staying at the hotel and is also available on a club membership basis to locals. Prices from £1,500 to £4,500.

The Lakeland Village has less of a Tropicana Club atmosphere than the Langdales and the air of luxury is more discreet, but some people belong to both so they obviously couldn't make up their minds either. They do a day membership too.

☆ **The Lakelands**, Lower Gale, Ambleside.
Tel: 05394 33777.

Substantial buildings, done in local stone by a local builder, which offers indoor pool, sauna and bistro. Much smaller than the first two developments. Price range is £2,150 to £4,300. The lease is for an initial 25 years, after which it becomes the property of the timeshare owners themselves, to sell or keep as they wish.

The same lot are also responsible for **The Quaysiders Club** at Waterhead (05394 33969). Self-catering apartments on a much-smaller site. Usual 80 year lease; prices £3,000 to £6,800.

☆ **Windermere Marina Village**, Nabwood, Bowness-on-Windermere. Tel: 05394 46551.

One of the newest timeshares, opened in 1987. Built on the site of a privately owned marina and it's all frightfully nautical. Purpose-built cottages and a £1.5m leisure centre, called the Spinnaker Club, overlook a busy yacht marina. The cottages are neat and homely, and if you own a boat you can moor it alongside for the duration of your stay. In the evening, you can sit out on your balcony and watch the sun go down over a forest of masts. Could be deafening if they don't all tie their halyards down.

The Spinnaker is very new and plush, but rather cramped. Everything is built practically on top of the swimming pool. In addition to the pool, there are jacuzzis, a sauna, the Commodore Bistro and a games room, featuring space invader machines. Membership of the club is restricted to timeshare owners, berth-holders on the marina and marina users on daily basis. Associate memberships are also available.

Prices are from £4,000 to £10,000 for 6 bed apartment. Leases run to 2040.

Chapter Sixteen

Surveys and Fascinating Facts

Tourism

☆ In 1991, nine million visitors made a day visit to the Lakes of at least 3 hours.
☆ Another 2.7 million stayed overnight - giving a total of 13.5 million bed nights.
☆ The day visitors spent £79 million
☆ The staying visitors spent £370 million

Where they come from: UK Visitors

North West	27%
South East	15%
North	14%
Yorkshire/Humberside	13%
West Midlands	7%
Other regions	32%

Overseas visitors: in 1991, total was 250,000

USA	34%
Australia	12%
Germany	8%
Canada	7%
France	7%
Other Countries	32%

Purpose of visit: UK visitors

Holidays	82%
Visiting friends or relations	8%
Business/conference	5%
Other	5%

Purpose of day trips

Visiting heritage attractions	5%
Visiting commercial outdoor attractions	3%
Informal outdoor recreation	38%
Sport	28%
Indoor entertainment	11%
Bathing/sunbathing	2%
Visiting friends/relatives	10%
Other	3%

It is interesting to note that general moving around and doing things (climbing a fell, sailing a boat or riding a horse) accounts for 66% of the figures. So much for needing more indoor visitor attractions in the Lakes.

The NPA asked people if there were any parts of the Lake District they no longer enjoyed, and if so why? Bowness and Windermere came top of the table, as the place people no longer enjoyed most. Some way behind came Keswick, Ambleside and Coniston. In all cases, the overriding reason was that they were too crowded (and not because they lacked facilities - interesting).

Who Comes to the Lakes:

age	
16-24	19%
25-35	17%
35-44	18%
45-54	14%
55-64	21%
65+	10%

Preferred Time of Year for Trips to Cumbria

Jan, Feb, March	14%
April, May, June	27%
July, Aug., Sept.	42%
Oct, Nov, December	16%

On a Spring Bank Holiday there may be as many as 7,000 tents in the National Park. (And there are about 1,800 holiday or second homes.)

Peers

Has Penrith got more hereditary peers associated with it than any other town of its size in the country? Well there's the Earl of Lonsdale (Head of the Lowther family), then Viscount Ullswater, Lord Howard of Penrith, Lord Inglewood of Hutton-in-the-Forest, and Viscount Whitelaw, Willie Whitelaw as was. So that's five. Beat that, any town.

Population

The Lake District National Park has 40,674 people. Almost 24% of these were retired folks. The number of young children (under 14 years) had fallen from 21% in 1971 to 15% in 1991.

The total population figure has in fact hardly changed at all in the last 30 years - in 1951 it was 40,500. But it is pretty obvious what's happening - we're all getting older. There are now 10% more elderly people than 10 years ago. Will the Lake District become a Museum - the people and not just the exhibits?

Cumbria's Most Visited Places: 1992

1	Tullie House, Carlisle	250,000
2	Sellafield	200,000
3	Grizedale Visitor Centre	160,000
4	Brockhole	150,000
5	World of Beatrix Potter	117,000
6	Cumberland Pencil Museum	102,000
7	Whinlatter Visitor Centre	100,000
8	Lowther Park	90,000
9	Dove Cottage	80,000
10	Holker Hall	75,000
11	Hill Top	70,000
12	Carlisle Castle	70,000
13	Border Regiment Museum	70,000
14	Muncaster Castle	60,000
15	Sizergh Castle	50,000
16	Cars of the Stars	50,000
17	Beatrix Pottery Gallery	47,000
18	Levens Hall	47,000
19	Brantwood	40,000
20	Windermere Steam Boat Museum	40,000
21	Lakeland Motor Museum	40,000
22	Rydal Mount	35,000
23	Mirehouse	30,000
24	Laurel and Hardy Museum	25,000
25	Townend	23,000

The new number one tourist attraction, not counting services, such as the Lake steamers, or beauty spots, such as Tarn Hows, or churches, such as Carlisle Cathedral where heads are only guessed at, or craft galleries which are really big shops, is . . . Tullie House, Carlisle. Not surprising, really, as it's had a £5 million face lift and the Queen did open it. It even beat Sellafield, which is totally free, of course, so that's cheating. Brockhole has also increased its number, thanks to giving free admission. The two Forestry Commission Visitor Centres, at Grizedale and Whinlatter, have benefited from recent refurbishments and also free admission.

Perhaps the best performance of all has been by a complete newcomer, the World of Beatrix Potter at the Old Laundry, Bowness, coming from nowhere to number five on the hit parade. Will they go even higher next time? Keswick's newcomer, Stars of the Cars, has also done well, and should zoom further up the table.

Of the old established attractions, the literary homes have stayed much the same, with Dove Cottage ahead of Hill Top (though Hill Top is trying if anything to reduce numbers) while Holker Hall still leads the stately homes.

Lakeland Transport: number of passengers, 1992.

Windermere Steamers	540,000
Lakeside and Haverthwaite Railway	140,000
Ravenglass and Eskdale Railway	134,000

Things People Have Asked

Some of the questions which have been put to the various Tourist Information Centres in the Lake District. Now that you know so much about Lakeland, you will of course know all the correct answers.

Can you direct me to the Beatrix Potteries?
How do you fill up the lakes?
Does it ever stop raining?
What time do the Windermere boats leave for the Isle of Man?
When is high tide on the lakes?
Can we visit the glass factory at Ravenglass?
Where's the rhinoceros pass?
Which mine does all the mint cake come from?
Have you got this week's Dorothy's journals?
Where are the Mountain Goats?
Where are the Kilt Factories?
Where can I see dryrot fencing?

Thirteen Things You Didn't Know about Kendal Mint Cake

1 Kendal Mint Cake was created in 1869 in a confectionary shop and factory, in Stricklandgate, Kendal, run by Joseph Wiper.

2 One theory of origin is that it was all a mistake. A standard sweet recipe went wrong, a pan over boiled, the contents spilt on the floor and quickly hardened, someone tasted it and though hmm, yummy.

3 The rival theory says it was nicked from an old women living nearby who made her own sweets.

4 The basic ingredients are sugar, glucose and water boiled in a copper pan, then peppermint oil is added. The secret is knowing the precise moment to pour it out.

5 The first expedition to carry Kendal Mint Cake as emergency supplies was the British Imperial Transantarctic Exploration of 1914, commanded by Sir Ernest Shackleton.

6 Almost every Everest Expedition has carried Kendal Mint Cake since 1922 when it was packed in an airtight case weighing 40 lbs, the maximum a Tibetan porter was allowed to carry up the mountain.

7 Other expeditions jolly thankful for Kendal Mint Cake include the Daily Mail's Abominable Snowman expedition of 1952, the Scottish Tierra del Fuego expedition 1977, Chris Bonnington's climbs, plus round the world yacht racers.

8 In the 1970s chocolate coated mint cake was introduced, which increased sales but appalled mint cake purists.

9 There are only four Kendal Mint Cake makers: Wipers, Wilson's (founded 1913), Quiggin (1920) and George Romney (1937). Romney's now owns Wipers.

10 George Romney's premises are in Mintsfeet Road, Kendal. No connection. The name comes from the River Mint, a tributary of the river Kent which flows through Kendal.

11 Own label mint cake is booming - firms order it specially with their name on, from the Ministry of Defence for ration packs to the folks at Balmoral for after dinner mints.

12 Over 800 tons of Kendal Mint Cake are produced every year, or roughly one million bars.

13 There is now a shop devoted to mint cake - The World Famous Kendal Mint Cake shop. In Kendal, of course, in the Westmorland Shopping Centre. Tel: 0539 720781.

ROMNEY'S EVEREST KENDAL MINT CAKE Manufactured by **GEORGE ROMNEY, LTD. IN KENDAL.** The Gateway to the English Lakes

Romney's Kendal Mint Cake was carried to the summit of MOUNT EVEREST on 29th May, 1953. "We sat on the snow and looked at the country far below us . . . . we nibbled Kendal Mint Cake." A member of the successful Everest Expedition wrote—"It was easily the most popular item on our high altitude ration—our only criticism was that we did not have enough of it."

Fascinating Facts

In 1855, 21,480 carrriages passd through Troutbeck Bridge on their way to Ambleside and areas North.

In 1789 William Chapman drew up plans to link Ullswater with the sea via a system of canals.

In 1797 the same William Chapman drew up plans for joining the North Sea and the Irish Sea by a navigable waterway passing through Cumbria. He estimated the cost at over £3,000 per mile. It would have needed over 100 locks to cope with hills.

In 1823, William Chapman's canal was opened (what price persistence?) which connected Carlisle to the sea. It emerged on the Solway Firth at Fisher's Cross, grandly renamed Port Carlisle, remaining open for 25 years, before being filled in to create a railway line. This means that Carlisle had a direct navigable connection with the sea for 1.25% of its recorded history.

The River Kent is said to be the swiftest flowing English river - it descends 1,000' in 25 miles (Kentmere to Levens).

In the seventeenth century Milnthorpe was recorded as Westmorland's only sea town.

In 1847-8, the Kendal-Windermere railway carried over 120,000 passengers.

In 1890, there was a minor scandal on Lake Windermere. An advertising yacht appeared on the Lake, together with a lakeside hoarding, commending the beneficial effects of Beechams Pills. After two local worthies were caught in the act of placing explosives under the yacht, Beechams agreed to remove the hoarding. The yacht had already sunk.

In June 1990, visitors to Lake Windermere felt a little bemused by the sight of an aeroplane moored on the water. It was a Sunderland Mk V Flying Boat, returning to its native waters after a gap of 45 years. They were built at White Cross Bay on Windermere.

Lakeland Book of the Year awards

An annual competition for the book which does most to promote interest in Cumbria. There are also other awards, all given out at a grand Literary Lunch held every Easter, usually in Windermere. Great speeches. Proceeds from the lunch to to a Cumbrian Charity. Tickets and further information from Lorna van Hove, Cumbria Tourist Board.

1984   'AA/OS Guide to the Lake District'
1985   'Fellwalking with Wainwright'
1986   'Lakeland from the Air' by Peter Thornton, jointly with 'Walking with a Camera in Herries' Lakeland' by Trevor Hayward.
1988   'The Bondage of Love', a biography of Coleridge, by Molly Lefebure
1989   'Country Diary' by Enid Wilson.
1990   'Dream Gardens' by Vivian Russell.
1991   'The Diaries of Anne Clifford', edited by David Clifford.
1992   'Coleridge Walks the Fells' by Alan Hankinson.

Lakeland Rock Climbs

Rock climbing as a sport was invented in the Lake District in the 1880s. Yet another world first. It started around Wastdale and when a new climb was made, the climber had the privilege of give it a name. In the early days, the names were rather boring such as 'North Climb on Pillar Rock'. After the First World War, something strange happened. The names of new climbs became weird, and rather wonderful.

Sodom and Gomorrah - on Pillar Rock, named by C. F. Holland, 1919. On the first ascent, he got in a rage when his plimsolls collapsed, his pipe fell down a crag and a small lump of rock hit him in the face.

Joas - on Gimmer Crag, named by Graham MacPhee, 1928. It stands for 'Just One Awful Sweat'.

Kipling Groove - on Gimmer Crag, named by Arthur Dolphin, 1948. He thought it was "Ruddy 'ard",

Cleopatra - on Buckstone Howe, 1949; *'Jezebel'* - on Miner's Crag, 1950; *Delilah* - on High Crag, 1951 - all named by Bill Peascod, a coal miner from Workington, later an eminent rock climber and artist. He liked to name his routes after notorious ladies from the past.

Eve - on Shepherds Crag, 1951, also named by Bill Peascod. This time after a living woman, Eve the bar maid at the Scafell Hotel climbers bar. Peascod and his friends got free drinks that evening.

Rigor Mortis - on Castle Rock, named by Paul Ross, 1959. 'Because we thought it a rather stiff problem'.

Incantations - on Great Gable; *Coroner's Crack* and *Dead on Arrival* - both on Eagle Crag: all named in the 1980s by Pete Whillance. He just happens to have a morbid taste in names.

Phone numbers

British Telecom have been busy bringing the Lake District into the 21st - pulse dialling - 10 digit-century. That's great for getting through, rotten for Good Guide researchers, and for all those villages who have now lost their own small exchanges.

A quick reference to the code areas and exchanges used in the Guide - and a lingering farewell to those wonderful sounding exchanges . . . .

0539	Kendal, Staveley, Selside
05394	Ambleside, Coniston, Grasmere, Hawkshead, Langdale, Windermere
05395	Cartmel, Crosthwaite, Flookburgh, Grange-over-Sands, Milnthorpe, Newby Bridge, Sedgwick, Witherslack
05396	Dent, Newbiggin-on-Lune, Sedbergh
0524	Burton, Carnforth, Lancaster, Silverdale

Cumbrian Names

So you think you might have local connections? If your surname is one of the following, you have Cumbrian or Border ancestors, so feel proud. On the other hand, they were probably Border Reivers, known for their stealing and looting.

Archibold	Graham	Potts
Armstrong	Gray	Pringle
Beattie	Hall	Radcliffe
Bell	Hedley	Reade
Burn	Henderson	Ridley
Carleton	Heron	Robson
Carlisle	Hetherington	Routledge
Carnaby	Hodgson	Rutherford
Carruthers	Hume	Salkeld
Chamberlain	Huntley	Scott
Charleton	Hunter	Selby
Charlton	Irvine	Shaftoe
Collingwood	Irving	Simpson
Crisp	Jameson	Tailor
Croser	Johnstone	Tait
Crozier	Kerr	Taylor
Cuthbert	Laidlaw	Thompson
Dacre	Little	Torey
Davison	Lowther	Trotter
Dixon	Maxwell	Turnbull
Dodd	Milburn,	Wake
Douglas	Musgrave	Watson
Dunne	Nixon	Wilson
Elliot	Noble	Woodrington
Fenwick	Ogle	Yarrow
Forster	Oliver	Young

Index

Acknowledgements

I am grateful to the following people for their help, interest, information and enthusiasm during the compiling of this edition: Pam Williamson, who did most of the really fiddly research on this edition, oh those boring new telephone numbers; Dr Bill Rollinson, George Bott, Vicki Robinson, Lorna van Hove, Bobbie Nunn, Alan Hankinson. Thanks also to Oliver Turnbull and staff at Titus Wilson for knocking the book into shape.

To All Readers

It is hoped that this book will be reprinted every two years, for ever and ever, and we plan to update almost everything in due course. It is meant to help everyone who loves the Lakes, either residents or visitors, so if you have any good news, new restaurants or new amenities, or bad news, places which you think we should not recommend any more, then do let us know. The more opinions that come in the better. Write to Hunter Davies, Loweswater, Cumbria, CA13 0RU.

To all Suppliers of Lakeland Services

Hotels, restaurants, museums, shops, mint cake middlemen, etc., whether you are mentioned in the book or not - please let us know of any changes, improvements, excitements you might be offering. We can't be expected to know everything. There is no charge for inclusion. If you would like to sell copies of this book or give it to guests or patrons, you could get an exceedingly good discount by ordering direct: from Tiptree Book Services, Colchester, CO5 0SR, tel: 0621 816 362; or from a Cumbrian wholesaler, such as Hills, Clay Flatts, Workington, CA14 2DR, tel: 0900 603031, or PR Books, Unit 1, Summerland Industrial Estate, Endmoor, Kendal. 0539 561059.

Chief Researcher Colin Shelbourn lives in Windermere and is a freelance writer and cartoonist. He was educated at York University where he read psychology. Cartoonist for *The Westmorland Gazette* and author of *Great Walks in the Lake District* and *What the Helvellyn?*

Author Hunter Davies comes from Carlisle, was educated at University College, Durham, and is a well-known author and broadcaster. He lives half of every year at Loweswater. He is married with three children and is the author of many books, including *A Walk Around the Lakes*, *Beatrix Potter's Lakeland* and a biography of Wordsworth.